GREAT FOODS
OF THE
WORLD

Joyce Goldstein, Gerald Hirigoyen
and Mary Beth Clark

First published in the U.S.A. in 1995 and 1996 by
Sunset Publishing Corporation

Originally published as
Bistro (copyright © 1995 Weldon Owen Inc.)
Taverna (copyright © 1996 Weldon Owen Inc.)
Trattoria (copyright © 1995 Weldon Owen Inc.)

Produced by

FOG CITY PRESS
Chief Executive Officer: John Owen
President: Terry Newell
Chief Operating Officer: Larry Partington
Associate Publisher: Hannah Rahill
Project Manager/Editor: Julie Stillman
Business Manager: Emily Jahn
Vice President International Sales: Stuart Laurence
Consulting Editor: Norman Kolpas
Copy Editor: Sharon Silva
Indexer: Michael D. Loo
Design: Patty Hill
Production Manager: Chris Hemesath
Digital Production: Lorna Strutt
Chapter Opener Illustrations: Michelle Stong,
    Ed Miller, Dorothy Reinhardt
Glossary Illustrations: Alice Harth
Cover Design: Sarah Gifford
Front Matter Design: Lorna Strutt

A Weldon Owen Production

Library of Congress Cataloging-in-Publication Data
is available.

ISBN 1-892374-44-7

Printed in China by
Leefung-Asco Printers Trading Ltd.

A Note on Weights and Measures:
All recipes include customary U.S., U.K., and metric measure-
ments. Conversions are based on a standard developed for these
books and have been rounded off. Actual weights may vary.

A Note on Language:
For Greek words transliterated into the Roman alphabet, we
have used common spellings that make phonetic pronunciation
the simplest. In the case of Turkish, we have not included the
special diacritical marks that indicate pronunciation.

GREAT FOODS

OF THE
WORLD

Over 150 Traditional Recipes from Italy,
France and the Mediterranean

Contents

INTRODUCTION

Cuisines of the sun. That poetic description has often been applied to the cooking of France, Italy and other lands with shorelines that touch the Mediterranean. Their often sun-drenched climate encourages a leisurely lifestyle and meals enjoyed in casual surroundings, whether a family kitchen table, an Italian trattoria, a French country bistro or a taverna in Greece, Turkey, Portugal or Spain. The abundant warmth also yields a wonderful bounty of rich, earthy ingredients.

This volume of *Great Foods of the World* celebrates Europe's cuisines of the sun in all their delightful variety. It presents over 150 authentic and well-tried recipes for delicious but unassuming specialties, from appetizers to desserts, using the wholesome and robust fare of the region. The book has been divided into three sections focusing on the diverse cuisines of Italy, France and the Mediterranean.

Italy

Wherever you travel in Italy, the cooking changes with the dialect. Each region has its own culinary style, with climate and geography still determining local specialties.

In general, cooks in the rich agricultural north use more butter, cow's milk cheeses, polenta, rice, fresh pasta, meat and game. You'll discover these influences in favorites like Spinach Gnocchi in Gorgonzola Cream Sauce (page 45) and Braised Veal Shanks with Lemon, Parsley and Garlic (page 60).

In the warmer south, olive oil, tomatoes, dried pasta, seafood and sheep and goat's milk cheeses pro-

vide the foundation. Such hallmarks are unmistakable in recipes including Swordfish Rolls Stuffed with Shrimp (page 79) or Sicilian Caponata with Pine Nuts and Raisins (page 92).

France

Throughout France, the French continue to favor simple, honest homestyle fare like Roast Chicken Stuffed with Bread and Garlic (page 184), Cassoulet (page 190), and French Apple Tart (page 210).

Rooted in tradition though they may be, French cooks also incorporate contemporary elements along with the classical. They employ lessons and techniques

derived from many different cultures—tropical fruit in Crab Salad with Mango (page 147) or Indian spices in Chicken Curry with Green Apple (page 177). Thus does a great cuisine continually renew itself.

The Mediterranean

Only the best, freshest seasonal ingredients are found in the Mediterranean kitchen. At restaurant kitchen doors and in the markets where homemakers shop, local farmers regularly stop by with a truckload of fresh vegetables and fruits, or perhaps a lamb or pig. Fishermen bring their daily catch, and cooks pull fresh greens from their own backyards.

This harvest, along with olive oil, aromatic herbs and abundant spices, is transformed into unpretentious yet irresistible food. The local touch shines through in dishes ranging from Spanish Garlic Shrimp (page 232) and Greek Spinach Filo Pie (page 252) to Turkish Grilled Lamb Skewers (page 316) and Portuguese Figs Stuffed with Chocolate and Almonds (page 331).

Bringing It Home

Throughout this book are features designed to make it simple to enjoy *Great Foods of the World* in your own home. Basic recipes for stocks, sauces and pasta dough enable you to prepare dishes easily from scratch. An illustrated glossary (pages 340–347) defines common ingredients, cooking procedures and equipment. Full-color photographs show you exactly how each finished dish should look.

So, whether you are making French Onion Soup Gratinée (page 126), Lasagne Bolognese (page 31), Paella (page 296) or Baklava (page 332), all the information you need to make an unforgettable dish is at your fingertips.

ITALY

Appetizers

Just inside the door of most Italian trattorias stands a table arrayed with the day's offering of *antipasti*—a warm welcome to all who enter. These appetizers glisten with freshness and hold the promise of a delectable meal to come. They are intended to whet the appetite, take the edge off the most ravenous hunger and complement the rest of the repast. This course may be limited to a single dish, or it may comprise two or three different selections made from those on display.

There are two basic categories of *antipasti,* those served cold and those presented hot. Both groups often reflect the region and season in which they are offered. *Antipasti* are usually based on vegetables, cheese or shellfish, with meat generally only a light accent. The most important characteristics of any *antipasti,* however, are that the preparations be simple and the ingredients perfectly fresh.

Whether you opt for a slice of toasted bread topped with tomatoes, a crisp salad or a skewer of grilled fresh shrimp, the *antipasto* offers a hint of the savory flavors to come. Enjoyed with an *aperitivo,* it is all you need to stave off the pangs of hunger until the first course arrives.

Sicilian Smoked Fish and Orange Salad

Typically Sicilian in its mixture of savory and sweet flavors, this dish is at its best in winter, when oranges are slightly tart and contrast vividly with the smoked fish and creamy cheese. Smoked trout makes an excellent substitute for the whitefish.

2   whole smoked whitefish, such as smoked chub, 1¼ lb (625 g) total weight

2   large juice oranges, peeled and all white pith removed

12 oil-cured black olives, pitted and cut in halves

6   oz (185 g) caciotta, provolone or Gouda cheese, rind removed and cut into ½-inch (12-mm) cubes

2   green (spring) onions, thinly sliced

2   tablespoons fresh oregano leaves or 2 teaspoons dried oregano

2   tablespoons extra-virgin olive oil
    Salt and ground white pepper

1   small head radicchio (red chicory), leaves separated

▣ Preheat an oven to 275°F (135°C).

▣ Wrap the fish in aluminum foil and place on a baking sheet in the center of the oven. Immediately reduce the heat to 225°F (105°C) and bake until warmed through, about 20 minutes. Remove from the oven and then from the foil.

▣ Transfer the fish to a cutting board and let cool briefly. Using a sharp knife, make 2 crosswise slashes, one below the gills and the other at the narrow part of the fish at the tail end, just until you reach the spine of the fish. Then, using the tip of the knife, make a lengthwise slash down the center of the fish, following the spine. Working from the center, lift off the skin and discard. Using the knife and a fork, lift one side of the fish fillet from the spine and transfer to a bowl. Lift the other side from the spine and transfer to the bowl. Turn the fish over and repeat with the other side. Flake the fish into bite-sized pieces.

▣ Slice each peeled orange crosswise into 3 thick rings. Cut each ring into small wedges by cutting between the membranes. Add to the bowl along with the olives, cheese, green onions, oregano and olive oil. Toss well. Season to taste with salt and white pepper.

▣ Place 1 or more radicchio leaves on each individual plate and top with an equal amount of the fish mixture. Serve at room temperature.

Serves 4

Bruschetta with Tomatoes, Beans and Fresh Herbs

In Tuscany, the city of Lucca is known for its outstanding olive oil, showcased here in the garlic-scented toast known as bruschetta. You can also serve the toasts topped with cured meats, marinated roasted peppers or other ingredients of your choosing.

TOPPING
1 cup (6 oz/185 g) seeded and diced ripe beefsteak tomato
¾ cup (5½ oz/170 g) well-drained cannellini beans (freshly cooked or canned)
¼ cup (1¼ oz/37 g) seeded and diced cucumber
2 tablespoons thinly sliced green (spring) onion
1 tablespoon fresh oregano leaves or 1½ teaspoons dried oregano
1 tablespoon chopped fresh basil or 1½ teaspoons dried basil
   Freshly ground pepper

BRUSCHETTA
8 slices country-style white or whole-wheat (wholemeal) bread, each 2½ inches (6 cm) wide and ½ inch (12 mm) thick
1 large clove garlic, cut in half
4 teaspoons extra-virgin olive oil

◼ To make the topping, in a bowl, combine all the topping ingredients, including pepper to taste. Toss well, cover and refrigerate for at least 1–2 hours or for up to 2 days to allow the flavors to blend.

◼ To make the bruschetta, preheat a broiler (griller) or prepare a fire in a charcoal grill. Arrange the bread slices on a rack on a broiler pan or on a grill rack and broil or grill for 2 minutes. Turn the bread slices over and continue to cook until golden,

1–2 minutes longer. Remove from the heat, rub a cut side of the garlic clove over one side of each warm bread slice and then brush with ½ teaspoon of the olive oil.

◼ Mound an equal amount of the topping on the garlic-rubbed side of each bread slice. Transfer to a platter and serve immediately.

Serves 4

16

Grilled Shrimp Wrapped in Prosciutto and Zucchini

Assembled in advance, quickly cooked and accompanied by bruschetta, these marinated and skewered shrimp are excellent fare for a backyard barbecue. Shrimp, and their close cousins, scampi, *are plentiful in the waters along Italy's lengthy coastline.*

MARINADE

1	tablespoon fresh lemon juice
2	tablespoons fruity Italian white wine
2	tablespoons extra-virgin olive oil
8	lemon zest strips, each about 2 inches (5 cm) long
½	teaspoon crumbled bay leaf
1	teaspoon fresh thyme leaves or ½ teaspoon dried thyme
3	large cloves garlic, crushed Freshly ground pepper

SHRIMP SKEWERS

1	lb (500 g) jumbo shrimp (prawns), peeled and deveined (12–16 shrimp)
1	lb (500 g) zucchini (courgettes), trimmed and cut lengthwise into slices ⅛ inch (3 mm) thick (12–16 slices)
6–8	paper-thin slices prosciutto, cut lengthwise into halves

BRUSCHETTA

8	slices country-style white bread, each ½ inch (12 mm) thick
1	large clove garlic, cut in half
4	teaspoons extra-virgin olive oil Small fresh thyme sprigs

To make the marinade, in a shallow nonaluminum bowl, combine all the marinade ingredients, including pepper to taste, and stir until blended.

To make the shrimp skewers, add the shrimp to the marinade and turn to coat. Cover and refrigerate for at least 4 hours or as long as overnight.

Remove the shrimp from the refrigerator about 30 minutes before you cook them. Meanwhile, soak 4 bamboo skewers in water to cover.

Preheat a broiler (griller) or prepare a fire in a charcoal grill. Arrange the zucchini slices on a rack in a broiler pan or on a grill rack and broil or grill for 3 minutes. Turn the slices over and continue to cook until limp, 2–3 minutes longer. Set aside to cool. Leave the broiler on or maintain the charcoal fire.

Remove the shrimp from the marinade, reserving the lemon zest strips. Drain the skewers. Wrap 1 piece of prosciutto around the center of each shrimp, and then wrap with a zucchini slice. Thread 3 or 4 wrapped shrimp onto each skewer and then garnish each skewer with 2 of the reserved lemon strips.

Arrange the skewers on the rack of the broiler pan or on the grill rack over hot coals. Broil or grill the shrimp for 3–4 minutes. Turn the shrimp over and continue to cook until pink and slightly curled, 2–3 minutes longer.

While the shrimp cook, make the bruschetta. Toast or grill the bread, turning once, until golden on both sides. Rub a cut side of the garlic clove over one side of each warm bread slice, then brush with ½ teaspoon of the olive oil.

To serve, arrange the bruschetta and skewers on a platter or divide among individual plates. Garnish with the thyme sprigs and serve at once.

Serves 4

Country–Style Spinach Crostini

Crostini, among the most typical Italian antipasti, are prevalent in Tuscany, where toppings may range from warm sautéed Swiss chard to simple stewed beans. Here, sautéed spinach is topped with creamy melted cheese to form crusty gratinéed toasts.

2 tablespoons extra-virgin olive oil

3 tablespoons finely chopped prosciutto

2 tablespoons chopped green (spring) onions

1 lb (500 g) spinach, stems removed and chopped

1 large egg

2 tablespoons freshly grated good-quality Italian Parmesan cheese

1 tablespoon heavy (double) cream
  Salt and ground white pepper
  Freshly grated nutmeg

8 slices country-style white or whole-wheat (wholemeal) bread, each 2½ inches (6 cm) wide and ½ inch (12 mm) thick

2 oz (60 g) Swiss or Emmenthaler cheese, cut into 8 equal slices

◻ In a frying pan over medium heat, warm the olive oil. Add the prosciutto and green onions and sauté until fragrant, about 1 minute. Raise the heat to high, add the spinach and sauté until barely wilted, 2–3 minutes. Transfer to a colander to drain, pressing against the spinach with a spoon to remove any excess liquid. Let cool.

◻ Preheat a broiler (griller).

◻ In a bowl, whisk the egg until blended. Whisk in the Parmesan cheese and cream until well mixed. Season to taste with salt, white pepper and nutmeg. Add the spinach mixture and stir until blended.

◻ Toast the bread until golden. Using a slotted spoon to drain off any excess liquid, arrange the spinach mixture on top of the toasted bread slices, dividing it evenly and making sure all edges of the toasts are covered to prevent burning. Lay a slice of cheese on top of each toast. Place on a rack in a broiler pan and broil (grill) until the cheese has just melted, 1–2 minutes.

◻ Transfer to a platter and serve immediately.

Serves 4

Sicilian Eggplant and Zucchini Rollatini

*The use of currants and pine nuts in this specialty of Palermo reflects the exotic influences—
Greek, Middle Eastern, North African—that have helped to shape Sicilian cooking. Eggplant
appears on many trattoria menus, in everything from pastas to grilled vegetable plates.*

1   large eggplant (aubergine),
     unpeeled

1   large zucchini (courgette)

3   tablespoons extra-virgin olive oil

STUFFING

⅔   cup (3 oz/90 g) dried bread
     crumbs

5   tablespoons (1¼ oz/37 g)
     chopped pine nuts

3   tablespoons dried currants

1½ oz (45 g) caciotta or provolone
     cheese, rind removed and
     chopped

3   tablespoons chopped fresh
     parsley

5   tablespoons (2 oz/60 g) diced
     Canadian bacon or smoked ham,
     optional

6   tablespoons (3 fl oz/90 ml)
     quick tomato sauce *(recipe on
     page 121)*

1   extra-large egg white, lightly
     beaten
     Salt and ground white pepper

TOPPING

1   cup (8 fl oz/250 ml) quick
     tomato sauce *(recipe on page 121)*

3   oz (90 g) caciotta or provolone
     cheese, rind removed and cut
     into 8 thin slices

◈ Preheat a broiler (griller). Slice the eggplant lengthwise into 8 slices each ¼ inch (6 mm) thick. Slice the zucchini lengthwise into 8 slices each ⅛ inch (3 mm) thick. Using about ¼ teaspoon of the olive oil for each side, lightly brush both sides of each eggplant and zucchini slice.

◈ Arrange the eggplant slices on a rack in a broiler pan and broil (grill) until barely cooked on one side, about 5 minutes. Turn the slices over and broil until lightly golden, 4–5 minutes longer. Remove from the broiler, transfer to a plate and let cool.

◈ Arrange the zucchini slices on the rack in the broiler pan and broil until barely cooked on one side, about 4 minutes. Turn the zucchini slices over and broil until just tender, 2–3 minutes longer. Remove the slices from the broiler, transfer to a plate and let cool.

◈ Position a rack in the middle of an oven and preheat to 400°F (200°C). Lightly brush the remaining olive oil over the bottom and sides of an 8-inch (20-cm) square nonmetal baking dish.

◈ To make the stuffing, in a bowl, stir together all the stuffing ingredients, including salt and white pepper to taste, until blended.

◈ To assemble the rollatini, on a clean work surface, lay 1 eggplant slice and place 1 zucchini slice on top of it. Using your fingertips, gently shape 2–3 tablespoons of the stuffing into a log and place in the center of the zucchini slice. Fold both ends of the eggplant and zucchini over the stuffing to cover fully, overlapping the ends. Place seam-side down in the prepared baking dish. Repeat with the remaining slices and stuffing.

◈ Cover the dish with aluminum foil and place in the center of the oven. Immediately reduce the heat to 350°F (180°C) and bake until heated through, 20–25 minutes.

◈ Spoon the tomato sauce evenly over the rolls and re-cover the dish. Bake until cooked through, 15–20 minutes. Divide the cheese slices evenly among the rollatini, placing them over the center of each roll. Bake, uncovered, until the cheese melts, 6–8 minutes.

◈ Remove from the oven and let stand for a few minutes. To serve, transfer 2 rolls to each warmed individual plate and serve immediately.

Serves 4

Stuffed Zucchini Flowers with Tomato-Mint Sauce

Gentle sautéing brings out the delightful peppery flavor of fresh zucchini flowers. In this simple preparation, the tender blossoms are filled with a sheep's milk cheese, then accented with a refreshing tomato-mint sauce. If you like, substitute mozzarella or Fontina for the caciotta or provolone.

16 zucchini (courgette) flowers, slightly closed

4 oz (125 g) caciotta or provolone cheese, rind removed

¼ cup (1½ oz/45 g) all-purpose (plain) flour

¼ cup (2 fl oz/60 ml) sunflower or safflower oil

TOMATO-MINT SAUCE

1 cup (8 fl oz/250 ml) quick tomato sauce *(recipe on page 121)*

2 large fresh mint leaves, thinly sliced, or ⅛ teaspoon dried mint

◈ Trim off the long stems from the flowers and carefully spread apart the petals slightly. Cut the cheese into 16 rectangles ½ inch (12 mm) wide by ½ inch (12 mm) thick by 1 inch (2.5 cm) long, or long enough to fit snugly inside the flowers. Insert 1 piece of cheese into each flower and close the petals over the cheese.

◈ Spread the flour on a plate. Gently roll each flower in the flour, carefully turning to coat lightly but evenly. Transfer to a plate.

◈ In a large frying pan over medium heat, warm the oil. When hot, add the stuffed flowers in a single layer and sauté for 2–3 minutes. Using 2 forks, carefully turn over the flowers and sauté until barely golden brown on the edges and the cheese has begun to melt, 1–2 minutes longer. The flowers should remain soft.

◈ Meanwhile, make the sauce. In a small saucepan over medium heat, warm the tomato sauce to a simmer. Add the mint and simmer for 1 minute longer.

◈ Using 2 forks, remove the flowers from the pan, draining any excess oil. Transfer to warmed individual plates, arranging 4 flowers on each plate with the stem ends toward the center. Spoon the tomato-mint sauce only over the stem end of each flower. Serve immediately.

Serves 4

Bocconcini Salad

*Bite-sized balls of mozzarella, known as bocconcini, are ideal for making this colorful salad.
Look for them in Italian delicatessens, or cut larger mozzarella balls into small chunks. If possible,
seek out* mozzarella di bufala, *made from water buffalo's milk; a specialty of central and
southern Italy, it is a softer, creamier mozzarella than that made from cow's milk.*

1	lb (500 g) mozzarella bocconcini
8	cherry tomatoes, cut in halves
½	cup (2½ oz/75 g) diced green bell pepper (capsicum)
½	cup (2½ oz/75 g) thickly sliced celery
½	cup (1½ oz/45 g) thickly sliced Belgian endive (chicory/witloof)
½	cup (1 oz/30 g) thickly sliced arugula (rocket)
1½	tablespoons fresh lemon juice
3	tablespoons extra-virgin olive oil
	Salt and freshly ground pepper
2	tablespoons fresh basil leaves or 1 tablespoon dried basil

◧ In a large salad bowl, combine the mozzarella, cherry tomatoes, bell pepper, celery, endive and arugula.

◧ Pour the lemon juice into a small bowl. Gradually add the olive oil, pouring it in a slow, steady stream and whisking constantly until emulsified.

◧ Pour the mixture over the salad and season to taste with salt and pepper. Toss until all the ingredients are thoroughly coated with the dressing.

◧ Sprinkle the basil over the salad and serve immediately.

Serves 4

First Courses

The *primo piatto* is arguably the most recognizably Italian course, for this is when the grain dishes—the pasta, risotto and polenta—are served. Italians pride themselves particularly on their pasta, which has long been a daily staple. It has sustained them through hardships and poverty, and has become so integral to the national diet that it is often eaten twice a day. According to reliable sources, there are more than 100 different varieties of pasta served in Italy today.

Also popular as a first course in northern and central Italy are risottos, made by slowly cooking short-grained Arborio, Vialone Nano or Carnaroli rice in flavorful broths. Stone-ground corn in the form of polenta is served in these regions as well, where it might appear topped with a ragù of roasted vegetables.

Soups, listed on menus as *minestre,* likewise make excellent first courses. Great Italian soups range from a summertime blend of tomatoes and bread to a heartier concoction of pasta and beans. And for those days when you want a simpler meal, all of these *primi piatti* are well suited for serving as a light main course.

Lasagna Bolognese

In Italy, small portions of lasagna are customarily served as a first course, but this hearty dish would also make an excellent main dish for four. The combination of a creamy white sauce, Parmesan cheese and a rich meat sauce—ragù bolognese—is typical of Bologna.

1   recipe spinach pasta dough *(recipe on pages 118–119),* or 1 lb (500 g) dried lasagne noodles

RAGÙ BOLOGNESE
3   tablespoons sunflower, safflower or canola oil
⅓   cup (2 oz/60 g) diced carrots
⅓   cup (2 oz/60 g) diced celery
⅓   cup (2 oz/60 g) diced yellow onion
6   oz (185 g) pancetta, coarsely ground (minced) or finely chopped
¾   lb (375 g) coarsely ground (minced) or finely chopped pork butt or shoulder
6   oz (185 g) coarsely ground (minced) or finely chopped veal
2   cans (28 oz/875 g each) plum (Roma) tomatoes, drained and chopped, plus juice from 1 can
     Salt and freshly ground pepper
     Freshly grated nutmeg

1   recipe white sauce *(recipe on page 32)*
     Ice water, as needed
½   lb (250 g) good-quality Parmesan cheese, freshly grated
     Salt and freshly ground pepper

◻ Make the spinach pasta dough, if using. Cover and let rest for 1 hour as directed, then roll out the dough about 1⁄16 inch (2 mm) thick. Cover with a damp cloth and set aside.

◻ To make the ragù, in a deep pot over low heat, warm the oil. Add the carrots and celery and sauté until the edges of the celery become translucent, about 5 minutes. Add the onion and sauté until almost translucent, about 5 minutes. Add the pancetta and cook, stirring occasionally, for 10 minutes. Then add the pork and veal and cook, stirring occasionally, until cooked but not browned, about 15 minutes. Add the tomatoes and juice and simmer, uncovered, stirring occasionally, until very thick, 2–2½ hours. Season to taste with salt, pepper and nutmeg.

◻ Cut the fresh pasta sheets, if using, into sixteen 4-by-10-inch (10-by-25-cm) strips. Prepare the white sauce and set aside.

◻ Fill a deep pot three-fourths full with salted water and bring to a rolling boil. Add the pasta all at once and gently stir to prevent the pasta from sticking together. Cook until not yet al dente, about 2 minutes for fresh pasta and 6 minutes for dried. Drain in a colander and immediately plunge the pasta into ice water to halt the cooking. Drain again and lay flat in a single layer on kitchen towels to dry briefly.

◻ Preheat an oven to 450°F (230°C). Select a 9-by-12-inch (23-by-30-cm) baking dish.

◻ Spread ½ cup (4 fl oz/125 ml) ragù over the bottom of the baking dish. Arrange a single layer of the pasta on top, being careful not to overlap. Spread ⅓ cup (2½ fl oz/80 ml) of the white sauce over the top and then top with another ½–⅔ cup (4–5 fl oz/125–160 ml) ragù. Sprinkle with 3–4 tablespoons of the Parmesan cheese, then season to taste with salt and pepper. Repeat with the pasta, sauces and cheese to make 7 pasta layers in all. Then arrange a final pasta layer on top and spread with only white sauce and cheese.

◻ Place in the center of the oven and immediately reduce the heat to 400°F (200°C). Bake until bubbling and golden brown, 35–45 minutes. Remove from oven and let stand for 5 minutes before cutting.

◻ To serve, cut into pieces and transfer to warmed individual plates.

Serves 8 as a first course, 4 as a main course

31

Cannelloni

*The meat-and-ricotta filling for these filled pasta tubes can also be used to stuff ravioli,
and the white sauce, known in Italian as* besciamella, *may be replaced by quick tomato sauce
(recipe on page 121). To simplify preparation further, use purchased pasta sheets.*

½ recipe basic egg pasta dough *(recipe on pages 118–119)* or 5 oz (155 g) purchased thin fresh pasta sheets

FILLING
2 teaspoons sunflower, safflower or canola oil
2 tablespoons minced yellow onion
¼ lb (125 g) ground (minced) pork shoulder or butt or ground veal
¼ lb (125 g) mortadella, ground (minced)
2 oz (60 g) prosciutto, ground (minced)
2 cups (1 lb/500 g) ricotta cheese
¾ cup (3 oz/90 g) freshly grated good-quality Parmesan cheese
Salt and ground white pepper
Freshly grated nutmeg

WHITE SAUCE
¼ cup (2 oz/60 g) unsalted butter
⅓ cup (2 oz/60 g) all-purpose (plain) flour
3 cups (24 fl oz/750 ml) milk, heated almost to a boil
Salt and ground white pepper
Freshly grated nutmeg

Ice water, as needed
cup (2 oz/60 g) freshly grated good-quality Parmesan cheese

◻ Make the basic pasta dough, if using. Cover with a bowl to prevent drying and set aside.

◻ To make the filling, in a small frying pan over medium heat, warm the oil. Add the onion and sauté until almost translucent, about 3 minutes. Add the pork or veal and simmer, stirring occasionally, for 5 minutes; do not allow to brown. Transfer to a colander to drain and let cool.

◻ In a bowl, combine the cooled meat mixture, mortadella, prosciutto and ricotta and Parmesan cheeses and mix well. Season to taste with salt, white pepper and nutmeg. Set aside.

◻ Roll out the basic pasta dough, if using, ⅟₁₆ inch (2 mm) thick. Cut the fresh or purchased sheets into eight 4½-inch (11.5-cm) squares. Set aside.

◻ To make the white sauce, in a saucepan over low heat, melt the butter. Whisk in the flour until blended, then gradually add the hot milk, whisking constantly. Simmer, whisking constantly and scraping the sides and bottom of the pan with a spatula as necessary to avoid burning, until the raw flour flavor dissipates, about 5 minutes. Remove from the heat and season to taste with salt, white pepper and nutmeg.

◻ Fill a deep pot three-fourths full with salted water and bring to a boil. Add the pasta all at once and stir gently to prevent sticking. Cook until not yet al dente, about 2 minutes. Drain, then plunge into ice water to halt the cooking. Drain again and lay flat in a single layer on kitchen towels to dry briefly.

◻ Preheat an oven to 450°F (230°C). Select a 9-by-12-inch (23-by-30-cm) baking dish. Spread 1 cup (8 fl oz/250 ml) of the white sauce over the bottom of the baking dish. To make the cannelloni, form about ⅓ cup (2 oz/60 g) of the filling into a log shape on the center of each pasta square and roll up into a cylinder. Place the rolls, seam side down, in a single layer in the dish. Evenly spread the remaining white sauce over the top. Sprinkle evenly with the cheese.

◻ Place in the center of the oven and immediately reduce the heat to 400°F (200°C). Bake until bubbling and golden brown on top, 30–35 minutes. Remove from oven and let stand for 5 minutes before serving.

◻ To serve, using a spatula, carefully transfer the cannelloni to warmed individual plates. Serve immediately.

Serves 8 as a first course, 4 as a main course

Orecchiette with Broccoli Rabe, Garlic and Pine Nuts

*A variety of small, round pasta shaped like little ears, orecchiette are typically found in southern
Italian trattorias, especially those in Apulia. Broccoli rabe has longer stems, smaller flower heads and
a somewhat more bitter flavor than regular broccoli, which can be substituted.*

1	lb (500 g) broccoli rabe
¾	lb (375 g) dried orecchiette
1	tablespoon unsalted butter
2	tablespoons extra-virgin olive oil
½	cup (2½ oz/75 g) finely chopped yellow onion
½	cup (2½ oz/75 g) pine nuts
1–2	fresh small red chilies, seeded and sliced into thin rings
4	teaspoons chopped garlic
1½	cups (12 fl oz/375 ml) vegetable or meat stock *(recipes on pages 120–121)*
2	tablespoons chopped fresh parsley
1	cup (1 oz/30 g) fresh cilantro leaves (fresh coriander), optional
	Salt and freshly ground pepper
	Freshly grated good-quality Italian Parmesan or pecorino romano cheese

◙ Trim any tough portions from the broccoli rabe, then cut the stems and leaves into 1-inch (2.5-cm) lengths; leave the florets whole. Place the stems on a steamer rack over (not touching) gently boiling water; cover and steam for 2–3 minutes. Add the leaves and florets and steam until cooked through yet firm when pierced with a fork, 2–3 minutes longer. Remove from the rack and set aside.

◙ Fill a deep pot three-fourths full with salted water and bring to a rolling boil. Add the pasta and stir gently to prevent the pasta from sticking together. Cook until al dente, 10–12 minutes or according to package directions.

◙ Meanwhile, in a large frying pan over medium heat, melt the butter with the olive oil. Add the onion and pine nuts and sauté until the onion is translucent and the pine nuts are lightly golden, about 3 minutes; do not allow the onion to brown. Add the chilies and garlic and sauté for a few seconds until very fragrant. Add the broccoli rabe and sauté for 2 minutes. Add the stock, bring to a boil, then reduce the heat to low and simmer for 1 minute.

◙ Drain the orecchiette briefly in a colander and immediately add it to the frying pan. Toss well. Add the parsley and cilantro, if using, and toss well again. Season to taste with salt and pepper.

◙ Transfer to a warmed serving bowl and sprinkle with the cheese. Serve immediately.

Serves 4

Penne with Arugula in Tomato–Cream Sauce

Combining tomato sauce with cream produces a delicate-looking rose-colored sauce whose mild, sweet flavor complements the slight saltiness of prosciutto and the pleasant pepperiness of arugula. Other tubular pastas, such as rigatoni, can be used in place of the penne.

3 oz (90 g) prosciutto, finely diced

1¾ cups (14 fl oz/440 ml) quick tomato sauce *(recipe on page 121)*

1 cup (8 fl oz/250 ml) heavy (double) cream

3 oz (90 g) arugula (rocket), stems removed and chopped
   Salt and ground white pepper

1 lb (500 g) dried penne

In a saucepan over medium heat, combine the prosciutto and tomato sauce. Bring to a simmer and simmer for 3–4 minutes. Pour in the cream, stir until blended and simmer for 1 minute. Add the arugula and cook just until wilted, about 1 minute longer. Season to taste with salt and white pepper.

Meanwhile, fill a deep pot three-fourths full with salted water and bring to a rolling boil. Add the pasta and stir gently to prevent the pasta from sticking together. Cook until al dente, 8–10 minutes or according to package directions. Drain the pasta briefly in a colander and immediately add it to the saucepan. Stir to mix well, coating the pasta with the sauce.

Transfer to a warmed serving platter or individual bowls and serve immediately.

Serves 4

Eggplant and Walnut Ravioli in Tomato-Pesto Sauce

Combine Genoa's signature pesto sauce with tomato sauce and you create pesto corto,
which tops these eggplant-stuffed ravioli and is also good on the region's local pasta ribbons, trenette.

FILLING

1	large eggplant (aubergine), peeled and cut crosswise into slices ½ inch (12 mm) thick
¼	cup (1 oz/30 g) walnuts, finely chopped
1	cup (8 oz/250 g) ricotta cheese
¼	cup (1 oz/30 g) freshly grated good-quality Parmesan cheese
4	teaspoons minced fresh parsley
2	tablespoons minced fresh basil
1	tablespoon minced fresh sage
	Salt and ground white pepper
1	recipe basic egg pasta dough *(recipe on pages 118–119)* or ¾ lb (375 g) purchased thin fresh pasta sheets

TOMATO-PESTO SAUCE

½	cup (½ oz/15 g) firmly packed fresh basil leaves
1½	teaspoons pine nuts
1	teaspoon finely chopped walnuts
1	clove garlic
3	tablespoons freshly grated Italian Parmesan cheese
⅓	cup (3 fl oz/80 ml) extra-virgin olive oil
	Salt and ground white pepper
1	tablespoon unsalted butter
¾	cup (6 fl oz/180 ml) quick tomato sauce *(recipe on page 121)*
1	wedge, 2 oz (60 g) Italian Parmesan cheese

◓ To make the filling, preheat a broiler (griller). Arrange the eggplant slices on a rack in a broiler pan and broil (grill) until lightly browned, 3–4 minutes. Turn the slices over and broil (grill) on the second side until lightly browned and tender, 2–3 minutes.

◓ Transfer the eggplant to a cutting board and cut into small pieces; you should have about 1 cup (8 oz/250 g). Place on kitchen towels to drain off any excess liquid and let cool.

◓ In a food processor fitted with the metal blade or in a blender, combine the eggplant, walnuts and ¼ cup (2 oz/60 g) of the ricotta cheese and purée until smooth. Transfer to a bowl and add the remaining ricotta and Parmesan cheeses, parsley, basil and sage and stir until blended. Cover and refrigerate for at least a few hours or for up to 1 day before using. Just before using, season to taste with salt and white pepper.

◓ Meanwhile, make the basic pasta dough, if using. Cover and let rest for 1 hour as directed, then roll out the dough ⅛ inch (3 mm) thick.

◓ Using a cookie cutter 2½ inches (6 cm) in diameter, cut out 64 disks from the fresh or purchased pasta sheets. Cover the disks with a damp kitchen towel to prevent drying; reserve any remaining pasta for another use. Place 1 teaspoon filling in the center of a disk, brush the edges of the disk with a little water, and top with a second disk. Gently press the edges together, sealing well. Place in a single layer on a rack until slightly dry to the touch, 1–2 hours.

◓ Meanwhile, make the pesto for the sauce. In a food processor fitted with the metal blade, purée the basil, pine nuts, walnuts and garlic. Add the cheese and blend well. With the processor on, pour in the oil in a steady stream until thick. Season to taste with salt and pepper.

◓ Fill a deep pot three-fourths full with salted water and bring to a rolling boil. Add the ravioli all at once. Gently stir to prevent sticking. Boil until al dente, 3–4 minutes.

◓ Meanwhile, in a large frying pan over medium heat, melt the butter and stir in the tomato sauce. Just before the ravioli are done, stir in the reserved pesto sauce.

◓ Drain the ravioli briefly in a colander and immediately add to the sauce. Stir gently to coat and arrange on warmed individual plates.

◓ Using a small, sharp knife or a vegetable peeler, shave thin slices from the Parmesan wedge and sprinkle over the ravioli. Serve at once.

Serves 8 as a first course, 4 as a main course

Genoa Pansotti with Artichokes

Along the Ligurian coast on the Gulf of Genoa in northwestern Italy, herbs grow in profusion.
They add their distinctive fragrance to a wealth of local fish and pasta dishes, including these pansotti
cloaked with an herb-laced butter sauce. Spinach or watercress may be substituted for the arugula.

FILLING

2 oz (60 g) steamed fresh artichoke hearts *(see glossary, page 340)* or thawed, frozen artichoke hearts

¼ cup (2 oz/60 g) ricotta cheese

2 tablespoons mascarpone cheese

½ cup (2 oz/60 g) freshly grated good-quality Italian Parmesan cheese

1 teaspoon minced arugula (rocket)

1 teaspoon minced fresh parsley

¼ teaspoon minced garlic
   Salt and ground white pepper
   Freshly grated nutmeg

½ recipe basic egg pasta dough *(recipe on pages 118–119)* or ½ lb (250 g) purchased thin fresh pasta sheets

SAUCE

¼ cup (2 oz/60 g) unsalted butter

½ cup (2½ oz/75 g) chopped steamed fresh artichoke hearts *(see glossary, page 340)* or thawed, frozen artichoke hearts

2 tablespoons chopped fresh parsley, basil, thyme, marjoram, sage or chives, or a mixture

¼ cup (½ oz/15 g) thinly sliced arugula (rocket)
   Salt and ground white pepper

▨ To make the filling, in a blender or in a food processor fitted with the metal blade, combine the artichokes and ricotta cheese and purée until smooth. In a bowl, combine the artichoke mixture, mascarpone and Parmesan cheeses, arugula, parsley and garlic. Using a spoon, stir until very smooth. Cover and refrigerate for at least 2 hours or for up to 1 day. Just before using, season to taste with salt, white pepper and nutmeg.

▨ Make the basic pasta dough, if using. Cover and let rest for 1 hour as directed, then roll out the dough ⅛ inch (3 mm) thick.

▨ Cut the fresh or purchased pasta into forty-eight 2-inch (5-cm) squares. Cover the squares with a damp kitchen towel to prevent them from drying; reserve any remaining pasta for another use. Place about ½ teaspoon filling in the center of each square. Brush the edges of the square with a little water and fold each square in half, forming a triangle and covering the filling completely. Stretch the pasta, if necessary, so the points of the triangle meet. Gently press the edges together, sealing well. Place in a single layer on a rack until slightly dry to the touch, 1–2 hours.

▨ Fill a deep pot three-fourths full with salted water and bring to a rolling boil. Add the pansotti all at once. Gently stir to prevent the pansotti from sticking together. Boil until al dente, 2–3 minutes.

▨ Meanwhile, make the sauce. In a large frying pan over low heat, melt the butter. Add the chopped artichoke hearts and sauté until heated through, about 1 minute. Drain the pasta briefly in a colander and immediately add it to the artichokes. Raise the heat to high and toss the pasta gently. Add the herbs and arugula and toss again until mixed.

▨ Season to taste with salt and white pepper. Transfer to warmed plates and serve immediately.

Serves 8 as a first course, 4 as a main course

41

Tagliatelle with Seafood, Sun–Dried Tomatoes and Olives

*Tagliatelle, a classic pasta of Bologna and the surrounding Emilia-Romagna region,
forms a delicate bed for a sauce of quickly sautéed seafood from the Adriatic coast. Fettuccine,
generally thicker and slightly narrower than tagliatelle, may be substituted.*

1	recipe basic egg pasta dough *(recipe on pages 118–119)* or 1 lb (500 g) purchased fresh or dried fettuccine

SAUCE

1	tablespoon unsalted butter
2	tablespoons minced shallots
2	cups (16 fl oz/500 ml) heavy (double) cream
¼	cup (2 fl oz/60 ml) dry Italian white wine
6	oz (185 g) medium shrimp (prawns), peeled, deveined and cut in halves lengthwise
¼	lb (125 g) sea scallops, sliced crosswise ¼ inch (6 mm) thick
½	cup (4 oz/125 g) oil-packed sun-dried tomatoes, drained and cut into thin julienne strips
½	cup (3 oz/90 g) oil-cured black olives, pitted and cut in halves
½	cup (2 oz/60 g) freshly grated good-quality Italian Parmesan cheese
	Salt and ground white pepper
	Freshly grated nutmeg

◼ Make the basic pasta dough, if using. Cover and let rest for 1 hour as directed, then roll out the dough about ¹⁄₁₆ inch (2 mm) thick. Cut into noodles ¼ inch (6 mm) wide. Separate the pasta strands and toss gently to prevent sticking. Set aside to dry for at least 30 minutes.

◼ To make the sauce, in a large frying pan over medium heat, melt the butter. Add the shallots and sauté until almost translucent, about 3 minutes. Pour in the cream and bring to a boil. Reduce the heat to medium and simmer, uncovered, until slightly thickened, about 6 minutes. Add the wine and simmer for 1 minute.

◼ Meanwhile, fill a deep pot three-fourths full with salted water and bring to a rolling boil. Add the pasta all at once. Gently stir to prevent the pasta from sticking together. Boil until al dente, 2–3 minutes for fresh pasta and 6–8 minutes for dried or according to package directions.

◼ While the pasta is cooking, add the shrimp, scallops and sun-dried tomatoes to the sauce and simmer for 1 minute. Add the olives and Parmesan cheese. Raise the heat to high and bring to a boil.

◼ Drain the pasta briefly in a colander and immediately add it to the sauce. Toss well and cook briefly until the pasta is very hot.

◼ Season to taste with salt, white pepper and nutmeg. Transfer to warmed individual plates and serve immediately.

Serves 4

Spinach Gnocchi in Gorgonzola Cream Sauce

On northern Italian trattoria tables during winter, you'll frequently find these little dumplings served as a warming, satisfying first course. For the lightest gnocchi, use yellow-fleshed potatoes such as Yukon Gold or Finnish Yellow; white-fleshed potatoes produce denser, but no less delicious, results.

SPINACH GNOCCHI

1¼ lb (625 g) fresh spinach, stems removed, or 1 package (10 oz/ 315 g) thawed, frozen leaf spinach

26 oz (815 g) yellow- or white-fleshed potatoes *(see note)*, unpeeled, cut into large pieces

2½ cups (12½ oz/390 g) all-purpose (plain) flour, plus ½ cup (2½ oz/ 75 g) flour for dusting

1 extra-large egg

GORGONZOLA SAUCE

2 cups (16 fl oz/500 ml) heavy (double) cream

2 oz (60 g) sweet Gorgonzola cheese, crumbled

3 tablespoons fruity Italian white wine

1 teaspoon Cognac or other brandy, optional
Salt and ground white pepper
Freshly grated nutmeg

To make the gnocchi, if using fresh spinach, place the spinach on a steamer rack over (not touching) boiling water. Cover and steam until wilted and tender, 3–4 minutes. Transfer the steamer rack holding the spinach to a sink to drain and let cool.

Using your hands, gather the cooled or thawed, frozen spinach into a ball; squeeze out any excess moisture. In a food processor fitted with the metal blade, purée the spinach until smooth. Transfer to paper towels, squeeze to remove any remaining moisture and set aside.

Place the potatoes on a steamer rack over (not touching) boiling water, cover and steam until tender, 8–10 minutes. Remove the potatoes from the steamer rack. While still hot, peel the potatoes, then pass them through a ricer onto a clean work surface, forming a broad, low mound. Sprinkle the 2½ cups (12½ oz/390 g) flour on top and quickly and gently "fluff" the potato and flour together with your fingertips.

Place the puréed spinach on top and, using a fork or your fingertips, begin to work it into the potato and flour mixture to form a dough. Place the egg on top and lightly mix it in. Press the dough together, then knead just until a dough forms.

Scrape the work surface clean. Sprinkle a little more flour on the work surface. Divide the dough into 6 equal portions; cover 5 of the portions with a kitchen towel to prevent drying. Form the sixth portion into a log ¾ inch (2 cm) in diameter. Cut crosswise into pieces ¾ inch (2 cm) wide. If the pieces are sticky, lightly coat them with some of the remaining flour. Repeat with the remaining 5 portions.

Fill a deep pot three-fourths full with salted water and bring to a rolling boil. Add the gnocchi all at once. Gently stir to prevent the gnocchi from sticking together. Boil until just cooked through, 12–15 minutes.

Meanwhile, make the Gorgonzola sauce. In a frying pan over high heat, bring the cream to a boil. Boil until slightly thickened, about 4 minutes. Stir in the cheese and reduce the heat to medium. Stir in the wine and simmer for 1 minute. Stir in the brandy, if using. Season to taste with salt, white pepper and nutmeg.

Drain the gnocchi and immediately add them to the sauce. Toss well to coat. Spoon onto warmed individual plates and serve immediately.

Serves 8 as a first course, 4 as a main course

Risotto with Saffron

*In Lombardy and the Piedmont, short-grained rice varieties such as Arborio, Vialone
Nano and Carnaroli are grown specifically for making risotto. If you like, prepare the risotto
partially in advance and finish the cooking about 15 minutes before serving.*

3	tablespoons unsalted butter
2	tablespoons minced shallots
1	cup (7 oz/220 g) rice *(see note)*
2½	cups (20 fl oz/625 ml) meat or vegetable stock *(recipes on pages 120–121)*, or as needed, heated
½	cup (4 fl oz/125 ml) dry Italian white wine, plus white wine to taste
	Generous pinch of powdered saffron (one 125-mg packet), optional
¼	cup (1 oz/30 g) freshly grated good-quality Italian Parmesan cheese, or to taste
	Salt and ground white pepper
	Freshly grated nutmeg

◙ In a deep saucepan over low heat, melt 2 tablespoons of the butter. Add the shallots and sauté until almost translucent, about 2 minutes. Stir in the rice, coating it thoroughly with the butter. Cook, stirring, until the edges of the grains are translucent, about 2 minutes.

◙ Add 1 cup (8 fl oz/250 ml) of the stock and simmer over medium heat, stirring occasionally, until the rice absorbs most of the stock and there is only a little visible liquid remaining, 5–6 minutes.

◙ Add another 1 cup (8 fl oz/250 ml) stock, stir to mix and again allow the rice to absorb most of the liquid, another 5–6 minutes. (At this point, you can remove the risotto from the heat and set aside for up to 2 hours.)

◙ Reduce the heat to medium-low, add the ½ cup (4 fl oz/125 ml) wine and saffron and stir to distribute the saffron evenly. Allow the rice to absorb most of the wine, stirring occasionally to prevent sticking. Add another ½ cup (4 fl oz/125 ml) stock and continue to simmer, stirring, for 4–5 minutes.

◙ Stir in the Parmesan cheese, the remaining 1 tablespoon butter and season to taste with salt, white pepper and nutmeg. The risotto should be al dente at this point. If it is too moist, simmer for a few minutes longer; if it is too dry, stir in a little additional stock to achieve the desired consistency. Taste and adjust with more wine, cheese and seasonings.

◙ Remove from the heat when there is a little more liquid than the desired amount, as the rice will continue to absorb it. To serve, mound the risotto in warmed shallow bowls and serve immediately.

Serves 4

47

Seafood Risotto

Laden with fresh mussels, shrimp and scallops, creamy rice and seafood stews like this one abound in the trattorias of Italy's coastal villages. To serve as a generous main dish, double all of the ingredients and increase the cooking time by about 10 minutes.

MUSSELS

1	tablespoon olive oil
1	tablespoon minced shallots
1	tablespoon minced garlic
½	cup (4 fl oz/125 ml) dry Italian white wine
48	mussels in the shell, beards removed and scrubbed

RISOTTO

2	tablespoons unsalted butter
2	tablespoons minced shallots
1	teaspoon minced garlic
1	cup (7 oz/220 g) Vialone Nano, Arborio or Carnaroli rice
1¾	cups (14 fl oz/440 ml) fish stock *(recipe on page 120),* or as needed, heated
⅔	cup (5 fl oz/160 ml) dry Italian white wine
4	small dried chilies, optional
1	cup (6 oz/185 g) peeled, seeded and chopped ripe plum (Roma) tomatoes (fresh or canned)
¼	lb (125 g) shrimp (prawns), peeled, deveined and chopped
¼	lb (125 g) sea or bay scallops, chopped
	Salt and ground white pepper
2	teaspoons chopped fresh parsley

To prepare the mussels, in a large frying pan over medium heat, warm the olive oil. Add the shallots and garlic and sauté for 1 minute. Pour in the wine and add the mussels, discarding any that do not close to the touch. Cover, raise the heat to high, and cook until the mussels open, 3–4 minutes. Remove from the heat and discard any mussels that did not open.

Transfer 32 mussels in their shells to a bowl; cover to keep warm. Remove and discard the shells from the remaining mussels, cover and set aside separately. Strain the broth through a fine-mesh sieve lined with cheesecloth (muslin) into another bowl; set aside.

To make the risotto, in a deep saucepan over low heat, melt the butter. Add the shallots and garlic and sauté until the shallots are almost translucent, about 2 minutes. Stir in the rice and cook, stirring, until the edges of the grains are translucent, about 2 minutes. Add enough fish stock to the mussel broth to make 2½–3 cups (20–24 fl oz/625–750 ml).

Add 1 cup (8 fl oz/250 ml) of the broth mixture to the rice and simmer over medium heat, stirring occasionally, until only a little visible liquid remains, 5–6 minutes. Stir in another ½ cup (4 fl oz/125 ml) of the broth

mixture and again allow the rice to absorb most of the liquid, another 3–4 minutes.

Add ½ cup (4 fl oz/125 ml) of the wine and the chilies, if using, and simmer over low heat, stirring occasionally, for 3–4 minutes. Stir in the tomatoes and simmer for 3 minutes. Add another 1 cup (8 fl oz/250 ml) broth mixture and simmer, stirring occasionally, for 5 minutes. Stir in the shrimp, scallops and shelled mussels and simmer for 2 minutes.

Stir in the remaining wine. Season to taste with salt and white pepper. The risotto should be al dente at this point. If it is too moist, simmer for a few minutes longer; if it is too dry, stir in a little additional stock to achieve the proper consistency. Remove and discard the chilies. Taste and adjust the seasoning.

Remove from the heat when there is still a little more liquid than desired, as the rice will continue to absorb it. Mound in warmed shallow bowls and surround each serving with 8 mussels. Sprinkle with the parsley and serve immediately.

Serves 4

Polenta with Roasted Vegetable Ragù

Creamy cooked polenta is a popular primo piatto. *You can also cook the polenta as directed, spread it on a baking sheet to a thickness of about ½ inch (12 mm) and let cool until set. Then cut it into 3-inch (7.5-cm) squares, bake, broil or fry until heated through and serve as a side dish or with a savory topping.*

ROASTED VEGETABLE RAGÙ

1   small butternut (pumpkin) squash, cut in half and seeds removed
1   small turnip, parsnip or rutabaga (swede), peeled and quartered
1   small zucchini (courgette), quartered
1   small eggplant (aubergine), peeled and quartered lengthwise
1   small green bell pepper (capsicum), halved and seeded
4   ripe tomatoes, about 1 lb (500 g)
1   leek, cut in half lengthwise and carefully washed
3   oz (90 g) fresh white mushrooms
2   tablespoons olive oil
1   cup (8 fl oz/250 ml) vegetable or meat stock *(recipes on pages 120–121)*
2   tablespoons dry white wine
    Salt and ground black pepper

POLENTA

4   cups (32 fl oz/1 l) water
2   tablespoons unsalted butter
1   cup (5 oz/155 g) coarse-grind polenta (quick-cooking or regular)
3   tablespoons fresh herbs, such as oregano, thyme and/or marjoram, or 1½ tablespoons dried herbs
¾   cup (3 oz/90 g) freshly grated good-quality Italian Parmesan cheese
    Salt and ground white pepper

☒ To roast the vegetables for the ragù, preheat an oven to 450°F (230°C). Put the butternut squash in a baking pan and place in the center of the oven. Bake, uncovered, until soft but not mushy when pierced, about 1 hour.

☒ About 40 minutes before the squash is ready, place all the other vegetables in a large baking pan, keeping each vegetable separate, and cover with aluminum foil. Place the second baking pan in the oven and bake for 15–20 minutes. Uncover and continue to bake until tender when pierced with a fork, 20–25 minutes longer. Remove all the vegetables from the oven and let cool.

☒ Peel the butternut squash. Cut the squash; turnip, parsnip or rutabaga; zucchini; eggplant; bell pepper and tomatoes into ½-inch (12-mm) dice. Thinly slice the leek crosswise, and quarter the mushrooms. Keep the vegetables separate.

☒ To make the ragù, in a saucepan over medium heat, warm the olive oil. Add the turnip, parsnip or rutabaga and leek and sauté for 1 minute. Raise the heat to high and add the zucchini, eggplant, bell pepper and mushrooms and sauté for 2 minutes. Add the squash and sauté for 1 minute. Add the tomatoes and sauté for 1 minute longer. Add the stock and bring to a boil, then reduce the heat to medium and simmer until the flavors are blended, 2–3 minutes. Add the wine and simmer for 1 minute longer. Season to taste with salt and black pepper. Keep warm.

☒ To make the polenta, in a deep saucepan over high heat, bring the water and butter to a boil. Slowly pour in the polenta while stirring continuously with a whisk. Allow the mixture to bubble, whisking constantly, for 1–2 minutes as it thickens. Reduce the heat to low and continue to simmer, whisking constantly to prevent burning and lumps from forming, until the polenta grains swell and are tender like porridge, about 5 minutes for quick-cooking polenta and 20 minutes for regular polenta or according to package directions. During the last few minutes of cooking, stir in the herbs and cheese and season to taste with salt and white pepper.

☒ Ladle the polenta onto warmed individual plates. Make a well in the center of each serving, ladle the ragù over the top and serve.

Serves 4

Four Seasons Pizza

Arguably the most popular pizza in Italy, the quattro stagioni *pie represents the four seasons in its use of toppings: artichokes for spring, olives for summer, mushrooms for autumn and prosciutto for winter.*

PIZZA DOUGH
2   teaspoons active dry yeast
⅔   cup (5 fl oz/160 ml) warm water, 105°–115°F (40°–46°C)
¼   teaspoon sugar
2   cups (10 oz/315 g) unbleached all-purpose (plain) flour, plus flour for dusting
     Salt and ground white pepper
1   tablespoon extra-virgin olive oil

PIZZA SAUCE
1   cup (8 fl oz/250 ml) quick tomato sauce *(recipe on page 121)* or purchased tomato sauce
2   teaspoons minced garlic
2   teaspoons fresh oregano leaves
1   tablespoon fresh basil leaves

     Cornmeal or semolina

TOPPING
2   tablespoons freshly grated good-quality Italian Parmesan cheese
3   oz (90 g) mozzarella cheese, thinly sliced
3   oz (90 g) smoked mozzarella cheese, thinly sliced
4   thin slices prosciutto or baked ham, halved lengthwise
4–8 fresh shiitake, cremini or white mushrooms, stems removed and brushed clean
6   oil-cured black olives, pitted and cut in halves
4   artichoke hearts, quartered lengthwise (drained, canned or thawed, frozen)

To make the pizza dough, in a small bowl, stir together the yeast, warm water and sugar and let stand until foamy, about 5 minutes.

Place the 2 cups (10 oz/315 g) flour and salt and white pepper to taste in a mixing bowl or in a food processor fitted with the metal blade. Add the oil, then the yeast mixture while stirring or processing continuously until the mixture begins to gather into a ball.

Transfer the dough to a lightly floured work surface and knead a few times until the dough feels smooth. Form into a ball and place in a bowl. Cover the bowl tightly with plastic wrap and let the dough rise in a warm place until doubled, about 1½ hours.

To make the pizza sauce, make ½ recipe (1 cup/8 fl oz/250 ml) quick tomato sauce, if using, adding the garlic, oregano and basil as directed. Set aside to cool. If using purchased tomato sauce, pour the sauce into a small saucepan and bring to a boil. Add the garlic, oregano and basil, reduce the heat to low and simmer for 2 minutes. Set aside to cool.

Sprinkle some cornmeal or semolina on a rimless baking sheet. Place the dough on the sheet and, using your fingertips, press and stretch the dough into a round 12 inches (30 cm) in diameter, forming a slight rim at the dough edge. Cover with a kitchen towel and let rise again in a warm place until tripled in height, about 1½ hours.

Place a pizza stone, if you have one, on the middle rack of an oven and preheat to 475°F (245°C).

Using a fork, pierce the dough in even intervals to allow steam to escape during cooking. Spread the tomato sauce over the dough round. Then, for the topping, scatter the Parmesan evenly over the sauce. Place the mozzarella cheeses in an even layer over the Parmesan cheese. Arrange the prosciutto, mushrooms, olives and artichokes on top, overlapping them with the cheeses.

Place the pizza in the center of the oven or, if you are using a pizza stone, slide the pizza from the sheet onto the stone. Immediately reduce the oven temperature to 425°F (220°C) and bake until the dough is cooked and the cheese is light golden brown, 25–30 minutes. Remove the pizza from the oven and let stand for a few minutes before serving.

To serve, slice into wedges and transfer to individual plates.

Serves 4

Tuscan Vegetable Soup

The addition of a grain imparts body and rich, earthy flavor to this hearty country soup. Spelt,
an ancient variety of wheat known in Italy as farro, *is highly prized in Tuscany for its pleasantly nutty*
flavor and slightly crunchy texture. Look for it in well-stocked Italian shops or health-food stores.

1 cup (7 oz/220 g) spelt, barley or long-grain white rice

4–5 cups (32–40 fl oz/1–1.25 l) water

2 broccoli stalks

1 small leek, white part only

1 small celery stalk

1 large carrot, peeled

2 tablespoons extra-virgin olive oil, plus olive oil for garnish

1 cup (4 oz/125 g) chopped yellow onion

1½ cups (9 oz/280 g) peeled, seeded and chopped plum (Roma) tomatoes (fresh or canned)

½ cup (2½ oz/75 g) peeled and thinly sliced white turnip

5 cups (40 fl oz/1.25 l) vegetable or meat stock *(recipes on pages 120–121)*

¾ cup (3½ oz/105 g) diagonally sliced green beans

1 small zucchini (courgette), cut in half lengthwise, then thinly sliced crosswise

Salt and freshly ground pepper

Freshly grated good-quality Italian Parmesan cheese

⊠ In a bowl, combine the spelt, barley or rice and 3 cups (24 fl oz/750 ml) of the water. Let stand for 1 hour.

⊠ Meanwhile, cut the broccoli, leek, celery and carrot into slices ¼ inch (6 mm) thick; set aside.

⊠ In a soup pot over low heat, warm the 2 tablespoons olive oil. Add the onion and sauté until translucent, about 5 minutes. Add the tomatoes and sauté for 2 minutes. Drain the spelt, barley or rice and add it to the pot, along with the turnip, broccoli, leek, celery and carrot. Cook, stirring, for 3 minutes.

⊠ Add the stock and another 1 cup (8 fl oz/250 ml) of the water. Bring to a boil, reduce the heat to low, cover and simmer for 15 minutes.

⊠ Add the green beans and zucchini, cover, and continue to simmer, stirring occasionally, until the vegetables are soft yet retain their shape and the grain is tender, 35–40 minutes. If the soup becomes too thick, stir in the remaining 1 cup (8 fl oz/250 ml) water. Season to taste with salt and pepper.

⊠ To serve, ladle the soup into warmed individual soup bowls. Lace each serving with a thin drizzle of olive oil and sprinkle the cheese on top. Serve immediately.

Serves 4

Summer Tomato-Bread Soup

*When summer's tomatoes are at their peak, Florentine trattorias combine them with stale bread
and fruity olive oil to make this seasonal soup. To capture the true Italian character of this rustic dish,
use a dense country-style white, whole-wheat (wholemeal) or mild brown loaf.*

1	lb (500 g) country-style bread *(see note)*
3	tablespoons extra-virgin olive oil, plus olive oil for garnish
2	small cloves garlic, thinly sliced
5–5½	lb (2.5–2.75 kg) ripe plum (Roma) or beefsteak tomatoes, peeled, seeded and chopped (7 cups/2⅔ lb/1.3 kg)
1	fresh sage leaf, minced
½	teaspoon minced fresh basil
	Salt and freshly ground pepper
3–4	cups (24–32 fl oz/750 ml–1 l) vegetable or meat stock *(recipes on pages 120–121)*
2	teaspoons red wine vinegar

◘ Trim off the crusts from the bread and cut the bread into 1-inch (2.5-cm) cubes; you should have about ½ lb (250 g). Place in a single layer on a tray and let dry, uncovered, overnight.

◘ In a deep, heavy-bottomed soup pot over low heat, warm the 3 table-spoons olive oil. Add the garlic and sauté until fragrant but not brown, about 1 minute. Add the bread and sauté for 2 minutes; do not allow to brown. Add the tomatoes and cook, stirring occasionally, until they begin to soften, about 5 minutes. Add the sage and basil and season to taste with salt and pepper.

◘ As the bread absorbs the tomatoes, add some of the stock as needed to keep the mixture soupy. At the same time, use a spoon to mash the bread so the soup is thick and the bread blends into the tomato sauce.

◘ Cook the soup, stirring occasionally to prevent burning, until thickened and no chunks of bread remain, 30–40 minutes. Remove from the heat and let rest for 30–60 minutes to allow the flavors to blend and develop.

◘ Return the pot to low heat and stir in the vinegar. Bring to a simmer and simmer until the sharp fumes of the vinegar have evaporated, about 1 minute. Taste and adjust the seasoning.

◘ To serve, ladle into warmed individual bowls and lightly drizzle olive oil on top.

Serves 4

Main Courses

The classic Italian meal builds to *il secondo piatto,* the main course. Literally translated as "the second plate," it follows gracefully on the heels of the more delicate *primo piatto* and is often accented with the full range of Mediterranean flavors—herbs, tomatoes, garlic, olives, capers and lemon.

During much of the year, poultry, meat and fish are rather simply prepared for this course, generally grilled, broiled or sautéed to preserve their fresh tastes and enticing aromas. In the winter, however, robust roasts, stews and braised dishes are more common fare. These are usually served family style in generous portions on platters or in bowls that are set in the center of the table for everyone to share. Grains and vegetables are traditionally offered on the side.

A variation is the *piatto unico,* or meal-in-one-dish: a balanced union of meat or fish and vegetables on a single plate. The southern Italian specialty of veal chops topped with bitter greens typifies such a preparation. Contemporary Italian cooking, in which swordfish rolls might conceal small caches of shrimp, has greatly expanded the repertoire of trattoria main courses.

59

Braised Veal Shanks with Lemon, Parsley and Garlic

Outside of Italy, ossobuco often lacks its distinctive topping of gremolata, a heady mixture of lemon zest, garlic and parsley. Offer polenta (recipe on page 50) instead of the risotto, if you like, and don't overlook the marrow concealed within the veal bones; spread it on toast for a delectable finale.

VEAL SHANKS

½   cup (2½ oz/75 g) unbleached all-purpose (plain) flour

4   veal shanks, about 4 lb (2 kg) total weight, each about 2 inches (5 cm) thick

2   tablespoons unsalted butter

2   tablespoons extra-virgin olive oil

½   cup (2½ oz/75 g) chopped yellow onion

½   cup (2½ oz/75 g) peeled, diced carrot

½   cup (2½ oz/75 g) diced celery

⅓   cup (2 oz/60 g) diced fennel

1   teaspoon minced garlic

2   teaspoons fresh marjoram leaves

2   teaspoons fresh thyme leaves

1   bay leaf

1¼ cups (8 oz/250 g) peeled, seeded and chopped tomatoes

1   cup (8 fl oz/250 ml) dry Italian white wine

2–3 cups (16–24 fl oz/500–750 ml) meat stock *(recipe on page 120)*
    Salt and freshly ground pepper

    Risotto with saffron *(recipe on page 47)*

GREMOLATA

½   cup (¾ oz/20 g) chopped fresh Italian (flat-leaf) parsley

1½ teaspoons minced lemon zest

½   teaspoon minced garlic

◼ To prepare the veal shanks, spread the flour on a plate and evenly coat the veal shanks with the flour, shaking off any excess.

◼ In a large frying pan or pot over medium-high heat, melt the butter with the olive oil. When hot, add the veal shanks and lightly brown on both sides, about 4 minutes per side. Remove the veal shanks from the pan and set aside.

◼ Reduce the heat to medium-low and add the onion, carrot, celery and fennel. Sauté until the edges of the onion are translucent, 3–4 minutes; do not allow to brown. Add the garlic, marjoram, thyme and bay leaf and stir until blended. Add the tomatoes and bring to a boil. Return the veal to the pan and cook for 1 minute. Raise the heat to high, pour in the wine and deglaze the pan by stirring to dislodge any browned bits from the pan bottom.

◼ When the mixture boils, add about 2 cups (16 fl oz/500 ml) of the stock; the liquid should reach three-fourths of the way up the sides of the veal shanks. Reduce the heat to medium-low, cover partially and simmer, turning the shanks over occasionally. Continue cooking, adding more stock as needed to keep the mixture moist, until the veal is tender when pierced with a fork and there are about 2 cups (16 fl oz/500 ml) of liquid and vegetables remaining, about 2½ hours. If there is too much liquid, uncover and boil gently to concentrate the broth. Season to taste with salt and pepper.

◼ While the stew is cooking, make the risotto. Just before serving, make the *gremolata* by tossing together the parsley, lemon zest and garlic in a small bowl until evenly mixed.

◼ To serve, discard the bay leaf. Place a mound of risotto on each individual plate. Place 1 veal shank on top of each mound of risotto. Spoon the broth and vegetables on top. Sprinkle with the *gremolata* and serve immediately.

Serves 4

Neapolitan–Style Braised Beef Braciole

A favorite dish in the trattorias of central and southern Italy is tender braciole,
beef slices concealing a filling of cheese and vegetables. Open a good Chianti or other
robust red wine both for cooking and enjoying with the meal.

1   lb (500 g) top beef round, cut into 4 thin slices

¼   lb (125 g) smoked baked ham, cut into 4 thin slices

¼   lb (125 g) provolone cheese, cut into 4 thin slices

2   tablespoons chopped fresh parsley

4   teaspoons minced garlic

3   tablespoons chopped, peeled carrot

4   teaspoons plus 2 tablespoons chopped celery

3   tablespoons extra-virgin olive oil

¼   cup (1½ oz/45 g) chopped red (Spanish) onion

½   cup (4 fl oz/125 ml) plus 2 tablespoons Italian red wine *(see note)*

2   cans (28 oz/875 g each) plum (Roma) tomatoes, drained and puréed (3½ cups/28 fl oz/875 ml purée)

Salt and freshly ground pepper

◻ Place each beef slice between 2 sheets of plastic wrap and, using a meat pounder, pound until ⅛ inch (3 mm) thick. Place 1 ham slice on top of each beef slice, and then top with a cheese slice.

◻ In a small bowl, mix together the parsley, 2 teaspoons of the garlic, 1 tablespoon of the carrot and the 4 teaspoons celery. Sprinkle the mixture evenly over the center of each cheese slice. Beginning at one end of each beef slice, tightly roll up and secure the seam with toothpicks. Seal the ends with toothpicks as well, to keep the filling from spilling out.

◻ In a deep saucepan over medium heat, warm the olive oil. Add the beef rolls and brown well on all sides, 4–5 minutes. Reduce the heat to medium-low, add the remaining 2 tablespoons carrot, 2 tablespoons celery and the onion and sauté for 2 minutes. Add the remaining 2 teaspoons garlic and sauté until fragrant, 1–2 minutes.

◻ Raise the heat to high, add the ½ cup (4 fl oz/125 ml) red wine and deglaze the pan by stirring to dislodge the browned bits from the pan bottom. Boil for 1 minute, then add the tomato purée. Return to a boil, then reduce the heat to low and simmer, uncovered, until the beef is tender when pierced with a fork, about 1½ hours.

◻ Add the remaining 2 tablespoons red wine and continue to simmer for 2 minutes longer. Season to taste with salt and pepper. Spoon onto warmed individual plates, remove the toothpicks, and serve immediately.

Serves 4

Roman Roast Lamb with Rosemary and Garlic

The appearance of roast lamb on trattoria menus, especially around Rome, traditionally signals the coming of spring. Cooking lamb in this manner yields especially tender, succulent results. To make carving easier, ask your butcher to crack the bones between the ribs.

2 racks of lamb, 8 chops per rack and about 4 lb (2 kg) total weight, cracked

¼ cup (2 fl oz/60 ml) sunflower or canola oil

Small fresh rosemary sprigs

Garlic cloves, cut into quarters lengthwise

2 cups (16 fl oz/500 ml) full-bodied Italian white wine, or as needed

Freshly ground pepper

Salt

Lemon wedges

▨ Using a sharp knife, score the fat on the top surface of the lamb to prevent curling and shrinking. In a large frying pan over high heat, warm the oil. When hot, add a lamb rack and brown on all sides, about 5 minutes. Place the rack, bone side down, in a large roasting pan. Repeat with the other rack.

▨ Preheat an oven to 450°F (230°C). Place rosemary and garlic between the chops, pushing them to the bottom where the bones are cracked and using whatever amount suits your taste. Stud the scored surface with rosemary and garlic as well. Pour white wine over the chops into the pan to a depth of ¼ inch (6 mm) and grind pepper over the racks.

▨ Place in the center of the oven, immediately reduce the heat to 400°F (200°C) and roast, basting once with the wine, until golden brown, about 1 hour.

▨ Remove the pan from the oven, baste the lamb again with the wine and cover with aluminum foil. Return to the oven and continue to roast for 20 minutes. Remove the foil, baste again, and continue to roast the lamb, uncovered, until the surface is deep brown and crisp, about 10 minutes longer.

▨ Transfer the lamb to a cutting board and let stand for 15 minutes before carving. If the lamb becomes cool, warm in a 225°F (105°C) oven for 2–3 minutes just before carving.

▨ Carve into chops and distribute among warmed individual plates. Season to taste with salt and pepper and garnish with lemon wedges.

Serves 4

Grilled Veal Chops with Salad

*Nothing could be more rustic and elegant at the same time: a succulent veal
chop straight from the charcoal grill, topped with an assortment of fresh bitter greens
and thinly sliced artichokes. The meat juices marry superbly with the greens,
forming the ideal trattoria piatto unico, or "meal in one dish."*

VEAL CHOPS
4 veal loin chops with bone, ½ lb
   (250 g) each
2 cloves garlic, cut in halves
   lengthwise
   Freshly ground pepper
4 teaspoons extra-virgin olive oil

SALAD
1 small bunch arugula (rocket),
   stems removed
2 radicchio (red chicory) leaves,
   sliced into thin shreds
4 Belgian endive (chicory/witloof)
   leaves, sliced into thin shreds
2 small artichokes, trimmed (raw or
   thawed, frozen), optional
1 wedge, 1 oz (30 g), good-
   quality Italian Parmesan cheese

4 lemon wedges
   Extra-virgin olive oil

▣ To prepare the veal chops, using a
sharp knife, slash the fat along the
edge of each chop in 3 places to
avoid curling during cooking. Place
each chop between 2 sheets of plastic
wrap and, using a meat pounder,
pound ½ inch (12 mm) thick. Rub
each chop all over with half of a garlic
clove, pepper to taste and 1 teaspoon
of the olive oil. Let stand at room
temperature for 1 hour.

▣ Preheat a broiler (griller) or prepare a fire in a charcoal grill.

▣ Arrange the chops on a rack in a
broiler pan or place on a grill rack
over hot coals. Broil or grill, turning
once, until done to your liking. For
rare, cook 2–3 minutes on the first
side and 1–2 minutes on the second;
for medium, cook 4–5 minutes on
the first side and 3–4 minutes on the
second; for well-done, cook 6–7
minutes on the first side and 5–6
minutes on the second.

▣ Transfer the chops to warmed
individual plates and scatter an equal
amount of arugula, radicchio and
endive over the top of each chop.
Thinly slice the artichokes lengthwise, if using, and scatter over the
salad. Using a sharp knife or vegetable peeler, shave off paper-thin
slices of the Parmesan and scatter
over the greens. Place a lemon
wedge on each plate and pass the
olive oil for drizzling over the top.

Serves 4

Broiled Chicken with Oregano, Lemon and Olives

This Mediterranean-inspired dish offers a wonderfully fragrant and subtly spicy way to serve broiled chicken. Because it is best served at room temperature, you can make it up to 1 hour in advance and serve as an al fresco dish for a picnic. If you like, substitute fresh rosemary leaves for the oregano.

1   chicken, 4 lb (2 kg)

MARINADE

2   tablespoons extra-virgin olive oil

2   tablespoons dry Italian white wine

6   large cloves garlic, crushed

4–6 teaspoons fresh oregano leaves or 2–3 teaspoons dried oregano
     Red pepper flakes or small whole red chilies (fresh or dried)

GARNISH
     Fresh oregano sprigs
     Zest from 1 lemon, cut into thin julienne strips

12   oil-cured black olives

12   cracked Sicilian green olives
     Red pepper flakes or small whole red chili peppers (fresh or dried)
     Salt

◼ Cut the chicken into 10 serving pieces.

◼ To make the marinade, in a large nonaluminum dish, combine all the marinade ingredients, including red pepper flakes or chilies to taste. Stir well, then add the chicken pieces. Toss to coat evenly, then cover and refrigerate for a few hours or as long as overnight. Remove from the refrigerator 1 hour before cooking.

◼ Preheat a broiler (griller) or prepare a fire in a charcoal grill.

◼ Place the chicken pieces, skin side down, on a rack in a broiler pan or on a grill rack over hot coals. Broil or grill until golden around the edges, 20–22 minutes. Turn the chicken over and continue to cook until golden brown around the edges on the second side and opaque throughout when cut with a knife, about 20 minutes longer.

◼ Transfer the chicken to a large serving platter and garnish with oregano sprigs, lemon zest, black and green olives and red pepper flakes or chilies to taste. Let rest for at least 30 minutes, to blend the flavors. Season to taste with salt and serve at room temperature

Serves 4

Stuffed Chicken Breasts in Mushroom–Wine Sauce

To make these easier to fill and roll, select the broadest chicken breasts you can find. Slices of turkey or veal can also be used for making this dish. If you like, you can assemble the rolls up to 2 hours in advance, cover and refrigerate, then flour and cook just before serving.

FILLING
2   teaspoons unsalted butter
2   tablespoons finely chopped yellow onion
1   teaspoon minced garlic
¾   lb (375 g) spinach, stems removed and chopped
3   tablespoons drained and chopped, oil-packed sun-dried tomatoes
2   tablespoons freshly grated good-quality Italian Parmesan cheese
    Salt and ground white pepper

4   skinless, boneless chicken breast halves, about ¼ lb (125 g) each
4   thin slices Emmenthaler cheese
2   tablespoons canola oil
½   cup (2½ oz/75 g) all–purpose (plain) flour

MUSHROOM-WINE SAUCE
2   teaspoons unsalted butter
⅛   cup (½ oz/15 g) thinly sliced yellow onion
½   lb (250 g) fresh white mushrooms, stems removed and thinly sliced
¼   cup (2 fl oz/60 ml) fruity Italian white wine
½   cup (4 fl oz/125 ml) meat or vegetable stock *(recipes on pages 120–121)*
¼   cup (2 fl oz/60 ml) heavy (double) cream
    Salt, ground white pepper and freshly grated nutmeg

▣ To make the filling, in a frying pan over medium heat, melt the butter. Add the onion and sauté for 1 minute. Raise the heat to medium-high, add the garlic and spinach and sauté until the spinach is wilted, 2–3 minutes. Stir in the sun-dried tomatoes. Transfer the spinach mixture to a colander and, using the back of a wooden spoon, press gently against the mixture to remove any excess moisture, then let cool. Wipe the frying pan clean and set aside.

▣ Transfer the spinach mixture to a bowl. Stir in the Parmesan cheese and season to taste with salt and white pepper. Set aside.

▣ Place each chicken breast between 2 sheets of plastic wrap and, using a meat pounder, pound until ¼ inch (6 mm) thick. Place 1 cheese slice on top of each pounded breast. Spoon one-fourth of the spinach filling onto the bottom center of each cheese slice and shape the filling into a log, being careful that it does not protrude over the edges. Fold the sides in toward the center and then, beginning at the bottom end, roll up tightly. Secure with toothpicks.

▣ Preheat an oven to 425°F (220°C). In the frying pan over medium-high heat, warm the oil. While the oil is heating, spread the flour on a plate.

Roll the stuffed chicken breasts in the flour, coating lightly and evenly. Add the chicken to the pan and brown lightly on all sides, 5–7 minutes.

▣ Using a slotted spatula, transfer the chicken to a baking dish. Place in the center of the oven and immediately reduce the heat to 375°F (190°C). Bake until cooked through, 10–12 minutes. Transfer to warmed individual plates and let stand for a few minutes. Remove the toothpicks.

▣ While the chicken is baking, make the mushroom-wine sauce. In a small frying pan over medium heat, melt the butter. Add the onion and sauté until the edges begin to turn translucent, about 2 minutes. Add the mushrooms and sauté until barely limp, about 2 minutes. Pour in the wine and deglaze the pan by stirring to dislodge any browned bits from the pan bottom. Cook over medium heat until the wine is reduced by half, about 2 minutes. Add the stock and simmer until reduced by half, 3–4 minutes. Pour in the cream and simmer until the sauce thickens slightly, 1–2 minutes. Season to taste with salt, white pepper and nutmeg.

▣ Spoon the sauce over the chicken and serve immediately.

Serves 4

Cornish Hens with Roasted Vegetables

In Italy, this fragrant dish would be made with a faraona (guinea hen), a species first brought to the country from Africa at the time of the Roman Empire when it was known as a Carthaginian or Numidian chicken. Try to find a young balsamic vinegar, aged only about five years, for the marinade.

2   fresh Cornish hens (spatchcocks), 3–4 lb (1.5–2 kg) total weight

MARINADE
⅓   cup (3 fl oz/80 ml) extra-virgin olive oil
½   cup (4 fl oz/125 ml) balsamic vinegar
1   tablespoon chopped garlic
3   tablespoons chopped shallots
4   teaspoons fresh rosemary leaves or 2 teaspoons dried rosemary
15   fresh sage leaves or 1 teaspoon ground dried sage
2   bay leaves
    Freshly ground pepper

VEGETABLES
2   large broccoli florets
2   large cauliflower florets
1   zucchini (courgette)
1   whole head garlic
2   yellow onions, cut in halves
1   cup (8 fl oz/250 ml) water, or as needed

❖ Cut each hen in half. To make the marinade, in a shallow nonaluminum dish, combine all the marinade ingredients, including pepper to taste. Place the hens in the marinade, turning to coat evenly. Cover and refrigerate overnight, turning once.

❖ To prepare the vegetables, preheat an oven to 450°F (230°C). Cut the broccoli and cauliflower florets lengthwise into smaller florets each about 2–3 inches (5–7.5 cm) in diameter. Cut the zucchini in half lengthwise and then cut in half crosswise to make quarters. Remove some outside layers of papery skin from the head of garlic and cut off the top one-fourth of the head, exposing the cloves.

❖ Arrange all the vegetables, including the onions, in the bottom of a deep roasting pan. Pour in the water to a depth of ⅛ inch (3 mm). Cover with aluminum foil. Place the pan in the center of the oven and immediately reduce the heat to 400°F (200°C). Roast for 15 minutes.

❖ Remove the pan from the oven, remove the foil and rest a flat roasting rack on the edges of the pan over (not touching) the vegetables. Remove the hens from the marinade, reserving the marinade, and place the hen halves on the rack, skin side down. Place in the center of the oven and continue roasting for 45 minutes.

❖ Remove the pan from the oven and drain off any excess water, leaving ⅛ inch (3 mm) in the bottom of the pan. Turn the vegetables over, and then turn the hen halves over, skin side up, and baste with the reserved marinade.

❖ Continue to roast until the hens are a deep brown and cooked through when cut with a knife and the vegetables are tender, about 30 minutes. (Check the vegetables during the last 15 minutes of roasting and remove them from the oven if done to your liking.)

❖ Remove the hens from the oven and let stand for 10 minutes. To serve, transfer to warmed individual plates, dividing the hens and vegetables evenly among them.

Serves 4

Duck with Vin Santo

Vin Santo, Italy's popular sherrylike wine, reputedly got its name in Florence around 1440, when Cardinal Bessarione sipped it at a banquet and declared, "Ma questo è un vino santo"—"Now there is a holy wine!" This dish can be served in two courses, with the sauce—thinned with 1 cup (8 fl oz/250 ml) meat stock—spooned over fettuccine as a first course, followed by the braised duckling pieces.

1	White Pekin or Long Island duckling, 5 lb (2.5 kg), preferably with giblets
2	tablespoons extra-virgin olive oil
¾	cup (4 oz/125 g) peeled, diced carrot
¾	cup (4 oz/125 g) diced celery
½	cup (4 fl oz/125 ml) water, or as needed
¾	cup (4 oz/125 g) diced yellow onion
3	oz (90 g) lean prosciutto, trimmed of fat and chopped
1	teaspoon minced garlic
2	fresh sage leaves or ¼ teaspoon dried sage
1	teaspoon fresh thyme leaves or ½ teaspoon dried thyme
1	teaspoon fresh marjoram leaves or ½ teaspoon dried marjoram
1	teaspoon fresh rosemary leaves or ½ teaspoon dried rosemary
½	bay leaf
1⅔	cups (13 fl oz/410 ml) Vin Santo
2½	cups (20 fl oz/625 ml) meat stock *(recipe on page 120)*

◉ Set the duck giblets aside, if included. Cut the duckling into 12 serving pieces. In a 5-qt (5-l) pot over medium-high heat, warm the olive oil. Add the duckling and brown evenly on all sides, 10–12 minutes. Transfer the duckling to a plate and pour off all but 1 tablespoon of the fat and oil from the pot.

◉ In the same pot over medium heat, add the carrot and celery and sauté, stirring occasionally and adding a little of the water as needed to prevent burning, until the edges of the celery begin to turn translucent, about 5 minutes. Add the onion and prosciutto and sauté, stirring occasionally and adding more water as needed to prevent burning, until the vegetables are barely soft but not browned, about 4 minutes.

◉ Return the duckling to the pan, along with the giblets, if using, the garlic, sage, thyme, marjoram, rosemary and bay leaf. Raise the heat to high, add the Vin Santo and deglaze the pan by stirring to dislodge any browned bits from the pan bottom.

Bring to a boil, reduce the heat to low, cover partially and simmer, stirring occasionally, for 15 minutes.

◉ Turn the duckling pieces over, add the stock and continue to simmer, partially covered, until the duckling is tender and there are about 2 cups (16 fl oz/500 ml) sauce remaining, about 2 hours. Remove the bay leaf and the giblets.

◉ To serve, skim off any fat from the surface and spoon the duckling and sauce into warmed individual serving dishes. Serve immediately.

Serves 4

Mediterranean Scallop Stew with Crostini

Scallops are harvested in abundance from the waters of the northern Adriatic Sea. In this dish, they are combined with the flavors of orange, fennel and herbs. Like many of the classic Italian seafood stews, this one is spooned over garlic-scented toasts known as crostini before serving.

1½ lb (750 g) bay or sea scallops
2   tablespoons extra-virgin olive oil, plus extra for brushing on bread
1⅓ cups (4 oz/125 g) sliced leeks, white part only
½   cup (2 oz/60 g) thinly sliced yellow onion
6   oz (185 g) pancetta, trimmed of fat and cut into thin strips
4   cloves garlic, thinly sliced, plus 1 clove garlic, cut in half
2   cups (12 oz/375) peeled, seeded and chopped plum (Roma) tomatoes (fresh or canned)
1½ cups (12 fl oz/375 ml) fruity Italian white wine
5   cups (40 fl oz/1.25 l) fish stock *(recipe on page 120)*
½   pound fresh white mushrooms, stems removed and sliced
4   tablespoons chopped fresh parsley
1   bay leaf
2   orange zest strips, each 2 inches (5 cm) long and ½ inch (12 mm) wide
½   teaspoon fresh thyme leaves
¼   teaspoon fennel seeds
⅛   teaspoon powdered saffron
    Salt and ground white pepper
4   slices country-style white bread
    Small fresh basil leaves
    Freshly grated good-quality Italian Parmesan cheese

◙ If using sea scallops, cut crosswise into slices ½ inch (12 mm) thick. Set aside.

◙ In a large saucepan or stockpot over medium heat, warm the 2 tablespoons olive oil. Add the leeks and onion and sauté until barely translucent, about 3 minutes; do not allow to brown. Add the pancetta and sauté for about 2 minutes to blend the flavors. Add the sliced garlic and tomatoes and sauté for 1 minute.

◙ Raise the heat to high, add 1¼ cups (10 fl oz/310 ml) of the wine and deglaze the pan by stirring to dislodge any browned bits from the pan bottom. Bring to a boil and add the stock, mushrooms, parsley, bay leaf, orange zest, thyme, fennel seeds and saffron. Return to a boil, then reduce the heat to medium and simmer, uncovered, for 15–20 minutes, to blend the flavors.

◙ Add the scallops and cook until not quite opaque in the center, 2–3 minutes. Add the remaining ¼ cup (2 fl oz/60 ml) wine and simmer until the scallops are just opaque throughout, about 1 minute longer. Remove the bay leaf and season to taste with salt and pepper.

◙ Meanwhile, toast the bread slices until golden. Rub a cut side of the halved garlic clove over one side of each warm bread slice and then brush with olive oil to taste.

◙ To serve, place 1 bread slice, garlic-rubbed side up, in the bottom of each of 4 warmed individual bowls. Ladle the stew over the bread slices. Garnish with the basil leaves and Parmesan cheese and serve immediately.

Serves 4

Swordfish Rolls Stuffed with Shrimp

Nearly any seaside trattoria in Sicily would be likely to have some variation of this skewered specialty on its menu. The skewers may be either baked, broiled or grilled.

4 boneless swordfish steaks, about 6 oz (185 g) each and ¾ inch (2 cm) thick

SHRIMP FILLING
¼ lb (125 g) shrimp (prawns)
¼ cup (1 oz/30 g) pine nuts
¼ cup (1 oz/30 g) freshly grated pecorino romano cheese
⅔ cup (3 oz/90 g) dried bread crumbs
2 tablespoons minced yellow onion
1 teaspoon minced garlic
2 teaspoons capers, rinsed
2 tablespoons chopped fresh parsley
⅓ cup (1 oz/30 g) chopped fresh white mushrooms
2 tablespoons white wine
2 teaspoons chopped fresh oregano
3 tablespoons chopped fresh basil
1 large egg, lightly beaten
Salt and ground white pepper

1 cup (4 oz/125 g) dried bread crumbs
½ cup (4 fl oz/125 ml) olive oil
12 bay leaves
1 cup (3½ oz/105 g) sliced yellow onion
3 cups (12 oz/375 g) sliced yellow squash or zucchini
1 cup (4 oz/125 g) sliced green bell pepper (capsicum)
¼ cup (2 fl oz/60 ml) white wine
8 oil-cured black olives, pitted
Salt and ground white pepper
Lemon wedges

■ Place 4 bamboo skewers in water to cover and let soak for about 30 minutes. Remove the skin from the swordfish steaks and discard. Place each steak between 2 sheets of plastic wrap and, using a meat pounder, pound ¼ inch (6 mm) thick. Then cut each piece in half to make 8 pieces in all. Set aside.

■ To make the filling, peel and devein the shrimp. Chop the shrimp and pine nuts and place them in a bowl. Add all the remaining filling ingredients, including salt and pepper to taste. Stir until well blended.

■ Place an equal portion of the filling in the center of each swordfish piece and gently shape it into a log; do not allow the filling to protrude over the edges of the fish. Roll up the swordfish to enclose the filling.

■ Spread the bread crumbs on a plate. Brush the swordfish rolls with ¼ cup (2 fl oz/60 ml) of the olive oil and then coat evenly with the bread crumbs. Drain the skewers and thread 2 rolls on each skewer, placing a bay leaf between each roll and a bay leaf on either end as well.

■ If baking the rolls, place the skewers in a baking pan. Preheat an oven to 450°F (230°C). Place the pan in the center of the oven and immediately reduce the heat to 400°F (200°C). Bake for 12 minutes. Turn over the rolls and continue to bake until the fish is opaque throughout, 12–14 minutes longer.

■ If broiling or grilling the rolls, preheat a broiler (griller) or prepare a fire in a charcoal grill. Place on a rack in a broiler pan or on a grill rack over hot coals and cook as directed for baked rolls.

■ In a frying pan over medium heat, warm the remaining olive oil. Add the onion and sauté until fragrant, about 1 minute. Add the squash or zucchini and sauté until almost tender when pierced, 3–4 minutes; do not brown and add a little water if needed to prevent sticking. Stir in the bell pepper and sauté for 1 minute. Raise the heat to high, add the wine and boil until the wine is reduced by half and the vegetables are tender but not mushy, 2–3 minutes. Stir in the olives and salt and white pepper to taste.

■ To serve, spoon the vegetables onto warmed individual plates and arrange the skewered rolls and a lemon wedge alongside. Serve hot.

Serves 4

Monkfish with Potatoes and Artichokes

Italian country cooks recognize the natural affinity between potatoes and artichokes, a marriage that is enhanced here by the mild sweetness of fennel and the mellow richness of monkfish. For the monkfish, you can substitute medallions of halibut, baby cod or haddock, or slices of mahi-mahi fillet.

4	small artichokes, trimmed *(see glossary, page 340)*
4	new potatoes
1½	lb (750 g) monkfish fillets
2	tablespoons unsalted butter
1	tablespoon extra-virgin olive oil
¼	cup (2 fl oz/60 ml) dry Italian white wine
2	tablespoons minced shallots
2	teaspoons thinly sliced garlic
⅓	cup (2 oz/60 g) diced fennel
4	ripe plum (Roma) tomatoes, peeled, seeded and cut into ½-inch (12-mm) dice
½	cup (4 fl oz/125 ml) fish stock *(recipe on page 120)*
	Salt and ground white pepper

❖ Place the trimmed artichokes and potatoes on a steamer rack over (not touching) boiling water. Cover and steam until tender when pierced with a fork, 5–7 minutes for the artichokes and 8–10 minutes for the potatoes. Remove the vegetables from the steamer rack. When cool enough to handle, cut the artichokes lengthwise into quarters; peel the potatoes and cut crosswise into slices ¼ inch (6 mm) thick.

❖ Preheat an oven to 225°F (105°C).

❖ Trim off any thick outer membrane of the monkfish and cut into medallions ½ inch (12 mm) thick. At the top of each individual plate, arrange 6–8 potato slices in a fan, overlapping them slightly. Place 4 artichoke quarters in a fan below them, overlapping the potatoes. Keep warm in the oven.

❖ In a large frying pan over medium-high heat, melt the butter with the olive oil. When the pan is hot, add the monkfish and cook until white on the first side, about 1 minute. Turn the monkfish over and cook for 1 minute longer. Pour in the wine, reduce the heat to medium, cover and simmer until the monkfish is just cooked through and tender, 2–3 minutes; do not overcook or the monkfish will become chewy. Remove the pan from the heat and transfer the monkfish to the plates, arranging the medallions at the base of the artichoke fan. Place in the warm oven.

❖ In the same pan over medium heat, add the shallots and garlic and sauté until fragrant, just a few seconds. Add the fennel and sauté for 1 minute. Raise the heat to high, add the tomatoes and sauté for 1 minute longer. Pour in the stock and cook over medium heat until reduced by one-third, or until the sauce thickens slightly and the fennel is cooked yet slightly firm, 2–3 minutes.

❖ Remove the sauce from the heat, season to taste with the salt and white pepper and spoon over the monkfish, artichokes and potatoes. Serve immediately.

Serves 4

Side Dishes

Vegetables are a traditional part of every Italian meal. They appear, usually combined with other ingredients, in the *antipasti, primi* and *secondi,* but they assume their proper status when listed under their own menu category of *contorni.* From these choices on the trattoria menu, diners order vegetables to accompany their main dishes.

Trattoria chefs employ simple cooking methods—roasting, baking, sautéing—to produce a wealth of classic vegetable dishes year-round. The featured ingredients usually represent the best the market has to offer that day, so little embellishment is needed to bring out the full, rich flavors. Vegetables are often cooked with a touch of onion, garlic and herbs and perhaps a light lacing of butter, olive oil or wine, so that the finished dish enhances rather than overwhelms the main-course selection.

While every region in Italy emphasizes its own special preparations for locally grown produce, fresh vegetables are universally appreciated. Sometimes a *contorno* even becomes the main dish. During the heat of summer, or when the main meal is eaten at lunchtime, Italians find a plate of cooked vegetables refreshingly restorative at the end of the day.

Oven-Roasted Potatoes with Rosemary and Garlic

All over Italy, trattorias prepare potatoes in this simple manner. For the best flavor, select yellow-fleshed potatoes such as Finnish Yellow or Yukon Gold, or white-fleshed Maine potatoes. Serve the potatoes with Roman roast lamb with rosemary and garlic (recipe on page 64), grilled veal chops with salad (page 67) or Cornish hens with roasted vegetables (page 72).

¼ cup (2 fl oz/60 ml) extra-virgin olive oil

12 large cloves garlic, lightly crushed

1½ lb (750 g) yellow-fleshed potatoes, peeled and cut into 1-inch (2.5-cm) pieces

8 fresh rosemary sprigs, or to taste
Salt and freshly ground pepper

◙ Preheat an oven to 425°F (220°C).

◙ In a metal baking pan over low heat, warm the olive oil and the garlic until the oil is hot and garlic flavor is released into the oil, 1–2 minutes. Remove from the heat.

◙ Meanwhile, fill a saucepan three-fourths full with water and bring to a boil. Place the potatoes in the boiling water for 10 seconds, then drain and immediately transfer the potatoes to the baking pan holding the garlic and oil, leaving a little water still dripping from the potatoes. (This step helps to prevent the potatoes from breaking during roasting.)

◙ Sprinkle the rosemary sprigs over the potatoes. Toss gently to coat the potatoes and rosemary thoroughly with the oil. Spread the potatoes out in a single layer in the baking pan.

◙ Place the pan in the center of the oven and immediately reduce the heat to 375°F (190°C). Roast, stirring 2 or 3 times for even browning, until the potatoes are golden brown with crisp edges and tender when pierced with a fork, about 1 hour. Season to taste with salt and pepper.

◙ To serve, transfer to a warmed serving dish and serve immediately.

Serves 4

Baked Fennel

Literally translated as cooking "in a bag," al cartoccio is a superb way to steam vegetables in their own juices, with virtually no added fat. Here, fennel, a native of the Mediterranean, comes out tender and moist, and with its licoricelike flavor wonderfully mellowed.

2   fennel bulbs, about 2 lb (1 kg) total weight
1½ teaspoons extra-virgin olive oil
4   cloves garlic, lightly crushed (optional)
    Salt and ground white pepper

▣ Preheat an oven to 450°F (230°C).

▣ If the stalks and feathery tops of the fennel bulbs are still intact, cut them off and reserve for another use or discard. Trim the stem ends and remove any bruised outer leaves. Cut each bulb lengthwise into sixths; the core portion will hold each wedge intact. Coat one side of a large sheet of aluminum foil with the olive oil.

▣ Arrange the fennel wedges on the oiled side of the foil, tuck the garlic, if using, among the wedges and season to taste with salt and white pepper. Fold the foil over, bring the edges together and fold them over twice to make a double seal. Place on a baking sheet.

▣ Place the baking sheet on a rack in the center of the oven and immediately reduce the heat to 400°F (200°C). Bake for 15 minutes. Turn the pouch over and bake until fragrant and the fennel is tender when pierced with a fork, 10–15 minutes longer. To test for doneness, remove the pouch from the oven, unfold one corner and test with a fork. Seal and bake for a few more minutes longer if the fennel is not tender.

▣ To serve, remove the fennel from the pouch and transfer to a warmed serving dish. Serve warm.

Serves 4

Venetian-Style Beans with Swiss Chard

Combining beans, fresh herbs, anchovies and garlic, this Venetian side dish offers new flavors with every bite. Serve it as an antipasto *or a vegetarian* secondo piatto *accompanied with broiled mushrooms and tomatoes or steamed vegetables and garlic-rubbed bruschetta (recipe on page 16).*

BEANS

1½	cups (8 oz/250 g) dried borlotti or cranberry beans
1	carrot
1	celery stalk
½	yellow onion
1	bay leaf

DRESSING

4	tablespoons (2 fl oz/60 ml) extra-virgin olive oil
1	lb (500 g) Swiss chard leaves (silverbeet), stems trimmed and leaves cut into strips 2 inches (5 cm) wide
3	tablespoons minced shallots
2	tablespoons minced garlic
1	oil-packed anchovy fillet, rinsed and mashed (optional)
¾	cup (6 fl oz/180 ml) vegetable stock *(recipe on page 121)*
3	tablespoons chopped fresh parsley
2	tablespoons chopped fresh basil
2	teaspoons chopped fresh mint or 1 teaspoon dried mint
2	teaspoons chopped fresh sage or 1 teaspoon dried sage
2	teaspoons fresh thyme leaves or 1 teaspoon dried thyme
2	teaspoons fresh marjoram leaves or 1 teaspoon dried marjoram
1½	tablespoons red wine vinegar
	Salt and freshly ground pepper

Chopped fresh basil or parsley

◼ To prepare the beans, sort through them and discard any misshapen beans or stones. Rinse and place in a bowl. Add water to cover and let stand for 2–3 hours. Drain. In a saucepan, combine the beans with water to cover. Bring to a boil, then drain immediately. Re-cover with water, again bring to a boil and drain.

◼ Return the beans to the pan and add the carrot, celery, onion, bay leaf and water just to cover. Bring to a boil, then reduce the heat to low and simmer, uncovered, until the beans are tender but not mushy, 25–30 minutes. Remove from the heat and let cool for 10 minutes, then drain and discard the liquid, vegetables and bay leaf. Set the beans aside.

◼ To make the dressing, in a frying pan over medium heat, warm 3 tablespoons of the olive oil. Add the Swiss chard and sauté until almost limp, 3–4 minutes. Add the remaining 1 tablespoon olive oil, the shallots and garlic and sauté until fragrant, about 30 seconds; do not allow to brown. Add the anchovy, if using, and stir for a few seconds until fragrant. Add the stock and bring to a boil. Add the reserved beans and stir until hot, 2–3 minutes.

◼ Add the parsley, basil, mint, sage, thyme and marjoram and stir until blended. Add the vinegar and stir for a few seconds to release the sharp vinegar fumes. Remove from the heat and season to taste with salt and pepper. Let cool, cover and refrigerate overnight to allow the flavors to develop.

◼ The next day, transfer to a serving dish, garnish with basil or parsley and serve at room temperature.

Serves 4

Sautéed Mushrooms with Onion, Garlic and Parsley

The term trifolati *comes from the old Umbrian word for truffle,* trifole, *suggesting the rich aromas that result from cooking any mushrooms with a mixture of onion, garlic, parsley and wine. Select a diverse mixture of fresh mushrooms, including white mushrooms, portobellos, cremini and any wild varieties. Serve as a side dish to roasted meats or spoon atop bruschetta (recipe on page 16) or veal scaloppine.*

1   package (¾ oz/20 g) dried porcini
1   cup (8 fl oz/250 ml) cool water
1   tablespoon extra-virgin olive oil
2   tablespoons minced yellow onion
1   tablespoon minced garlic
1   lb (500 g) assorted fresh mushrooms *(see note)*, stems removed, brushed clean and sliced
¼   cup (½ oz/15 g) minced fresh parsley
¼   cup (2 fl oz/60 ml) dry Italian white wine
     Salt and freshly ground pepper

In a bowl, combine the porcini and water. Let stand until softened, about 20 minutes. Remove the porcini, reserving the liquid. Clean the porcini, if needed, and chop coarsely. Strain the porcini liquid through a fine-mesh sieve lined with cheesecloth (muslin) into a clean container, then discard all but ¼ cup (2 fl oz/60 ml) of the liquid.

In a frying pan over medium heat, warm the olive oil. When hot, add the onion and garlic and sauté until fragrant, about 30 seconds; do not allow to brown. Add the porcini and fresh mushrooms and continue to sauté over medium heat, stirring continuously to prevent burning, until slightly limp, about 3 minutes.

Add the ¼ cup (2 fl oz/60 ml) reserved porcini liquid and simmer for 3 minutes. Add the parsley and white wine and simmer over medium heat until there is only ¼ cup (2 fl oz/60 ml) liquid remaining, 8–10 minutes.

Season to taste with salt and pepper. Transfer to a warmed serving dish and serve immediately.

Serves 4

Sicilian Caponata with Pine Nuts and Raisins

This traditional Sicilian eggplant dish gets its delicate sweet-sour flavor from the combination of sugar, raisins, vinegar and capers. Every village on the island prepares its own version of the mixture, adding ingredients according to local custom.

1 large eggplant (aubergine),
   1½ lb (750 g), unpeeled, cut
   into 1½-inch (4-cm) cubes
   Salt
   Sunflower or canola oil
1 yellow onion
1 zucchini (courgette)
2 celery stalks, cut into slices
   ½ inch (12 mm) thick
2 cups (16 fl oz/500 ml) quick
   tomato sauce *(recipe on page 121)*
3–4 teaspoons sugar
2 tablespoons red wine vinegar
¼ cup (1 oz/30 g) pine nuts
¼ cup (1½ oz/45 g) raisins
2 teaspoons capers, rinsed and
   patted dry (optional)
   Salt and freshly ground pepper

◼ Place the eggplant cubes in a colander and sprinkle with salt, tossing to coat evenly. Let stand for 1 hour to release any excess moisture. Pat dry with paper towels.

◼ In a large frying pan, pour in the oil to a depth of ½ inch (12 mm). Heat to 400°F (200°C) on a deep-fat frying thermometer, or until a cube of eggplant dropped into the oil begins to brown immediately. Add the eggplant and fry, turning, until golden on all sides, 12–15 minutes.

◼ Using a slotted spoon, transfer the eggplant to a colander to drain for about 20 minutes. Using paper towels, gently blot the eggplant to remove any excess oil. Set the eggplant aside. Pour off all but 1 tablespoon of the oil and set the frying pan aside; reserve the remaining oil for other uses.

◼ Cut the onion crosswise into 3 thick rings and then cut into 1-inch (2.5-cm) cubes. Quarter the zucchini lengthwise, then cut into 1-inch (2.5-cm) cubes.

◼ Place the frying pan used for cooking the eggplant over medium heat. Add the onion and sauté for 1 minute. Add the zucchini and sauté

for another minute. Then stir in the celery and sauté for 1 minute longer. Stir in the tomato sauce and bring to a boil over medium heat, stirring occasionally. Add the eggplant, sugar to taste and vinegar and mix well. Reduce the heat to low and simmer, uncovered, until the sauce is thick and the vegetables are tender, 25–30 minutes.

◼ Meanwhile, toast the pine nuts. Preheat an oven to 325°F (165°C). Spread the nuts in a single layer on a baking sheet and toast, stirring occasionally, until golden, 8–10 minutes.

◼ Remove the eggplant mixture from the heat and stir in the toasted pine nuts, raisins and the capers, if using. Season to taste with salt and pepper. Let cool, then cover and chill for at least 1 day or for up to 3 days to blend the flavors.

◼ Before serving, using a large spoon, remove any oil that has solidified on the surface, then taste and adjust the seasonings. Serve at room temperature.

Serves 4

Desserts

A symbol of every family-operated trattoria are the pastries of *la nonna,* sweets made in the style of a grandmother and passed down through the generations. In many of Italy's best small restaurants, these pastries, along with other *dolci,* are presented on a long banquet table or a cart positioned in the center of the dining room to tempt visitors throughout the meal.

Seasonal fruits poached or made into a *sorbetto* or crisp *biscotti* dipped into dessert wines are favorite ways to conclude a meal. And although cheese is also increasingly popular as part of large repasts, it is more commonly offered as an *intermezzo*—that is, before the dessert.

A fresh peach *crostata,* filled with fruit marmalade and made with a traditional flaky butter pastry or a crispier olive oil–based alternative, exemplifies the Italian mastery of simple yet elegant desserts. Reserve the peach juice from the marmalade and use a few drops to flavor a sparkling white wine for enjoying along with the tart. A dessert of buttery lemon wafers, layered with a creamy filling that has been infused with chamomile and surrounded by berries, is an ideal conclusion to any summer meal, while a warm chocolate torte is the perfect ending for most winter repasts.

Sweet Gorgonzola with Baked Figs and Honey

Serving cheese as dessert, or just preceding dessert, is a European tradition. Here, the rich flavors of the cheese and the baked figs are offset by an extraordinary balance of sweet honey and the peppery nature of arugula. Select a sweet, not salty, cheese at its peak of ripeness. Offer thinly sliced walnut bread on the side and accompany with a sweet wine such as a Moscato or Malvasia.

4   firm yet ripe figs

1½   teaspoons extra-virgin olive oil

10   oz (315 g) sweet Gorgonzola cheese, rind removed and cut into 4 equal pieces

4   tablespoons (3 oz/90 g) acacia or wildflower honey

12   arugula (rocket) sprigs

◎ Preheat an oven to 475°F (245°C).

◎ Snip off the pointed tips of the figs and brush the fruits with the olive oil. Arrange in a small baking pan. Place in the center of the oven and immediately reduce the heat to 425°F (220°C). Bake until puffed and aromatic, about 10 minutes. Remove from the oven and let cool.

◎ Cut an X in the top of each fig and fold the corners back to resemble a flower, or split in half lengthwise. On each plate, attractively arrange 1 piece Gorgonzola, 1 fig and 3 arugula sprigs and drizzle with 1 tablespoon honey. Serve immediately.

Serves 4

Poached Autumn Pears with Mascarpone and Ginger

In Italy, autumn's choicest pears are often poached with sugar in a dry white or red wine. This recipe departs from convention, cooking them instead in a naturally sweet dessert wine. One of the best wines to use is Moscato d'Asti from Piedmont, which is made in both sparkling and still forms, and becomes a delicious honeylike syrup when reduced. If unavailable, any light, fruity dessert wine would do nicely.

POACHED PEARS
2   large ripe pears
1½ cups (12 fl oz/375 ml)
    Moscato d'Asti wine *(see note)*
1   stick cinnamon, 3 inches (7.5 cm)
    long, broken in half
½   teaspoon allspice berries or
    1 whole clove

TOPPING
½   cup (3 oz/90 g) mascarpone
    cheese
2   teaspoons confectioners' (icing)
    sugar, or to taste
1   teaspoon milk
2   teaspoons chopped candied
    ginger
4   fresh mint sprigs, optional

To poach the pears, cut the pears in half lengthwise, then core and peel the halves. In a saucepan, combine the wine, cinnamon and allspice berries or the clove and bring to a boil.

Place the pears in the liquid, cored side down, reduce the heat to medium-low and simmer for 4–5 minutes. Turn the pears over and poach until barely soft when pierced with a sharp knife, 4–5 minutes longer. Using a slotted spoon, carefully place each pear half, cored side down, in the center of an individual plate.

Reduce the poaching liquid over medium heat until it forms a thick syrup, about 5 minutes. Strain through a fine-mesh sieve into a clean container. Discard the contents of the sieve.

To make the topping, in a small bowl, whisk together the mascarpone, sugar and milk until smooth.

To serve, cut each pear half into a fan shape: Hold a paring knife at a 45-degree angle to the pear, and make slashes completely through it, but leave the top intact. Gently press on the slices to spread them out, and then drizzle the reduced syrup over the top. Put a dollop of the mascarpone mixture at the top of each pear. Sprinkle evenly with the candied ginger and garnish with the mint sprigs, if desired.

Serves 4

Fresh Peach Tart

Pasta frolla, *the classic Italian pastry dough, may also be made with butter for a flakier crust: use*
¾ cup (6 oz/185 g) chilled unsalted butter, cut into pieces, for the oil, only 1 egg and omit the vinegar.

FILLING
3½ lb (1.75 kg) ripe yet firm
     yellow peaches, peeled, pitted
     and chopped
½   cup (4 oz/125 g) sugar or ⅓ cup
     (3½ oz/105 g) honey, or to taste
½   cup (4 fl oz/125 ml) dry Italian
     white wine

PASTRY
¼   cup (1 oz/30 g) slivered blanched
     almonds
½   cup (4 oz/125 g) sugar
2   cups (10 oz/315 g) all-purpose
     (plain) flour
     Pinch of baking soda (bicarbon-
     ate of soda)
     Pinch of salt
2   extra-large eggs
2   teaspoons vanilla extract (essence)
¾   teaspoon minced lemon zest
¾   teaspoon minced orange zest
⅓   cup (2½ fl oz/80 ml) mild-
     flavored extra-virgin olive oil
1   teaspoon distilled white vinegar

▨ To make the filling, in a bowl, toss together the peaches and sugar or honey; let stand for 1 hour. Then, in a saucepan, combine the peaches and wine. Bring to a boil, reduce the heat to low and simmer, uncovered, until soft, 60–70 minutes. Drain and let cool.

▨ To make the pastry, in a food pro-cessor fitted with the metal blade or in a blender, combine the almonds and a little bit of the sugar. Process until finely ground. If using a blender, pour the nut mixture into the bowl of an electric mixer. To the processor or mixer, add the remaining sugar, the flour, baking soda and salt. Pulse or beat briefly until blended.

▨ In a small bowl, whisk together the eggs, vanilla and lemon and orange zests; set aside. Turn the pro-cessor on or set the mixer on low speed (using a paddle attachment if you have one) and pour in the oil, then the vinegar, and finally the egg mixture, mixing for only a few sec-onds until a ball of dough forms. Divide into 2 portions, one twice as large as the other. Cover and refrig-erate the smaller portion.

▨ Preheat an oven to 425°F (220°C). Place the larger dough portion be-tween 2 sheets of flour-dusted waxed paper. Roll into a round about 11 inches (28 cm) in diameter and ⅛ inch (3 mm) thick. Peel off one piece of paper and transfer the round, paper side up, to a tart pan with a removable bottom 9 inches (23 cm) in diameter and 1¼ inches (3 cm) deep. Remove the remaining paper and press the pastry into the pan; trim off the overhang. Spread the filling over the pastry.

▨ Roll out the remaining dough portion in the same manner, forming a round 9 inches (23 cm) in diameter. Using a fluted or plain pastry wheel, cut into strips ½ inch (12 mm) wide. Using longer strips near the center, place half of the strips about ½ inch (12 mm) apart on top of the pie. Place the remaining strips at a right angle to the first strips, forming a lat-tice; trim off any overhang. Press the strips against the rim to seal securely.

▨ Place on a baking sheet and put in the center of the oven. Reduce the heat to 375°F (190°C) and bake for 25–30 minutes. Rotate the tart to ensure even browning and reduce the heat to 300°F (150°C). Continue to bake until the crust is golden and the filling puffs slightly, 20–25 min-utes longer. Let cool before serving.

Makes one 9-inch (23-cm) tart; serves 8–10

Almond Biscotti

Biscotti means "twice-baked"; the first baking cooks the loaf of cookie dough and the second baking dries out and crisps the sliced cookies. Throughout Italy, an assortment of biscotti and other sweets are traditionally served with a glass of Vin Santo or an espresso or cappuccino for dipping.

½ cup (4 oz/125 g) unsalted butter, chilled

1 cup (8 oz/250 g) sugar

2 extra-large eggs, at room temperature

2⅓ cups (11½ oz/360 g) unbleached all–purpose (plain) flour

1 cup (4½ oz/140 g) slivered blanched almonds, chopped

2 teaspoons minced lemon zest

2 teaspoons fresh lemon juice

2¼ teaspoons aniseeds

1½ teaspoons baking powder

¼ teaspoon salt

1 tablespoon vanilla extract (essence)

1 teaspoon almond extract (essence)

◙ Preheat an oven to 375°F (190°C). Line 2 baking sheets with parchment (baking) paper.

◙ In a mixing bowl, using an electric mixer set on medium speed, beat together the butter and sugar until light and fluffy, 2–3 minutes. Beat in the eggs, one at a time, beating well after each addition. Gradually add the flour, beating until well mixed. Then add the almonds, lemon zest and juice, aniseeds, baking powder, salt, and vanilla and almond extracts and continue to beat until blended.

◙ Shape the dough into 4 logs, each one about 2 inches (5 cm) wide and ¾ inch (2 cm) high, and place on the prepared baking sheets. Place in the center of the oven and immediately reduce the heat to 325°F (165°C). Bake until light golden brown, puffy and a little firm when pressed on top, 25–30 minutes.

◙ Remove the baking sheets from the oven and immediately slice the logs crosswise on the sheets into pieces ½ inch (12 mm) thick. Separate the pieces on the sheets, keeping them upright and spacing them so that the air can circulate around them.

◙ Reduce the oven temperature to 275°F (135°C). Place the sheets in the center of the oven and bake until the biscotti are dry and crisp, 20–30 minutes. Transfer the biscotti to racks and let cool completely. Store in an airtight container.

Makes about 4 dozen cookies

Lemon Cialde with Chamomile Cream and Berries

Infused in cream, chamomile bestows its soothing character on an elegant dessert.
The recipe yields more wafers than you'll need for layering; store the remainder for teatime.

CHAMOMILE CREAM
1¼	cups (10 fl oz/310 ml) milk
1	tablespoon granulated sugar
4	extra-large egg yolks
3	chamomile tea bags
2	teaspoons powdered gelatin
2	tablespoons water
1	cup (8 fl oz/250 ml) heavy (double) cream, chilled

LEMON WAFERS
2	extra-large egg whites, at room temperature
½	cup (4 oz/125 g) granulated sugar
¼	cup (1½ oz/45 g) all-purpose (plain) flour
2	teaspoons minced lemon zest
¼	cup (2 oz/60 g) unsalted butter, melted and cooled

RASPBERRY SAUCE
1	cup (4 oz/125 g) raspberries
3–4	tablespoons confectioners' (icing) sugar, or to taste
1	tablespoon *grappa,* optional
1	cup (4 oz/125 g) strawberries, raspberries and/or blackberries, plus berries for garnish
3–4	teaspoons confectioners' (icing) sugar
	Fresh mint leaves

❖ To make the chamomile cream, in a small saucepan over medium heat, combine the milk and sugar and bring almost to a boil. Remove from the heat. In a small bowl, stir together the egg yolks until blended. Stir a few tablespoons of the hot milk into the yolks. Slowly pour the yolks into the hot milk, stirring continuously. Return to low heat and cook, stirring continuously, until thickened to a custard, 1–2 minutes; do not boil. Pour the custard through a fine-mesh sieve into a bowl. Add the tea bags and let stand for 30 minutes. Remove the tea bags, squeezing the liquid from them into the custard.

❖ In a small pan over low heat, sprinkle the gelatin over the water; stir until dissolved. Pour into the custard and stir to mix. Let cool slightly.

❖ Meanwhile, in a bowl, beat the cream until soft peaks form. Gently fold the cream into the cooled custard. Cover and refrigerate until firm, 4–6 hours or for up to 1 day.

❖ To make the wafers, preheat an oven to 375°F (190°C). Butter and flour 2 baking sheets. In a clean bowl, beat the egg whites until soft peaks form. Slowly add the sugar and continue beating until the peaks are stiff and glossy, 3–4 minutes. Fold in the flour and lemon zest alternately with the melted butter just until blended. Let rest for 10 minutes.

❖ For each wafer, using a spoon, place 2 teaspoons of the batter on a prepared baking sheet. Using the back of the spoon, spread into a disk 2¼ inches (5.5 cm) in diameter and ⅛ inch (3 mm) thick. You should have 24 disks in all. Place in the center of the oven and immediately reduce the heat to 325°F (165°C). Bake until pale gold and crisp, 10–12 minutes. While hot, using a spatula, carefully transfer to a rack to cool.

❖ To make the sauce, in a food processor fitted with the metal blade, purée the raspberries. Pass through a fine-mesh sieve into a bowl. Stir in the sugar and the *grappa,* if using.

❖ To assemble, set aside 12 of the wafers; store the remainder in an airtight container for another use. Spoon the custard into a pastry (piping) bag fitted with a star tip. Pipe a small dollop onto the center of a plate. Press a wafer on top. Pipe some custard over the center and arrange a row of berries around the edge. Cover with another wafer and again top with the custard and berries. Sprinkle a third wafer with ¾ teaspoon of the confectioners' sugar and place on top. Garnish with a swirl of custard, a berry and a mint leaf. Repeat until all have been assembled. Drizzle some berry sauce on each plate and serve immediately.

Serves 4

Tiramisù

Literally translated "pick-me-up," tiramisù appropriately lightens the mood at the end of any dinner party. Store-bought pound cake may be used instead of the ladyfingers, and instant espresso or very strong coffee will do if an espresso machine is not at hand.

5 extra-large egg yolks

5 tablespoons (2½ oz/75 g) sugar

1⅔ cups (13 oz/410 g) mascarpone cheese, chilled

1¾ cups (14 fl oz/440 ml) heavy (double) cream, chilled

¼ cup (2 fl oz/60 ml) brewed strong espresso, at room temperature

¼ cup (2 fl oz/60 ml) coffee-flavored liqueur

24 good-quality chocolate or plain ladyfingers

Raspberries, optional

Dutch-processed cocoa

◪ In a bowl, using an electric mixer set on high speed, beat together the egg yolks and sugar until pale yellow, smooth and shiny, 5–7 minutes. Add the mascarpone and beat until thickened and smooth, 3–4 minutes.

◪ In another bowl, using clean beaters or a whisk, whip the cream until soft peaks form. Using a rubber spatula or whisk, fold the whipped cream into the yolk mixture until thoroughly blended, breaking apart any lumps.

◪ In a small bowl, stir together the espresso and liqueur.

◪ Arrange the ladyfingers in a single layer over the bottom of a decorative serving bowl 10 inches (25 cm) in diameter. Brush some of the espresso mixture evenly over the ladyfingers. Turn the ladyfingers over and brush again until each one is almost soaked through with the espresso mixture. If using the raspberries, arrange around the edge. Spoon some of the mascarpone mixture over the ladyfingers to make an even layer ½ inch (12 mm) thick. Place the remaining ladyfingers in a single layer over the mascarpone and brush their tops with the remaining espresso mixture. Again, arrange raspberries around the edge, if using. Spoon the remaining whipped mascarpone on top, smoothing to cover completely. Cover and chill for at least 6 hours or for up to 2 days before serving.

◪ To serve, using a fine-mesh sieve, sift a light dusting of cocoa over the top. Using a large serving spoon, scoop portions of the tiramisù onto individual plates.

Serves 8

Plum Cake

Most trattorias take advantage of the abundance of seasonal fruits by offering them in desserts. In place of the plump summer plums that crown this delectable cake, you can use apricots, nectarines or blueberries. Whatever your selection, make sure the fruit is ripe but firm, as it will soften during baking.

6   tablespoons (3 oz/90 g) unsalted butter, at room temperature

⅓   cup (3 oz/90 g) plus 1 teaspoon granulated sugar

2   extra-large eggs, separated, at room temperature

1   cup (5 oz/155 g) unbleached all-purpose (plain) flour

2½   teaspoons baking powder

¼   cup (2 fl oz/60 ml) heavy (double) cream

¼   cup (2 fl oz/60 ml) water

2   teaspoons almond extract (essence)

1½   teaspoons vanilla extract (essence)

2   ripe plums, peeled, pitted and sliced into sixths

     Confectioners' (icing) sugar

◼ Preheat an oven to 400°F (200°C). Butter and flour a 9-inch (23-cm) cake pan or a tart pan with a removable bottom.

◼ In a bowl, using an electric mixer set on medium speed, beat together the butter and the ⅓ cup (3 oz/90 g) granulated sugar until smooth and fluffy, 2–3 minutes. Add the egg yolks and beat until very smooth.

◼ In a small bowl, stir together the flour and baking powder. In another small bowl, stir together the cream, water and almond and vanilla extracts. Stir the flour mixture into the butter mixture alternately with the cream mixture, beginning and ending with the flour mixture. Do not overmix.

◼ In a clean bowl, using clean beaters, whip the egg whites until they form very soft peaks. Sprinkle in the 1 teaspoon granulated sugar and continue to beat until semisoft peaks form. Using a rubber spatula or whisk, fold the beaten egg whites into the batter, breaking apart any lumps. Pour the batter into the prepared pan and level the surface.

◼ Arrange the plums in a circle on the top of the batter. Place in the center of the oven and immediately reduce the heat to 350°F (180°C). Bake until the cake pulls away from the sides of the pan and a toothpick inserted into the center comes out clean, 35–40 minutes. Transfer to a rack and let cool slightly.

◼ If using a cake pan, run a knife blade around the edge of the pan to loosen the cake sides, invert onto the rack and then turn the cake right side up. If using a tart pan, remove the pan sides.

◼ Place the cake on a serving plate and using a fine-mesh sieve, sift confectioners' sugar evenly over the top. Serve warm or at room temperature.

Serves 8

Warm Chocolate Tortes with Raspberry Sauce

*Serve these miniature chocolate tortes soon after baking, as the warmth best
showcases their creamy, runny centers. For the smoothest texture and richest flavor,
purchase the best-quality European chocolate you can find.*

RASPBERRY SAUCE
1½ cups (6 oz/185 g) raspberries
3   tablespoons confectioners' (icing)
     sugar, or to taste

CHOCOLATE TORTES
3   teaspoons plus ¼ cup (2 oz/60 g)
     granulated sugar
3   oz (90 g) bittersweet (plain)
     chocolate
5   tablespoons (2½ oz/75 g)
     unsalted butter
3   extra–large egg yolks
1½ teaspoons minced orange zest
2   extra–large egg whites
¼   cup (1½ oz/45 g) all-purpose
     (plain) flour, sifted

¼   oz (7 g) white chocolate, cut
     into 8 pieces
1   small block white chocolate, for
     chocolate curls
     Raspberries

▨ To make the raspberry sauce, in a food processor fitted with the metal blade, purée the raspberries. Pass the purée through a fine-mesh sieve into a clean container. Stir in the confectioners' sugar.

▨ Preheat an oven to 425°F (220°C). To make the tortes, butter four standard-sized (½-cup/4-fl oz/125-ml) muffin tin cups, then sprinkle the bottom and sides with 2 teaspoons of the granulated sugar.

▨ Combine the bittersweet chocolate and butter in a heatproof bowl and set in a pan over (not touching) simmering water. Heat over medium heat, stirring continuously, just until the chocolate melts. Remove from the heat and let cool slightly.

▨ Meanwhile, in a bowl, using an electric mixer set on high speed, beat together the egg yolks and the ¼ cup (2 oz/60 g) granulated sugar until thick, about 4 minutes. Reduce the mixer speed to medium and slowly pour in the melted chocolate. Beat in the orange zest.

▨ In a clean bowl, using clean beaters, beat the egg whites until very soft peaks form. Sprinkle in the remaining 1 teaspoon granulated sugar and continue to beat until semisoft peaks form.

▨ Using a rubber spatula or whisk, fold the flour into the chocolate batter alternately with the egg whites, beginning and ending with the flour.

▨ Pour the batter into the prepared molds, filling to within ⅛ inch (3 mm) of the rims. Place 2 pieces of white chocolate on top of each mold; they will sink a little during baking.

▨ Place the pan in the center of the oven and immediately reduce the heat to 375°F (190°C). Bake until puffy and a thin but firm crust forms on top, 6–8 minutes. Do not open the oven door during the first 6 minutes of baking. Transfer the pan to a rack and let rest for 4–5 minutes to ease unmolding.

▨ Meanwhile, run a vegetable peeler along the block of white chocolate to form curls for garnishing the tortes. Keep the curls cool until serving.

▨ Run a sharp paring knife around the edge of each cup and quickly invert the tortes onto the rack. Transfer the tortes to individual plates, top sides down.

▨ Pour the raspberry sauce evenly over the tortes and then sprinkle with the chocolate curls. Scatter fresh raspberries around each torte. Serve immediately.

Serves 4

111

Chocolate–Hazelnut Torte

Candies, ice cream and tortes throughout Italy are flavored with gianduja, *the pleasing combination of hazelnuts and chocolate; those with the richest taste and most intense aroma come from Piedmont. This torte is typical of ones served in the charming Piedmontese town of Alba.*

1½ cups (7½ oz/225 g) hazelnuts (filberts)

1 cup (4 oz/125 g) confectioners' (icing) sugar

3 tablespoons potato starch (potato flour)

⅔ cup (3½ oz/105 g) unbleached all-purpose (plain) flour

1½ tablespoons unsweetened cocoa

2½ teaspoons baking powder
  Pinch of ground cinnamon

½ cup (4 oz/125 g) unsalted butter, cut into small pieces

2 extra-large eggs, lightly beaten, plus 1 extra-large egg yolk

2 teaspoons vanilla extract (essence)

◧ Preheat an oven to 325°F (165°C). Spread the hazelnuts in a single layer on a baking sheet and toast in the oven until they just begin to change color and the skins begin to loosen, 8–10 minutes. Spread the warm nuts on a kitchen towel. Cover with another kitchen towel and rub against the nuts to remove as much of the skins as possible. Let cool.

◧ Raise the oven temperature to 450°F (230°C). Butter and flour a cake pan 9 inches (23 cm) in diameter.

◧ In a food processor fitted with the metal blade or in a blender, combine ½ cup (2½ oz/75 g) of the peeled, cooled hazelnuts and the confectioners' sugar. Process just until the hazelnuts are finely ground, almost to a flour. (Do not overprocess.)

◧ In a bowl, combine the ground nut mixture, the potato starch, all-purpose flour, cocoa, baking powder and cinnamon. Using an electric mixer set on medium speed, beat for a few seconds to aerate the flour mixture. Add the butter and continue to beat until the butter is in very small pieces. Beat in the whole eggs and the egg yolk and the vanilla until blended.

Increase the speed to medium-high and beat until the mixture is fluffy and a light cocoa color, 2–3 minutes.

◧ Pour the batter into the prepared pan and level the surface. Place in the center of the oven and immediately reduce the heat to 400°F (200°C). Bake until a knife inserted in the center comes out clean, 30–35 minutes.

◧ While the cake is baking, place the remaining 1 cup (5 oz/150 g) hazelnuts in the food processor fitted with the metal blade or the blender. Process just until the hazelnuts are coarsely ground.

◧ When the cake is done, transfer it to a rack; let cool for 5 minutes. Run a sharp knife around the edge of the pan to loosen the cake sides and invert onto the rack. Then place, right side up, on a serving plate. Immediately sprinkle the ground hazelnuts evenly over the top and press lightly to adhere. Let cool completely and serve.

Serves 8

Cappuccino Gelato

*The Saracens are credited with introducing ice cream to the Italians, who have
made Italian gelato world famous. If you'd like this gelato to have a milder coffee flavor,
make it with the mixture of espresso and liqueur known as* caffè corretto. *The addition
of both white and bittersweet chocolate, although optional, is irresistible.*

1½ cups (12 fl oz/375 ml) milk
½ cup (4 fl oz/125 ml) light (single) cream
¼ cup (2 oz/60 g) sugar
4 extra-large egg yolks
2 teaspoons vanilla extract (essence)
2 tablespoons instant espresso coffee powder dissolved in 1 tablespoon milk, or 3 tablespoons brewed espresso mixed with 1 tablespoon coffee-flavored liqueur
1 oz (30 g) white or bittersweet (plain) chocolate pieces, or a mixture, optional
Espresso-roast coffee beans or edible flowers, optional

◻ In a saucepan over medium heat, combine the milk, cream and sugar and stir to dissolve the sugar. Bring almost to a boil (190°F/88°C), then remove from the heat.

◻ In a small bowl, stir together the egg yolks until blended. Stir a few tablespoons of the hot milk into the yolks. Then slowly pour the yolks into the hot milk, stirring constantly. Place over low heat and cook, stirring, until thickened, 1–2 minutes. Do not allow to boil.

◻ Immediately pour the mixture through a fine-mesh sieve into a bowl to remove any lumps. Stir in the vanilla and one of the espresso mixtures. Let cool, cover and chill well, at least 2 hours.

◻ If desired, stir in the chocolate pieces, and then transfer to an ice cream maker. Freeze according to manufacturer's instructions.

◻ To serve, spoon into bowls and, if desired, top with coffee beans or garnish with fresh flowers.

Serves 4

Melon Sorbet

Italy's first melons came to ancient Rome from Persia. They were soon being cultivated successfully near the city, in the town of Cantalupo, which gave its name to today's best-known melon variety, showcased here in a light and refreshing sorbet. For the freshest flavor and best consistency, make the sorbet no more than 1 day in advance of serving.

¼   cup (2 fl oz/60 ml) water
¼   cup (2 oz/60 g) plus 1 teaspoon sugar
2½ lb (1.25 kg) cantaloupes
2   extra-large egg whites

▨ In a deep saucepan, combine the water and the ¼ cup (2 oz/60 g) sugar and bring to a boil over high heat. Do not stir or the mixture will crystallize. Continue to boil until it becomes a thick and clear syrup, about 5 minutes. Remove from the heat and let cool.

▨ Cut the cantaloupes in half, then remove and discard the seeds. Cut off and discard the rind. Chop the pulp coarsely. You should have about 1½ lb (750 g) pulp. Working in batches if necessary, place the melon pulp in a food processor fitted with the metal blade or in a blender and purée until smooth. Transfer the puréed melon to a bowl, add the cooled syrup and stir until blended. Cover and chill well, at least 2 hours.

▨ Transfer the melon mixture to an ice cream maker and freeze according to the manufacturer's instructions.

▨ Meanwhile, using a clean bowl and an electric mixer set at high speed, beat the egg whites until frothy. Add the 1 teaspoon sugar and continue to beat until semisoft peaks form.

▨ When the melon mixture is slushy and a little frozen, add the egg whites to the mixture and then continue to freeze until solid.

▨ To serve, spoon into bowls and serve immediately.

Serves 4

BASIC RECIPES

Just a handful of essential recipes provide a foundation for casual Italian cooking. Few trattoria meals would be complete without a light egg or spinach pasta and a robust tomato sauce. And to enhance the flavor of soups, stews, sauces and braises, a good homemade stock should always be close at hand.

MAKING FRESH PASTA

The classic pasta dough, or sfoglia, of Emilia-Romagna requires only two ingredients, flour and eggs. Bleached all-purpose flour yields a more tender dough than the unbleached variety. The dough can be made by hand or in a food processor, then rolled out with a wooden rolling pin or by machine. You can make pasta dough up to 2 days ahead. Or, if short of time, purchase ready-made fresh pasta sheets and cut as directed in individual recipes.

BASIC EGG PASTA
2   cups (10 oz/315 g) all-purpose (plain) flour, or as needed
4   large eggs, plus beaten egg as needed

SPINACH PASTA *(see opposite page)*
1¾   lb (875 g) spinach, stems removed (14 oz/440 g trimmed)
3   cups (15 oz/470 g) all-purpose (plain) flour, or as needed
2   large eggs, plus beaten egg as needed

Mixing the Dough

◩ *To mix the basic egg pasta by hand,* on a clean work surface, place the 2 cups (10 oz/315 g) flour in a mound. Make a well in the center and add the 4 eggs to the well. Using a fork, beat the eggs, gradually incorporating small amounts of the flour from the interior wall of the well into the eggs. Working in a circular pattern, continue to incorporate flour, being careful to maintain the wall of flour so the eggs do not run over the edge.

◩ Work the flour into the eggs until a smooth dough forms. Depending on the humidity, a little less or a little more flour may be needed. If less flour is needed, simply don't incorporate all of it; if more is needed, sprinkle a little on top of the dough and knead it in.

◩ On a clean surface, knead the dough until smooth, velvety and elastic, 1–2 minutes. Cover with a bowl to prevent drying and let the dough relax for 1 hour before rolling it out.

◩ *To mix the basic egg pasta in a food processor,* place the 2 cups (10 oz/315 g) flour in a food processor fitted with the metal blade. In a bowl, lightly whisk the eggs just until blended. Turn on the food processor to aerate the flour briefly, then pour in the eggs. Continue to process for a few seconds until the dough can be pressed into a ball. If the dough is too dry, add beaten egg, 1 teaspoon at a time, and pulse until the correct consistency is achieved. If too moist, add flour, 2 tablespoons at a time, and pulse. Remove the dough from the processor and knead briefly until the surface is smooth, velvety and elastic, 1–2 minutes. Cover with a bowl to prevent drying and let the dough relax for 1 hour before rolling it out.

◩ Use the pasta dough immediately, or wrap airtight and refrigerate for up to 2 days. Before using, unwrap the dough, cover with a bowl to prevent drying and bring to room temperature.

Rolling and Cutting the Dough

◩ *To roll out and cut the dough with a pasta machine,* cut the dough in half or thirds. Cover unused dough with a bowl to prevent drying. Set the pasta machine rollers to their widest opening (number 1 on most machines) and feed one portion of the dough through the rollers. Roll through once, fold the dough crosswise into thirds, turn it a quarter turn and roll through again. Then roll the sheet through one more time to strengthen the dough. Set the rollers to the next smaller opening and roll the dough through once. Continue in this manner, progressively setting the rollers to the next smaller opening and rolling the dough through once. On the first, third and fifth settings (numbers 1, 3 and 5), roll through twice to strengthen the dough. Roll out the dough to a thickness of ⅛ or ¹⁄₁₆ inch (3 mm or 2 mm), the second-to-last and last settings on most machines, as specified in each recipe.

◩ If the dough ripples, too much dough is being pushed through the rollers or the dough isn't relaxed enough to be stretched. Cover the pasta sheet and allow it to relax for a few minutes, then return to the previous setting and roll through. If the dough repeatedly breaks, the gluten must be developed more. Knead the dough by hand and let it relax as before, then begin the rolling again.

For flat cuts such as pappardelle and tagliatelle, place the pasta sheet on a lightly floured board and let dry a little for easier cutting (15–20 minutes) while you roll out the remaining dough. Then adjust the blades to the desired width as directed in individual recipes and pass the sheets through the cutters. Gently separate the pasta strands and gather loosely into small piles. Let dry for 1 hour. Meanwhile, cut the remaining pasta sheets.

To roll out and cut the dough by hand, divide the dough in half or thirds. Cover unused dough with a bowl to prevent drying. On a lightly floured board, roll out one portion of the dough ⅛–1/16-inch (3–2-mm) thick, or as specified in each recipe.

For flat cuts such as pappardelle and tagliatelle, place the pasta sheet on a lightly floured board; let dry a little for easy cutting (15–20 minutes) while you roll out the remaining dough. Using 1 pasta sheet at a time and beginning at a long end, loosely roll up the dough, making folds every 2½ inches (6 cm). Cut the roll crosswise into slices the width of pasta specified in each recipe. Gently separate the pasta strands and gather loosely into small piles. Let dry for 1 hour. Meanwhile, cut the remaining pasta sheets.

For filled pasta, use the pasta sheets made by either the machine or hand method immediately to prevent drying, filling and cutting the pasta dough as directed in individual recipes.

Making Spinach Pasta

Rinse the spinach and place in a steamer rack over (not touching) boiling water. Cover and steam, stirring occasionally, until wilted and tender, 4–5 minutes. Transfer to a colander to drain, pressing against the spinach with the back of a spoon and then squeezing it with your hands to remove the excess water.

In a food processor fitted with the metal blade or in a blender, purée the spinach until smooth. Transfer to paper towels; squeeze to remove any remaining moisture. You should have about ¾ cup (5 oz/155 g) spinach.

Follow the directions for basic egg pasta, adding the spinach with the eggs if mixing the dough by hand and with the flour if mixing it in a food processor. Continue to roll and cut the dough as directed for basic egg pasta.

Makes about 17 oz (530 g) basic egg pasta and 1½ lb (750 g) spinach pasta

FISH STOCK
BRODO DI PESCE

Fish stock tastes best when made with a combination of fish and shellfish. Frozen fish stock, available in some well-stocked food stores, is the best substitute.

1   tablespoon unsalted butter

2   lb (1 kg) cod, halibut or haddock steaks

6   oz (185 g) shrimp (prawns) in the shell or scallops

1   celery stalk, cut in half

2   thick slices yellow onion

1   cup (8 fl oz/250 ml) fruity Italian white wine

5   cups (40 fl oz/1.25 l) cold water

1   bay leaf

½   teaspoon fresh thyme leaves or ¼ teaspoon dried thyme

8   fresh parsley stems

❖ In a deep saucepan over medium heat, melt the butter. Add the fish and shrimp or scallops and sauté until opaque, 2–3 minutes.

❖ Add the celery, onion and wine. Bring to a boil over high heat and boil for 1 minute. Add the water and return to a boil. Using a large spoon, skim any scum from the surface. Add the bay leaf, thyme and parsley stems. Reduce the heat to low and simmer, uncovered, for 18–20 minutes; do not overcook.

❖ Strain the stock through a fine-mesh sieve lined with cheesecloth (muslin) into a clean container. Use immediately, or let cool, cover and refrigerate for up to 12 hours or freeze for up to 2 weeks.

Makes about 5 cups (40 fl oz / 1.25 l)

MEAT STOCK
BRODO DI CARNE

A variety of raw meats imparts a subtle depth of flavor and lightness to this versatile stock. The caramelized onion, cheese rind and tomato add to the satisfying richness. Purchased beef stock can replace homemade when you are pressed for time.

1   yellow onion

1   chicken, 3 lb (1.5 kg), cut into 8 pieces

1   lb (500 g) beef shank with bone

½   lb (250 g) veal stew meat, cut into large cubes

1   large carrot, peeled

1   celery stalk

4   qt (4 l) cold water

2   small pieces rind from Italian Parmesan cheese, about 1 oz (30 g) total weight

1   plum (Roma) tomato

❖ Skewer the whole onion on a fork and hold it over an open flame on the stove top until its skin turns a dark gold. Alternatively, preheat a broiler (griller) and broil (grill) the onion until the edges are lightly browned.

❖ In a deep stockpot, combine the chicken, beef, veal, browned onion, carrot and celery. Add the water and bring to a boil over high heat. Using a large spoon, skim any scum from the surface. Reduce the heat to low, cover partially and simmer for 2 hours.

❖ Add the cheese rind and tomato and simmer, uncovered, for 1 hour longer to blend the flavors; do not overcook and do not allow to boil.

❖ Remove from the heat and strain through a fine-mesh sieve lined with cheesecloth (muslin) into a clean container. Use immediately, or let cool, cover and refrigerate for up to 5 days or freeze for up to 1 month. Before using the chilled stock, lift off and discard the fat congealed on the surface.

Makes about 2¾ qt (2.75 l)

VEGETABLE STOCK

BRODO DI VERDURA

You can use this full-bodied vegetable stock in place of any meat or fish stock. Purchased vegetable stock can be used in place of homemade when time is short.

2 tablespoons extra-virgin olive oil
1 cup (5 oz/155 g) diced carrot
¾ cup (4 oz/125 g) diced celery
¾ cup (2 oz/60 g) sliced leeks
1 small clove garlic
1 small red (Spanish) onion, cut in half
¾ lb (375 g) fresh white mushrooms, cut in halves
8 cups (64 fl oz/2 l) cold water
1 small plum (Roma) tomato
½ teaspoon fresh thyme leaves or ¼ teaspoon dried thyme
½ teaspoon fresh marjoram leaves or ¼ teaspoon dried marjoram
4 fresh parsley sprigs
Salt and freshly ground pepper

❖ In a saucepan over low heat, warm the olive oil. Add the carrot, celery and leeks and sauté until the leeks are slightly translucent, 3–4 minutes.
❖ Add the garlic, onion and mushrooms and sauté until the onion is slightly translucent, about 2 minutes.
❖ Pour in the water and bring to a boil over high heat. Using a large spoon, skim any scum from the surface, if necessary. Add the tomato, thyme, marjoram and parsley. Reduce the heat to low and simmer, uncovered, until the flavors are blended, about 1 hour.
❖ Strain the stock through a fine-mesh sieve lined with cheesecloth (muslin) into a clean container. Season to taste with salt and pepper. Use immediately, or let cool, cover and refrigerate for up to 3 days or freeze for up to 1 month.

Makes about 5 cups (40 fl oz/1.25 l)

QUICK TOMATO SAUCE

SALSA RAPIDA DI POMODORO

This fresh-tasting tomato sauce cooks in less than 1 hour. It will have its freshest flavor when served within a few hours of preparation, but it can be covered and refrigerated for 1–2 days or frozen for up to 2 weeks and still be delicious. If you like, add garlic and herbs and/or a few tablespoons of red or white wine to the sauce near the end of cooking.

2 tablespoons extra-virgin olive oil or sunflower or canola oil
¼ cup (1¼ oz/37 g) finely chopped yellow onion
Minced garlic, optional
Minced fresh or dried herbs, optional
6 cups (36 oz/1.1 kg) peeled, seeded, chopped and well-drained plum (Roma) tomatoes (fresh or canned)
Salt and ground white pepper

❖ In a saucepan over low heat, warm the oil. Add the onion and sauté until translucent, 4–5 minutes; do not allow to brown. Add garlic and herbs to taste (or as directed in individual recipes) and sauté until fragrant, about 1 minute.
❖ Add the tomatoes and bring to a boil over high heat. Reduce the heat to low and simmer uncovered, stirring occasionally, until thickened and the juices have evaporated, 30–35 minutes for canned tomatoes and 40–45 minutes for fresh tomatoes.
❖ Season to taste with salt and white pepper. Use immediately, or let cool, cover and refrigerate or freeze.

Makes about 2 cups (16 fl oz/500 ml)

FRANCE

First Courses

Meals in France traditionally open with a simple first course, designed to excite the senses and to prepare the diner for the heartier, and frequently more elaborate, main course that follows. Often served cold and always tasty and light, it aims, after all, not to fill, but merely to tantalize.

Fresh seasonal vegetables, briefly cooked then served cold with a vinaigrette or other light sauce, are a popular choice. Most bistros also offer a range of fresh shellfish, with mollusks usually served on the half shell nested in ice and crustaceans cracked but still in their armor. If a pâté or terrine is ordered, it commonly arrives at the table still in its earthenware vessel, with a loaf of fresh bread alongside for diners to help themselves. In the winter months, creamy soups and lightly browned gratins are favored.

More complex preparations are usually reserved for Sunday dining and special occasions. At such meals, the entrées display a bit more refinement than most daily offerings. One might begin with a crisp layered potato galette, for example, or a savory seafood salad. Dishes are often selected not only for their own individual characteristics, but also with a mind to the roles they play in the meal as a whole.

Onion Soup Gratinée

In the past, this hearty onion soup with melted cheese on top was served from the late-night hours into the early morning in the Les Halles market district of Paris. Now, it is served at all times of the day in France. Commonly referred to as one of the great soupes de santé, restorative "soups for the sick," this flavorful broth is said to work equally well on curing the flu as it does on relieving hangovers.

3 large white onions

½ cup (4 oz/125 g) unsalted butter

3 tablespoons all-purpose (plain) flour

8 cups (64 fl oz/2 l) beef stock, preferably homemade
  Salt and freshly ground pepper

½ day-old baguette

2 cups (8 oz/250 g) shredded Swiss cheese

⚜ Cut the onions in half through the stem end, then cut crosswise into thin slices.

⚜ In a large saucepan over medium heat, melt the butter. Add the onions and flour and sauté, stirring frequently, until golden brown, about 5 minutes.

⚜ Pour in the stock, add salt and pepper to taste and bring to a boil. Reduce the heat to medium and simmer, stirring often, until the onions are soft and translucent and the flavors have blended, about 15 minutes.

⚜ Meanwhile, preheat a broiler (griller). Cut the baguette on the diagonal into 6–8 large slices about ½ inch (12 mm) thick.

⚜ Ladle the soup into 6–8 ovenproof bowls placed atop a baking sheet. Place a bread slice on top of each serving of soup and scatter the Swiss cheese evenly over the top of the soup and the bread.

⚜ Place the baking sheet under the broiler and broil (grill) until the cheese melts and turns golden brown, 2–3 minutes.

⚜ Remove from the broiler and serve immediately.

Serves 6–8

126

Cream of Artichoke Soup

Catherine de' Medicis was the first to popularize artichokes in France when she came to the French court from Italy to marry King Henry II in the late 16th century. In this smooth and mellow soup, only the tender hearts of the artichokes are used. Armagnac adds an extra touch of refinement; if you don't have any on hand, Cognac or any good-quality dry brandy will do.

6 medium-sized artichokes

⅓ cup (3 fl oz/80 ml) olive oil

1 white onion, coarsely chopped

3 celery stalks, coarsely chopped

1 large russet potato, peeled and coarsely chopped

6 cups (48 fl oz/1.5 l) chicken stock *(recipe on page 224)*

⅓ cup (2 oz/60 g) hazelnuts (filberts)

1 tablespoon salt

1 teaspoon ground white pepper

2 cups (16 fl oz/500 ml) heavy (double) cream

⅓ cup (3 fl oz/80 ml) Armagnac

Working with 1 artichoke at a time, cut off the top half. Trim off the stem even with the bottom. Then snap or cut off all the tough outer leaves until you reach the pale green, tender leaves. Carefully spread the tender leaves open and, using a small spoon, remove the prickly choke, leaving the inner leaves intact. Cut each artichoke lengthwise into eighths and set aside.

Preheat an oven to 400°F (200°C).

In a large saucepan over medium-high heat, warm the olive oil. Add the onion and celery and sauté until golden brown, 8–10 minutes. Add the artichokes, potato and chicken stock and bring to a boil. Reduce the heat to medium, cover and simmer until thickened slightly and the flavors have blended, about 45 minutes.

While the soup is cooking, toast and skin the hazelnuts: Spread the nuts in a single layer on a baking sheet and toast in the oven for 5 minutes. Spread the warm nuts on a kitchen towel, cover with another kitchen towel and rub gently against the nuts to remove as much of the skins as possible. Let cool, then chop coarsely and set aside.

Working in batches, transfer the soup to a blender or to a food processor fitted with a metal blade and blend or process on high speed until smooth and creamy, about 1 minute. Strain the puréed soup through a fine-mesh sieve back into the saucepan to remove any fibers. Add the salt, white pepper, cream and Armagnac and bring to a simmer over medium heat, stirring to mix well.

Ladle the soup into warmed bowls and sprinkle with the chopped hazelnuts. Serve immediately.

Serves 6–8

Chestnut and Celery Soup

During the winter months, hot roasted chestnuts are often sold by vendors on the boulevards of Paris. The meaty nut is a popular ingredient in bistros around France, either fresh or as a canned purée. This rich soup—combining chestnut purée with celery, potato and cream— is a popular first course for Christmastime luncheons and New Year's celebrations.

2 cups (1 lb/500 g) prepared unsweetened chestnut purée or 1½ lb (750 g) fresh chestnuts

½ cup (4 oz/125 g) unsalted butter

2 white onions, chopped

3 celery stalks, coarsely chopped

1 large russet potato, peeled and coarsely chopped

6 cups (48 fl oz/1.5 l) chicken stock *(recipe on page 224)*

2 cups (16 fl oz/500 ml) heavy (double) cream

1 tablespoon salt

1 teaspoon ground white pepper

⚜ If you are using prepared chestnut purée, set aside. If you are using fresh chestnuts, preheat an oven to 400°F (200°C). Using a sharp knife, cut an X on the flat side of each chestnut. Spread the chestnuts in a shallow pan and roast until the nuts feel tender when pressed and the shells have curled where cut, 25–30 minutes. Remove from the oven and, using a small, sharp knife, remove the shells and the furry skin directly under them. (The nuts peel easiest when still warm.) Set aside.

⚜ In a large saucepan over medium-high heat, melt the butter. Add the onions and celery and sauté until golden brown, about 5 minutes.

⚜ Add the chestnut purée or roasted chestnuts, potato, chicken stock and cream, stir well and bring to a boil. Add the salt and white pepper, reduce the heat to medium-low and simmer, uncovered, until the soup thickens slightly, about 1 hour.

⚜ Working in batches, transfer the soup to a blender and blend on high speed until smooth and creamy, about 1 minute.

⚜ Return the soup to the saucepan and bring to a simmer over medium heat. Taste and adjust the seasoning. Ladle into warmed bowls and serve immediately.

Serves 6–8

131

Salmon Rillettes

Although classic rillettes are commonly prepared with fatty mixtures of pork or duck, this lighter and more contemporary version combines two forms of salmon with lemon juice and chives. Like traditional rillettes, the shredded mixture is served on small buttered toasts as a first course. This dish is excellent accompanied with a cold, crisp glass of Champagne or a dry white wine such as Chenin Blanc.

Salt and freshly ground pepper
13 oz (410 g) fresh salmon fillet, skin removed
½ cup (4 oz/125 g) plus 1½ tablespoons unsalted butter, at room temperature, cut into small pieces
2 eggs
1 teaspoon fresh lemon juice
1 tablespoon chopped fresh chives
7 oz (220 g) sliced smoked salmon, cut into small pieces
Buttered, toasted baguette slices

※ Rub salt and pepper to taste on both sides of the salmon fillet. Place on a steamer rack over (not touching) gently boiling water. Cover and steam until firm, pale pink and opaque throughout, about 7 minutes, depending upon the thickness. Alternatively, fill a shallow saucepan or sauté pan about half full with water (enough to cover the salmon). Add the salmon and poach until it tests done, about 10 minutes.

※ Transfer the steamed or poached salmon to a bowl. Shred the salmon thoroughly with a fork and remove any small bones. Cover and refrigerate until cool.

※ Place the butter in a large mixing bowl and work it with a rubber spatula until it is smooth and creamy. Add the eggs, lemon juice, chives and salt and pepper to taste and mix well. Add the cooled fresh salmon and the smoked salmon and mix together thoroughly.

※ Spoon the salmon mixture into a terrine or individual ramekins and cover with plastic wrap. Refrigerate for at least 3 hours or as long as overnight. Bring to room temperature before serving.

※ To serve, spread the salmon mixture on toasted baguette slices.

Serves 6–8

133

Chicken Liver Terrine

Served simply with a baguette or crackers, a liver terrine is a standard prelude to many classic French meals. In many neighborhood bistros, modest terrines like this one are often set right on the table with a loaf of bread, allowing the diners to help themselves before the main course arrives. Soaking the livers in milk overnight removes any bitter flavor and keeps them tasting fresh and rich.

1½ lb (750 g) chicken livers, trimmed of any connective tissue
Milk
1   teaspoon salt
½   teaspoon ground white pepper
1½ cups (12 fl oz/375 ml) heavy (double) cream
1   egg
2   fresh thyme sprigs
2   bay leaves
Toasted baguette slices or crackers (savory biscuits)

⚓ The night before you bake the terrine, combine the chicken livers in a shallow bowl with milk to cover. Cover and refrigerate overnight.

⚓ The next day, preheat an oven to 375°F (190°C).

⚓ Drain the chicken livers and place in a food processor fitted with the metal blade or in a blender. Add the salt, white pepper, cream and egg. Process or blend on high speed until smooth, about 1 minute.

⚓ Strain the liver purée through a medium-mesh sieve into a bowl, to remove any fibrous matter. Then pour the strained purée into a 9½-by-3½-by-3½-inch (24-by-9-by-9-cm) terrine. Lay the thyme sprigs and the bay leaves on top as a garnish.

⚓ Cover the terrine with its lid or aluminum foil. Place it in a baking pan and pour enough hot water into the pan to reach halfway up the sides of the terrine. Bake until a knife inserted into the center comes out clean, about 45 minutes. Remove the baking pan from the oven and then remove the terrine from the baking pan. Uncover and let cool. Then cover and refrigerate overnight.

⚓ Cut into slices and serve chilled or at room temperature. Accompany with toasts or crackers.

Serves 6–8

134

Onion Pie with Roquefort, Prosciutto and Walnuts

A staple of everyday French cooking, onions are a common ingredient in a variety of dishes featured on bistro menus. Embellished with Roquefort, prosciutto and walnuts, this recipe produces a somewhat more upscale version of the ever-popular onion pie. It is traditionally served either as a first course or alongside a crisp green salad for a light supper.

2 tablespoons olive oil

2 white onions, very thinly sliced

¼ cup (2 fl oz/60 ml) water

3 oz (90 g) Roquefort cheese, crumbled into small pieces
  Salt and freshly ground pepper

½ cup (2 oz/60 g) walnuts, coarsely chopped

1 tablespoon unsalted butter, melted

2 puff pastry sheets, each 11 by 15 inches (28 by 37.5 cm), fresh or thawed frozen

1 egg, lightly beaten

4 slices prosciutto, about 1 oz (30 g) each

❧ Place a baking sheet with sides in a freezer.

❧ In a sauté pan over medium-high heat, warm the olive oil. Add the onions and sauté until golden brown, about 10 minutes. Add the water and continue to sauté until all the moisture evaporates, about another 5 minutes. Add the Roquefort cheese and continue cooking, stirring occasionally, until melted, about 5 minutes longer. Season only lightly with salt, if needed, and add pepper to taste. Stir in the walnuts, then spread the mixture out onto the chilled sheet pan. Place in the freezer until the onions cool down completely, about 10 minutes.

❧ Preheat an oven to 450°F (230°C). Brush a baking sheet evenly with the melted butter.

❧ Place the puff pastry on a cutting board. Using the rim of a small plate about 5 inches (13 cm) in diameter as a guide, cut the pastry into 8 rounds. Discard the pastry scraps.

❧ Place 4 of the rounds on the prepared baking sheet. Brush their outer rims and tops with the beaten egg. Evenly distribute the cooled onion mixture onto the middle of each of the 4 rounds, leaving 1 inch (2.5 cm) uncovered around the edges. Place 1 prosciutto slice on top of each mound of the onion mixture. Cover each round with a second pastry round, making sure to pinch down firmly around the edges to seal in the filling. Brush the top of each "pie" with more of the beaten egg. Using a small, sharp knife, pierce the top of each pie once with a small slit.

❧ Bake until golden brown, about 20 minutes. Remove from the oven and serve immediately.

Serves 4

Potato and Goat Cheese Galette

Although many galettes take the form of sweet cakes, the traditional galette of the French countryside is often a savory creation made from finely sliced or puréed potatoes. In this refined first-course preparation, potato rings are filled with fresh goat cheese and then breaded and fried.

Peanut oil or vegetable oil for deep-frying
2 russet potatoes, well scrubbed
6–8 oz (185–250 g) fresh goat cheese
2 pinches of cayenne pepper
½ cup (2 oz/60 g) fine dried bread crumbs
2 oil-packed sun-dried tomatoes, drained and blotted dry
10 large European brine-cured black olives, such as Kalamata
2 tablespoons pure olive oil
1 teaspoon extra-virgin olive oil
4 fresh basil leaves
Freshly ground pepper

🌿 In a deep-fat fryer or a heavy saucepan, pour the peanut or vegetable oil to a depth of 3 inches (7.5 cm). Heat to 300°F (150°C) on a deep-fat frying thermometer, or until a drop of water added to the oil dances and pops on the surface.

🌿 Meanwhile, cut off the ends of the potatoes and discard. Slice the centers of the potatoes crosswise into disks ¾ inch (2 cm) wide. You should have 4 disks in all. Cut a hole out of the center of each potato disk, forming a sturdy "ring." Be sure to leave at least a ½-inch (12-mm) border of potato remaining around the hole.

🌿 Slip the potato rings into the oil and deep-fry until they start to turn golden brown, about 5 minutes. Using a slotted spoon, remove the potato rings from the oil and place on paper towels. Pat the rings dry with the paper towels, removing any excess oil.

🌿 Fill the center of each of the 4 rings with one-fourth of the goat cheese. Smooth the surfaces of the rings by carefully scraping off any protruding cheese with a spatula. Sprinkle both sides of the cheese-filled potato rings with cayenne pepper. Spread the bread crumbs on a plate and coat both sides of the rings with the crumbs. Place the coated rings in a single layer on another plate, cover with plastic wrap and refrigerate for at least 2 hours or for up to 1 day.

🌿 Just before serving, slice each sun-dried tomato into 8 pieces; cut each olive in half, removing the pit. Place the tomatoes and olives around the outer edges of individual plates, alternating them to form a colorful pattern.

🌿 In a large nonstick sauté pan, warm the pure olive oil. Add the potatoes and cook, turning once, just until they turn golden brown, 20–30 seconds on each side. Transfer the cooked potatoes to the garnished plates.

🌿 Swirl a little of the extra-virgin olive oil evenly over each of the potatoes and the garnish. Place a single basil leaf on the center of each potato and then sprinkle with a few turns of ground pepper. Serve immediately.

Serves 4

138

Foie Gras Poached in Sweet Wine

In France, the fresh plumped goose or duck liver known as foie gras is often reserved for special occasions. Although foie gras used to be difficult to find outside of France, it can now be purchased in specialty-food stores. Accompany with the same late-harvest sweet wine used for cooking.

1   foie gras, about 1½ lb (750 g)
1⅔ cups (13 fl oz/400 ml) late-harvest sweet wine
2   teaspoons plus 1 tablespoon salt
2   teaspoons ground white pepper
7   cups (56 fl oz/1.75 l) veal stock *(recipe on pages 224–225)* or purchased beef stock
Ice cubes
1   day-old baguette

✿ Split apart the 2 lobes of the foie gras and, using a small, sharp knife, remove any thick portions of the veinlike connective tissue running through the lobes.

✿ Place the lobes of foie gras in a dish and pour ⅔ cup (5 fl oz/150 ml) of the sweet wine over them. Sprinkle each lobe evenly on all sides with the 2 teaspoons salt and 1 teaspoon of the white pepper. Cover with plastic wrap and let marinate in a refrigerator for 2–6 hours (the longer the better), turning the lobes at least 2 or 3 times to ensure that they are evenly flavored.

✿ Remove the foie gras from the marinade, reserving the marinade, and place in the center of a large piece of cheesecloth (muslin). Wrap the cloth around the lobes and press them gently into a sausage shape. Using kitchen string, tie the cheesecloth-wrapped "roll" of foie gras firmly at both ends. Then tie along the length of the roll every 1½ inches (4 cm), forming a sausage shape about 7–8 inches (18–20 cm) long and 2–2½ inches (5–6 cm) wide.

✿ In a saucepan, combine the stock, the remaining wine and the reserved marinade. Bring to a boil over medium-high heat and add the remaining salt and white pepper. Then gently drop in the roll of foie gras. Return to a boil and poach gently until slightly tender to the touch, 4–5 minutes.

✿ Meanwhile, fill a bowl large enough to hold the roll with ice cubes and add a splash of water. When the foie gras is done, using tongs, remove it from the pan and promptly bury it in the bowl of ice to halt the cooking. Let stand for 1 minute, then remove the roll and place it in a deep rectangular terrine or bowl. Place the saucepan holding the stock in the bowl of ice to cool it down completely, about 15 minutes.

✿ Pour the cooled stock into the terrine or bowl to cover the roll completely. Cover and refrigerate for at least 24 hours or for up to 3 days.

✿ Just before serving, cut the baguette crosswise into thin slices and toast until golden brown.

✿ Remove the roll from the stock, snip off the strings, and unwrap the foie gras. To serve, heat a sharp knife by dipping it into hot water. Wipe the blade dry, then slice the foie gras into medallions ¼ inch (6 mm) thick. Arrange on a platter with the toasted baguette slices.

Serves 10–12

Macédoine de Légumes

Macédoine of Seasonal Vegetables

A macédoine is a mixture of fresh vegetables or fruits, cut into small, uniform cubes.
Use any combination of the vegetables called for here, or include your own favorites.

4 medium-sized artichokes
½ cup (2 oz/60 g) snow peas (mangetouts), trimmed
¾ cup (4 oz/125 g) shelled green peas
1 cup (5 oz/155 g) shelled fava (broad) beans
12 asparagus spears, trimmed
10 baby carrots, peeled
8 small golden beets (beetroots)
½ cup (2 oz/60 g) peeled, cubed green apple
2 tablespoons julienned fresh basil leaves
3 tablespoons finely chopped fresh chives
   Vinaigrette *(recipe on page 225)*
¼ cup (1½ oz/45 g) pine nuts
12 fresh chervil sprigs
   Salt and freshly ground pepper

🌿 Using a sharp knife, cut the tops off the artichokes just above the heart. Trim the stems even with the bottoms. Place in a steamer rack over gently boiling water, cover and steam until tender, about 25 minutes. Remove from the steamer and, when cool enough to handle, pull off all the leaves until you reach the pale green hearts. Carefully spread the tender leaves open and, using a small spoon, remove the prickly chokes. Set the cleaned artichoke hearts aside.

🌿 Place several ice cubes in a large mixing bowl; fill with water. Set aside.

🌿 Fill a saucepan three-fourths full with water and bring to a boil. Add the snow peas and boil until tender, about 3 minutes. Using a small sieve, scoop out the snow peas and immediately plunge them into the ice water to halt the cooking. Remove them from the ice water and set aside.

🌿 Toss the peas into the same boiling water and boil until tender, 6–8 minutes. Remove with the sieve, plunge into the bowl of ice water; set aside.

🌿 Toss the fava beans into the same boiling water and boil until tender, 3–5 minutes. Scoop them out and plunge them into the ice water. Remove them from the water and, using a small knife, slit the skin on the edge of each bean and "pop" the bean free of its skin. Set aside.

🌿 Drain the saucepan, fill it with clean water and again bring to a boil. Add more ice cubes, if needed, to the water in the bowl.

🌿 Toss the asparagus into boiling water and boil just until tender, 8–10 minutes. Scoop them out, immediately plunge them into the ice water and then remove them. Set aside.

🌿 Toss the baby carrots into the same boiling water and boil just until tender, 5–7 minutes. Plunge them immediately into the ice water, remove them and set aside.

🌿 Cut the stems off of the beets above the crown and toss the beets into the same boiling water. Boil just until tender, about 15 minutes. Plunge them immediately into the ice water, then remove them. Using a small knife, peel away the skins.

🌿 Cut the artichoke hearts and beets into relatively uniform ¾-inch (2-cm) cubes. Then cut the snow peas, asparagus and carrots into ¾-inch (2-cm) pieces. Combine them all in a large bowl. Add the peas, fava beans, apple, basil and chives. Drizzle on the vinaigrette and mix gently.

🌿 Scatter the pine nuts and chervil over the top, season to taste with salt and pepper and serve immediately.

Serves 4

Frisée Salad with Poached Eggs and Pancetta

This savory salad is served plain with only pancetta and croutons or in the style of Lyon, with poached eggs placed on top. The sturdy, curly-edged, bitter frisée lettuce remains an excellent base for either preparation and stands up well when tossed with the warm dressing. If you can't find frisée, spinach is the best substitute.

4	small heads frisée
4	slices pancetta, each about 2 oz (60 g) and ½ inch (12 mm) thick
12	baguette slices, each cut on the diagonal ½ inch (12 mm) thick
4	tablespoons olive oil
4	tablespoons sherry or red wine vinegar
4	eggs
2	tablespoons chopped fresh chives
	Freshly ground pepper

❧ Preheat an oven to 450°F (230°C).

❧ Wash the heads of frisée by soaking them in a bowl of water and then gently lifting them out. Repeat with clean water until the water is clear. Spin or pat the heads dry. Remove and discard the greener outer leaves; keep the whitest parts of the lettuce nearer to the heart, and trim off the tough core. Place the frisée in a large bowl and set aside.

❧ Unroll the pancetta slices and cut crosswise into strips ½ inch (12 mm) thick. Place in a small saucepan with water to cover. Bring to a boil, then remove from the heat. Drain, rinse with cold water; drain again. Set aside.

❧ Brush the baguette slices on both sides with 2 tablespoons of the olive oil and arrange on a baking sheet. Place in the oven and toast, turning once, until the edges are golden brown, 3–4 minutes. Set aside.

❧ Fill a saucepan three-fourths full with water. Add 2 tablespoons of the vinegar and return to a boil. Reduce the heat to medium-low so that the water is just below a boil. One at a time, break each egg into a saucer and slip it into the water. Work quickly so that the eggs all begin cooking at nearly the same time. Poach until the whites appear cooked and are slightly warm to the touch and the yolks are still liquid, about 3 minutes.

❧ Meanwhile, warm the remaining 2 tablespoons olive oil in another sauté pan over medium heat. Add the drained pancetta and sauté until golden brown, about 2 minutes. Add the remaining 2 tablespoons vinegar and deglaze by stirring to dislodge any browned bits from the pan bottom; continue to stir for about 45 seconds. Pour the vinegar mixture evenly over the frisée, add the chives and toss well. Divide the greens evenly among individual plates.

❧ Using a slotted spoon, immediately remove the eggs from the water, shaking off any excess water. Place them on top of the salads.

❧ Add a few turns of ground pepper to each salad and place the toasted baguette slices around the edges of the plates. Serve immediately.

Serves 4

Crab Salad with Mango

French chefs have long been innovators when it comes to pairing new and different ingredients. This salad—combining the sweetness of tropical fruit and the spiciness of cayenne pepper with the rich flavor of crab—is the type of dish one might find on the menu of a city bistro, where open markets daily provide a range of fresh and exotic ingredients.

10 oz (315 g) fresh-cooked crab meat, picked over for shell fragments

2 tablespoons mayonnaise

⅔ cup (4 oz/125 g) peeled and finely diced mango

⅓ cup (2 oz/60 g) roasted, peeled and diced red bell pepper (capsicum) *(see glossary, page 340)*

¼ teaspoon cayenne pepper

2 tablespoons chopped fresh chives
Salt and freshly ground black pepper

2 cups (2 oz/60 g) mesclun or other bitter greens

🌿 Wrap the crab meat tightly in a clean kitchen towel to absorb any excess water. Place the crab meat in a bowl and add the mayonnaise. Using a fork, mix together thoroughly.

🌿 Add the mango, bell pepper, cayenne pepper, 1 tablespoon of the chives and salt and black pepper to taste. Mix gently until all the ingredients are evenly distributed.

🌿 Scatter the salad greens evenly over individual plates. Divide the crab mixture equally among the plates, mounding it on top of the greens. Sprinkle the remaining 1 tablespoon chives evenly over the top and serve immediately.

Serves 4

Mussel Salad with Curry Mayonnaise

*Curry was not used in French cooking until the early 18th century when the East India
Trading Company introduced it to European kitchens. Here, the sharp spiciness of the curry combines
with the sweetness of apples as a complement to freshly cooked mussels. Served at room temperature
with a very dry white wine, this shellfish salad makes an excellent first course.*

1	russet potato, about 10 oz (315 g)
1½	lb (750 g) mussels in the shell, well scrubbed and beards removed *(see glossary, page 346)*
1	cup (8 fl oz/250 ml) water
1	red bell pepper (capsicum), roasted, peeled and seeded *(see glossary, page 340)*
1	large tart, green apple such as Granny Smith, peeled, cored and cut into ½-inch (12-mm) cubes
2	tablespoons minced shallots
1	tablespoon minced fresh basil
3	tablespoons chopped fresh parsley
3	tablespoons mayonnaise
½	teaspoon curry powder
	Salt and freshly ground pepper
4	dashes of cayenne pepper
4	small fresh basil sprigs

♣ Peel the potato and cut into ½-inch (12-mm) cubes. Fill a small saucepan two-thirds full with water and bring to a boil. Add the potato and boil until tender when pierced with a fork, about 8 minutes. Drain and set aside.

♣ Discard any mussels that do not close to the touch. In a large saucepan, bring the 1 cup (8 fl oz/250 ml) water to a boil. Add the mussels, cover and steam over high heat, stirring once or twice, until the shells open, 2–3 minutes. Drain the mussels and discard any that have not opened. Remove all but 4 mussels from their shells. Place the shelled mussels in a large bowl; set aside the mussels in their shells to use as garnish.

♣ Cut the roasted bell pepper into ½-inch (12-mm) squares. Add to the mussels in the bowl, along with the potato, apple, shallots, basil, parsley, mayonnaise, curry powder and salt and pepper to taste. Mix together gently but thoroughly.

♣ Divide the salad among individual plates and sprinkle each salad with a dash of cayenne. Top each salad with a mussel in the shell and garnish with a basil sprig. Serve immediately.

Serves 4

Fish and Shellfish

Bordered on three sides by vast blue waters and punctuated by numerous rivers and lakes, France has traditionally offered a wide range of fresh fish and shellfish on its restaurant menus. Bistros often feature simple shellfish preparations as a first course, with warm, more sophisticated presentations reserved for a small second course to precede the main dish. However, many of the recipes in this chapter will suffice as delectable main course dishes on their own.

The light, versatile flavors of fresh fish and shellfish are deliciously accepting of a variety of different cooking methods, and French chefs find ample ways in which to showcase them. Delicate steamed fillets are natural partners for a mild and creamy sabayon sauce. Sautéed shrimp are combined with the heartier flavors of tomatoes and garlic in the traditional Provençal style. And, because most bistro chefs stress simplicity, you will often find them pairing fresh or steamed *fruits de mer* with simple vinaigrettes or heady blends of fresh herbs.

Basque Calamari Salad

In this spicy salad, calamari is prepared in the Basque style with plenty of tomatoes, red peppers and garlic. To ensure the best flavor, slice the onions and peppers paper-thin, using a mandoline if available, and be sure not to overcook the calamari. Depending on how hungry you are, this salad can be served either as an appetizer or a main course. A chilled dry rosé is a delicious complement.

CALAMARI SALAD
1	lb (500 g) squid
¼	cup (2 fl oz/60 ml) olive oil
2	large red bell peppers (capsicums), seeded, deribbed and very thinly sliced
2	white onions, very thinly sliced
4	cloves garlic, thinly sliced
	Dash of cayenne pepper
	Salt and freshly ground black pepper

SPICY TOMATO VINAIGRETTE
⅓	cup (3 fl oz/80 ml) tomato and red pepper coulis *(recipe on page 226)*
1½	tablespoons sherry vinegar
4	tablespoons chopped fresh parsley
½	teaspoon cayenne pepper
½	teaspoon salt
¼	teaspoon ground white pepper
2	tablespoons olive oil

❧ To make the salad, first clean the squid. Cut off the tentacles above the eyes. Remove the hard round beak lodged in the base of the tentacles by pushing it out. Pull the entrails free of the body and discard. Then pull out the transparent cartilage, or quill, and discard. Rinse the body under cold running water, flushing the body tube well. Using your fingers, pull off the mottled skin covering the body. Cut the body into rings ¼ inch (6 mm) wide. Set the rings and tentacles aside.

❧ In a large sauté pan over high heat, warm the olive oil. Add the bell peppers, onions and garlic and sauté for 2 minutes. Stir in the cayenne and salt and black pepper to taste. Reduce the heat to medium-low, cover and cook, stirring occasionally, until the onions and peppers are very soft, about 30 minutes. Set aside.

❧ Bring a saucepan three-fourths full of water to a boil. Add the squid and cook until just firm, 2–3 minutes; do not overcook. Drain and rinse immediately under cold running water. Drain well and set aside.

❧ To make the vinaigrette, in a large bowl, whisk together the tomato and red pepper coulis, vinegar, parsley, cayenne pepper, salt and white pepper. Add the olive oil and whisk for about 30 seconds until well blended and emulsified.

❧ Add the squid and the onion-pepper mixture to the vinaigrette and toss gently but thoroughly. Taste and adjust the seasoning. Cover and refrigerate for at least 1 hour or for up to 1 day. Serve chilled.

Serves 6 as a first course; 4 as a main course

Lobster Salad with Lemon Vinaigrette

Since its shell turns a deep red during cooking, the lobster has been referred to in France as
"cardinal of the sea." Even were it not for the bright color of their shells, the succulent, dense quality
of lobster meat has made it a king among shellfish often reserved for special occasions.

LOBSTER SALAD
2   live lobsters, 1½ lb (750 g) each
1   teaspoon salt
1   lb (500 g) zucchini (courgettes)
½   cup (3 oz/90 g) peeled, seeded
    and diced papaya (pawpaw)
½   cup (3 oz/90 g) roasted, peeled
    and sliced red bell pepper (capsi-
    cum) *(see glossary, page 340)*
1   tablespoon fresh tarragon leaves
2   tablespoons julienned fresh basil
1   tablespoon chopped fresh chives

LEMON VINAIGRETTE
3   tablespoons fresh lemon juice
1   teaspoon salt
¼   teaspoon ground white pepper
5   tablespoons (3 fl oz/80 ml)
    olive oil

🌿 To make the salad, first cook the lobster. Fill a stockpot three-fourths full with water and bring to a boil. Slip the lobsters into the water, cover, and cook until the shells are red, about 8 minutes. Using tongs, remove the lobsters and set aside to cool.

🌿 When the lobsters have cooled, lay them on their backs on a cutting board. Using a sharp knife and starting at the head end, cut each lobster in half lengthwise. Discard the intestinal vein along the back of the tail. Break off the claws, crack them with a mallet and carefully pull away the shell pieces, leaving the claw meat whole. Remove the tail meat from the shells and set the tail and claw meat aside. Discard the shells.

🌿 Place several ice cubes in a large mixing bowl; fill with water. Set aside.

🌿 Fill a large saucepan three-fourths full with salted water; bring to a boil.

🌿 Meanwhile, trim the zucchini. Then, using a mandoline with the forked shredding attachment or a sharp knife, cut down the length of the zucchini into long, spaghetti-sized julienne strips.

🌿 Add the zucchini to the boiling water. When the water returns to a boil, drain the zucchini and plunge it immediately into the ice water to halt the cooking. Drain it again and place in a large salad bowl. Add the papaya, bell pepper, tarragon, basil and chives and toss gently to mix. Set aside.

🌿 To make the vinaigrette, in a small bowl, combine the lemon juice, salt and white pepper and whisk together thoroughly. Add the olive oil and whisk for about 30 seconds until well blended and emulsified.

🌿 Pour the vinaigrette into the salad bowl, and gently toss all the ingredients together to distribute the vinaigrette evenly.

🌿 Divide the zucchini mixture evenly among individual plates. Place a lobster tail half, cut side up, on top of each serving and set the claw meat in the center. Drizzle with any vinaigrette remaining in the bottom of the bowl and serve immediately.

Serves 4

Steamed Mussels with Fresh Herbs

*Along France's northern coast, where mussels prosper in the cold Atlantic waters,
the fresh mollusks are often served with little or no embellishment, save for a sprinkling of
herbs. For a delicious light supper, pair this dish with a side of crisp french fries (recipe
on page 186) and a full-bodied Alsatian wine such as a Gewürztraminer.*

½ cup (2½ oz/75 g) finely chopped shallots

⅓ cup (½ oz/15 g) julienned fresh basil

4 tablespoons fresh tarragon leaves

⅓ cup (½ oz/15 g) chopped fresh chives

⅓ cup (½ oz/15 g) chopped fresh parsley

1½ cups (12 fl oz/375 ml) vinaigrette *(recipe on page 225)*

4 lb (2 kg) mussels in the shell, well scrubbed and beards removed *(see glossary, page 346)*

1 cup (8 fl oz/250 ml) water

½ cup (3 oz/90 g) roasted, peeled and sliced red bell peppers (capsicums) *(see glossary, page 340)*

🌿 In a small bowl, combine the shallots, basil, tarragon, chives, parsley and vinaigrette. Stir to mix and set aside.

🌿 Discard any mussels that do not close to the touch. In a large saucepan, bring the water to a boil. Add the mussels, cover and steam over high heat, stirring once or twice, until the shells open, 3–5 minutes.

🌿 Drain the mussels and discard any that have not opened. Place them in a large serving bowl or divide equally among smaller individual bowls. Scatter the peppers evenly over the top(s).

🌿 Pour the vinaigrette-herb mixture directly over the mussels and peppers. Serve immediately or let cool and serve at room temperature.

Serves 4–6

Steamed Salmon with Potato and Garlic Sabayon

Salmon has been popular in French cooking since the Middle Ages, when it was commonly prepared potted, braised or salted, or as an ingredient in ragouts, soups and pâtés. French bistros today prefer to concentrate on its naturally distinctive flavor, often choosing to serve it either steamed or poached. This delicate sabayon sauce adds the wonderfully mellowed flavor of fresh garlic to this simple preparation.

1 russet potato, peeled and cut into eight pieces

8 cloves garlic

4 salmon fillets, about 5 oz (155 g) each, skin removed
Salt to taste, plus ½ teaspoon salt
Freshly ground white pepper to taste, plus ¼ teaspoon ground white pepper

2 tablespoons fresh lemon juice

¼ cup (2 fl oz/60 ml) warm water

¼ cup (2 fl oz/60 ml) olive oil

2 tablespoons chopped fresh parsley or 4 sprigs fresh chervil

In a saucepan, place the potato and add water to cover generously. Bring to a boil and boil until tender when pierced with a fork, about 20 minutes. While the potato is boiling, put the garlic cloves in a separate saucepan, add water to cover and boil until very soft when pierced with the tip of a knife, about 15 minutes.

Meanwhile, sprinkle both sides of the salmon fillets with salt and white pepper to taste and set them aside until you finish preparing the sauce.

Drain both the garlic cloves and the potato and place in a food processor fitted with a metal blade or in a blender. Add the lemon juice, the ½ teaspoon salt, the ¼ teaspoon white pepper and the warm water. Process or blend on high speed just until smooth and creamy, about 20 seconds. Add the olive oil and blend for another 15 seconds to combine. Taste and adjust the seasoning. Set aside, covered.

Place the salmon fillets on a steamer rack over (not touching) gently boiling water. Cover and steam until the salmon is firm, pale pink and opaque throughout when flaked with a fork, about 5 minutes.

Place a fillet of salmon in the center of each of 4 warmed plates. Pour the sauce directly over the fillets, dividing it equally.

Sprinkle each dish with an equal amount of the chopped parsley or garnish with a chervil sprig and serve immediately.

Serves 4

Sautéed Shrimp with Fried Garlic and Baked Tomato

Fresh shrimp, sautéed in butter, garlic and herbs, is a classic bistro standby. In this recipe, baked tomatoes give the dish still more substance and bright color. Vine-ripened tomatoes provide the best flavor. If they are difficult to find, you might consider substituting a bed of steamed spinach in their place. Serve a crusty baguette alongside for sopping up all the delicious juices.

4   tomatoes, about 1½ lb (750 g) total weight
    Salt and freshly ground pepper
6   tablespoons (3 fl oz/90 ml) olive oil
1   lb (500 g) medium-sized shrimp (prawns), peeled and deveined
1   tablespoon finely chopped garlic
1   tablespoon sherry vinegar
2   tablespoons chopped fresh parsley
    Dash of cayenne pepper

❧ Preheat an oven to 450°F (230°C).

❧ Cut the tomatoes in half and place them, cut side up, in a shallow baking dish. Season to taste with salt and pepper and drizzle 2 tablespoons of the olive oil over the tops. Bake until cooked through but still firm, about 15 minutes.

❧ About 3 minutes before the tomatoes are done, in a sauté pan over high heat, warm 1 tablespoon of the olive oil. Add the shrimp and salt and pepper to taste and sauté until pink and firm, 2–3 minutes.

❧ Transfer the baked tomatoes to individual serving dishes. Place the sautéed shrimp on top of the tomatoes, dividing them evenly.

❧ In a small saucepan over high heat, combine the garlic and the remaining 3 tablespoons olive oil and sauté until the garlic turns golden brown, about 1 minute.

❧ Add the vinegar and deglaze the pan by stirring to dislodge any browned bits from the pan bottom, about 30 seconds. Immediately pour the contents of the saucepan equally over each serving. Sprinkle with the parsley and cayenne. Serve at once.

Serves 4

Sea Scallops with Shaved Fennel

The faint aniseed flavor of fresh fennel adds a subtle complement to sautéed sea scallops in this simple dish. The key to this recipe is to slice the fennel paper-thin so that it appears "shaved." Use a mandoline or an extremely sharp knife for the desired effect. Serve this dish hot or at room temperature over a bed of hot white rice, if you like.

2   fennel bulbs
2   teaspoons salt
2   tablespoons olive oil
20   sea scallops, about 1 lb (500 g) total weight
1   cup (8 fl oz/250 ml) tomato and red pepper coulis *(recipe on page 226)*
    Pinch of ground white pepper
½   teaspoon cayenne pepper
2   tablespoons chopped fresh parsley

🌿 Remove and discard any bruised outer leaves from the fennel bulbs, then cut off any stalks and feathery tops. Using an electric slicer, a mandoline or a very sharp knife, slice the fennel bulbs crosswise as thinly as possible. Place the fennel slices in a sieve or colander and sprinkle with 1 teaspoon of the salt, tossing the fennel to distribute evenly. Let stand for 30 minutes to drain off any water drawn out by the salt. Then rinse under cold running water and dry thoroughly with paper towels.

🌿 In a large sauté pan over high heat, warm the olive oil. Add the scallops and cook, turning once, until golden brown, 1–1½ minutes per side.

🌿 Add the fennel and the tomato-pepper coulis and stir well. Then stir in the remaining 1 teaspoon salt and the white and cayenne peppers. Bring to a boil and cook, stirring, until the scallops are firm to the touch, 1–2 minutes longer.

🌿 Transfer to a warmed platter or individual plates and sprinkle with the chopped parsley. Serve at once.

Serves 4

Monkfish with Lemon and Coriander Seed

Monkfish is among the ugliest fish to look at, a fact that has earned it the nicknames
crapaud *(toad) and* diable de mer *(sea devil) among French cooks and fishermen. Despite
its unfortunate appearance, monkfish has a lean, rich and firm flesh that is often
compared to lobster meat. Any firm, white fish fillet may be substituted.*

2   teaspoons coriander seeds
2   tablespoons fresh lemon juice
2   tablespoons water
¼   cup (1½ oz/45 g) roasted, peeled
    and chopped red bell pepper
    (capsicum) *(see glossary, page 340)*
⅓   cup (3 fl oz/80 ml) olive oil
1   teaspoon salt, plus salt to taste
½   teaspoon ground white pepper,
    plus ground white pepper
    to taste
4   monkfish fillets, ¼ lb (125 g)
    each
2   tablespoons chopped fresh parsley

⚜ In a blender, combine the coriander seeds, lemon juice, water, bell pepper, olive oil, the 1 teaspoon salt and the ½ teaspoon white pepper. Blend at high speed until smooth and creamy, about 1 minute. Pour the purée through a fine-mesh sieve into a clean bowl. Set aside.

⚜ Trim off any thick outer membrane of the monkfish fillets and sprinkle both sides of each fillet with salt and white pepper to taste. Place on a steamer rack over (not touching) gently boiling water. Cover and steam until opaque throughout when pierced with a knife, 6–7 minutes.

⚜ Transfer the fillets to warmed individual plates. Spoon the sauce evenly over the top and sides of the fish. Sprinkle with the parsley and serve at once.

Serves 6–8 as an appetizer; 4 as a main course

Steamed Halibut with Braised Leek Vinaigrette

Bistro chefs often pair the sweet flavor of cooked onions with steamed fish fillets. In this recipe, two onion preparations—braised and fried—set this dish apart. Since the fried onions should remain crisp to contrast with the delicate texture of the fish, add them only at the last moment, or serve them on the side for diners to add as they like.

Vegetable oil for deep-frying
1 large white onion
 Ice cubes
1 teaspoon salt, plus salt to taste
2 leeks, halved lengthwise and carefully washed
½ cup (4 fl oz/125 ml) vinaigrette *(recipe on page 225)*
1 tablespoon chopped fresh chives
1 tablespoon chopped fresh parsley
 Freshly ground pepper
4 halibut fillets, about 5 oz (155 g) each

🌿 In a deep-fat fryer or a large, heavy-bottomed saucepan, pour in vegetable oil to a depth of 3 inches (7.5 cm). Heat to 350°F (180°C) on a deep-fat frying thermometer, or until a crust of bread becomes golden within moments of being dropped into the oil.

🌿 While the oil heats, using a mandoline or a sharp knife, slice the onion crosswise as thinly as possible; you should have about 2 cups (7 oz/ 220 g). Separate the slices into rings.

🌿 Slip the onion slices into the hot oil and stir gently to separate the rings. Fry until golden brown, 10–12 minutes. Using a slotted spoon, remove the onion from the oil and spread them out on paper towels to drain; set aside.

🌿 Fill a bowl with ice cubes and water and set aside. Fill a large saucepan two-thirds full with water. Add the 1 teaspoon salt and bring to a boil.

🌿 Cut the leeks into ½-inch (12-mm) dice; you should have about 3 cups (12 oz/375 g).

🌿 Add the leeks to the boiling water, return to a boil and boil until they are very tender, 4–5 minutes. Drain and immediately plunge them into the ice water to halt the cooking. Drain again.

🌿 In a sauté pan over high heat, combine the cooked leeks and vinaigrette and heat, stirring often, until warmed through, 1–2 minutes. Stir in the chives and parsley. Taste and adjust the seasoning with salt and pepper. Set aside.

🌿 Sprinkle both sides of the halibut fillets with salt and pepper to taste. Place on a steamer rack over (not touching) gently boiling water. Cover and steam until opaque throughout when pierced with a knife, about 5 minutes.

🌿 Using a slotted spoon, remove the leeks from the sauté pan. Place on warmed individual plates, dividing the leeks evenly.

🌿 Place a halibut fillet on top of each bed of leeks. Scatter the fried onion over the fish and serve immediately.

Serves 4

Crispy Fillet of Striped Bass with Pipérade

This true pipérade—a mixture of tomatoes, bell pepper, onions and seasonings—is a signature sauce of the Basque country in southwestern France. The crunchiness of the sautéed skin makes the bass fillets especially flavorful; if you prefer, however, you may remove the skin just before serving.

PIPÉRADE
2   white onions
¼   cup (2 fl oz/60 ml) olive oil
2   green bell peppers (capsicums), seeded, deribbed and thinly sliced crosswise
5   cloves garlic, crushed
2   tomatoes, coarsely chopped
1   teaspoon salt
½   teaspoon ground white pepper
½   teaspoon cayenne pepper
    Pinch of sugar

BASS FILLETS
1   tablespoon olive oil
    Salt and ground white pepper
4   striped bass fillets with skin intact, about ¼ lb (125 g) each

⚓ To make the pipérade, using a mandoline or a sharp knife, slice the onions crosswise as thinly as possible. Separate the slices into rings; you should have about 3 cups (10½ oz/ 330 g) rings.

⚓ In a sauté pan over high heat, warm the ¼ cup (2 fl oz/60 ml) olive oil. Add the onions, bell peppers and garlic and sauté until the vegetables are soft and golden brown, about 10 minutes.

⚓ Add the tomatoes, 1 teaspoon salt, ½ teaspoon white pepper, the cayenne pepper and sugar; stir until blended, then cover. Reduce the heat to medium and continue to cook, stirring occasionally, until soupy, about 15 minutes.

⚓ Meanwhile, cook the fillets. In a nonstick sauté pan over high heat, warm the 1 tablespoon olive oil. Sprinkle both sides of the bass fillets with salt and white pepper to taste.

Place the fillets in the hot pan, skin side down, and cook until the skins are crisp and golden brown, 2–3 minutes. Turn the fillets over and continue cooking until opaque throughout when pierced with a knife, 1–2 minutes longer.

⚓ Just before the fillets are ready, taste the pipérade and adjust the seasoning if necessary. Spoon the sauce onto the center of a warmed platter or individual plates. Promptly remove the fillets from the sauté pan and lay them on top of the sauce. Serve immediately.

Serves 4

Swordfish Steak with Spinach and Citrus Vinaigrette

Sautéed fish fillet served à la florentine *(on a bed of spinach) is a popular method for preparing seafood throughout France. This particular dish is distinquished by its zesty vinaigrette, which combines three types of citrus with the pan juices. The result is light yet extremely flavorful. A full-bodied white wine such as a white Burgundy would balance the sprightly flavors well.*

¼ cup (2 fl oz/60 ml) water

¼ cup (2 oz/60 g) unsalted butter

5 tablespoons (3 fl oz/80 ml) olive oil

1¼ lb (625 g) spinach leaves, stems removed and carefully washed
   Salt and freshly ground pepper

4 swordfish steaks, 5 oz (155 g) each
   Juice of ½ orange
   Juice of ½ lemon
   Juice of ¼ grapefruit

¼ cup (2 fl oz/60 ml) veal stock *(recipe on pages 224–225)* or purchased chicken stock

♨ In a large saucepan over high heat, combine the water, butter and 2 tablespoons of the olive oil. Once the butter has melted completely, add the spinach leaves and salt and pepper to taste. Cover and cook, stirring every 20–30 seconds, until wilted, about 2 minutes. Remove from the heat and set aside, covered.

♨ In a large sauté pan over high heat, warm 1 tablespoon of the olive oil. Sprinkle both sides of the sword-fish steaks with salt and pepper to taste. Place the swordfish steaks in the hot pan and cook, turning once, until done to your liking, 1–2 minutes on each side for medium-rare. Transfer the fish steaks to a plate and cover to keep warm.

♨ In a small bowl, stir together the orange, lemon and grapefruit juices.

♨ Pour off any oil remaining in the sauté pan and place over high heat. When the pan is hot, pour in the cit-rus juices and deglaze by stirring to dislodge any browned bits from the pan bottom. Boil until the liquid is reduced by half, then add the veal or chicken stock and salt and pepper to taste. Return to a boil and stir in the remaining 2 tablespoons olive oil. Remove from the heat.

♨ Drain the spinach in a sieve and divide equally among warmed indi-vidual plates. Place the swordfish steaks on top of the spinach and spoon the citrus mixture evenly over the steaks. Serve immediately.

Serves 4

Seared Tuna Steaks with Onion Marmalade

Onions, which gained a reputation with the potato as the primary and highly versatile ingredient of the French peasant, reach a new level of refinement in this slow-cooked marmalade for seared tuna steaks. The style in many contemporary bistros is to cook the tuna medium-rare, but you can adjust the doneness to suit your taste. A bed of tender cooked lentils makes a good accompaniment.

ONION MARMALADE

2   slices pancetta, 2 oz (60 g) each, or ¼ lb (125 g) thickly sliced bacon
¼   cup (2 fl oz/60 ml) olive oil
2   large white onions, thinly sliced
½   cup (4 fl oz/125 ml) balsamic vinegar
¼   cup (2 fl oz/60 ml) sherry vinegar
½   cup (4 fl oz/125 ml) water
1   teaspoon salt
¼   teaspoon ground white pepper
2   teaspoons sugar
½   teaspoon cayenne pepper

TUNA STEAKS

4   tuna steaks, about 5 oz (155 g) each
2   tablespoons olive oil
    Salt and ground white pepper

🐟 To make the marmalade, first unroll the pancetta, if using. Cut the pancetta or bacon crosswise into strips ½ inch (12 mm) thick.

🐟 In a sauté pan over high heat, warm the ¼ cup (2 fl oz/60 ml) olive oil. Add the pancetta or bacon and sauté until slightly crisp, about 2 minutes. Add the sliced onions and continue to sauté until the onions are golden brown, about 10 minutes.

🐟 Stir in the balsamic vinegar, sherry vinegar, water, salt, white pepper, the sugar and cayenne. Bring to a boil over medium heat, then continue to boil until the liquid evaporates completely, 12–15 minutes.

🐟 About 5 minutes before the marmalade is ready, cook the tuna steaks. In a separate sauté pan over high heat, warm the 2 tablespoons olive oil. Sprinkle both sides of the tuna steaks with salt and white pepper to taste. Place the steaks in the hot pan and cook, turning once, until done to your liking, 1–2 minutes on each side for medium-rare, depending upon the thickness of the steaks.

🐟 Transfer the tuna steaks to warmed individual plates. Top with the onion marmalade and serve immediately.

Serves 4

Poultry and Meat

F rench chefs are expert in marrying cuts of meat or poultry with the cooking techniques best suited to them. Nowhere is this fact more apparent than in the preparation of the main course. The tougher cuts regularly offered on bistro menus, such as beef short ribs and shoulder of pork or lamb, are made tender by braising or stewing in their juices often with a mixture of vegetables. Leaner meats, such as duck, chicken breast or pork tenderloin, are frequently sautéed or simply broiled as a means of sealing in their own flavorful juices.

Main dish selections traditionally vary according to the region, but most bistro menus are sure to include at least a half-dozen variations on the same French specialties that have been featured in these lively eateries for nearly two centuries. Among the highlights of these classic offerings are the robust cassoulet of Languedoc; whole roasted chicken; perfectly pan-fried steaks accompanied with thin, crisp *pommes frites;* and lightly browned rabbit blanketed in a creamy mustard sauce. Contemporary bistro chefs balance the hearty flavors of old favorites with a host of lighter dishes that make use of the growing availability of fresh ingredients.

175

Chicken Curry with Green Apple

When curry powder was introduced in France by spice traders in the 18th century, French cooks began to experiment with the highly versatile mix of as many as 10 different ground spices. Curry powders vary slightly from region to region; this recipe calls for a Madras blend, which is one of the best. Serve this quick-to-assemble stew with basmati rice and cold beer.

1 chicken, about 3 lb (1.5 kg)
3 tablespoons olive oil
1 white onion, chopped
1 carrot, peeled and coarsely chopped
1 celery stalk, coarsely chopped
1 cup (8 fl oz/250 ml) dry white wine
1 teaspoon Madras curry powder
2 cups (16 fl oz/500 ml) veal stock or chicken stock *(recipes on pages 224–225)*
  Salt and freshly ground pepper
1 Granny Smith or other tart green apple, peeled, cored and coarsely chopped

🌿 Cut the chicken into 8 serving pieces, discarding the wing tips and the tail.

🌿 In a large sauté pan over high heat, warm 2 tablespoons of the olive oil. Add the chicken pieces and brown on all sides, 2–3 minutes. Add the onion, carrot and celery, reduce the heat to medium-high and sauté until the vegetables are golden brown, about 2 minutes longer. Add the white wine and cook until the liquid evaporates, 5–8 minutes.

🌿 Stir in the curry powder and the veal or chicken stock; bring to a boil. Reduce the heat to medium and simmer, uncovered, until the chicken is cooked through when pierced with a knife, 8–10 minutes longer. Season to taste with salt and pepper.

🌿 Transfer the chicken to a serving dish and cover to keep warm. Continue to simmer the sauce over medium heat until reduced by half, 5–8 minutes longer.

🌿 Meanwhile, in a small sauté pan over medium-high heat, warm the remaining 1 tablespoon olive oil. Add the apple and sauté until tender but firm, 1–2 minutes. Pour the cooked apple over the chicken.

🌿 Strain the reduced sauce through a fine-mesh sieve into a clean container; discard the contents of the sieve.

🌿 Pour the sauce over the chicken and apple and serve immediately.

Serves 4

Breast of Chicken with Carrot and Cumin Broth

French gastronome Brillat-Savarin once said that "poultry is for the cook what canvas is for the painter." Bistro chefs tend to agree, often combining chicken with a wide variety of ingredients and preparations. This dish, pairing chicken breast with the flavors of the Middle East, reflects the light and sophisticated approach of the modern bistro.

6	large carrots, peeled and cut into thin slices
2½	tablespoons olive oil
⅔	cup (2½ oz/75 g) chopped white onion
2	cloves garlic, crushed
1	tablespoon peeled and finely diced fresh ginger
2	tablespoons fresh lemon juice
2	cups (16 fl oz/500 ml) water
½	teaspoon cumin seeds
2	tablespoons chopped fresh parsley
	Salt and freshly ground pepper
4	boneless chicken breast halves, about 6 oz (185 g) each

🌿 Fill a saucepan three-fourths full with water and bring to a boil. Add two-thirds of the carrots and return to a boil. Cook the carrots until they are tender when pierced with a knife, about 5 minutes. Drain and set aside.

🌿 In a sauté pan over medium-high heat, warm 1½ tablespoons of the olive oil. Add the onion and garlic and sauté until soft and translucent, 3–4 minutes. Add the ginger and sauté for 1 minute longer. Then add the remaining carrots and stir for 30 seconds. Add the lemon juice, water and cumin seeds and bring to a boil. Cover, reduce the heat to medium and simmer until the carrots are tender, 5–7 minutes.

🌿 Pour the contents of the sauté pan into a food processor fitted with a metal blade or a blender and process or blend on high speed until smooth, 1–2 minutes.

🌿 Pour the sauce through a fine-mesh sieve back into the sauté pan. Add the reserved boiled carrots and the parsley and bring to a boil. Reduce the heat to low, cover and keep warm while you cook the chicken.

🌿 In a large sauté pan over high heat, warm the remaining 1 tablespoon olive oil. Rub salt and pepper to taste onto both sides of the chicken breasts. Add the chicken to the hot pan, skin side down, and cook for 1–2 minutes. Reduce the heat to medium and continue to cook the chicken, turning it occasionally, until opaque throughout when pierced with a knife, 12–15 minutes.

🌿 Transfer the chicken breasts to the carrot-cumin broth, turning to coat them completely.

🌿 To serve, transfer the chicken breasts to warmed shallow bowls and spoon the carrot-cumin broth over the tops.

Serves 4

Duck Leg Confit with Warm Green Lentil Salad

The tradition of cooking and then storing duck in its own fat goes back to the Moors, who passed through southwest France in the 8th century A.D. Although confit was once prepared as a means to preserve meat over long periods of time, it is now prized for its succulence and intense flavor.

DUCK LEG CONFIT
1   tablespoon salt
1   teaspoon cracked pepper
4   duck legs, about ¾ lb (375 g) each
4   cloves garlic, crushed
4   fresh thyme sprigs
2   bay leaves, torn in half
5   lb (2.5 kg) duck or pork fat, cut into pieces

GREEN LENTIL SALAD
6   cups (48 fl oz/1.5 l) water
1½ cups (10 oz/315 g) dried green lentils
    Bouquet garni *(see glossary, page 340)*
1   teaspoon salt
½   teaspoon freshly ground pepper
1   cup (8 fl oz/250 ml) veal stock or chicken stock *(recipes on pages 224–225)*
    Vinaigrette *(recipe on page 225)*
2   tablespoons chopped fresh parsley

⚜ To make the confit, rub the 1 tablespoon salt and the cracked pepper evenly over the duck legs and place in a shallow glass dish. Place 1 clove garlic, a thyme sprig and half of a bay leaf on each leg. Cover with plastic wrap and refrigerate overnight.

⚜ The next day, to render the duck or pork fat, place the fat in a heavy-bottomed pan over low heat. Cook slowly until all the fat liquifies, any tissue has become crispy and the impurities sink to the bottom of the pan. This should take 2–3 hours. Pour the clear fat through a fine-mesh sieve lined with cheesecloth (muslin) into a large saucepan.

⚜ Cut the duck legs in half to separate the thighs and drumsticks. Place the meat, along with the thyme, garlic and bay leaves, into the melted fat. Bring to a boil, then reduce the heat to medium-low and simmer, uncovered, until the meat is easily pierced with a fork and the juices run clear, about 2½ hours.

⚜ Using tongs, carefully transfer the meat to a deep earthenware bowl or terrine. Line a fine-mesh sieve with cheesecloth (muslin) and strain enough of the fat through the sieve to cover the meat completely. Let cool until the fat hardens fully. Make sure that the duck pieces are totally sealed in the fat so that no air can reach them. Cover and refrigerate for at least 24 hours or for up to 3 weeks.

⚜ Preheat an oven to 450°F (230°C).

⚜ To make the lentil salad, bring the water to a boil in a large saucepan. Rinse the lentils under cold running water. Add the lentils, bouquet garni, the 1 teaspoon salt and the pepper to the boiling water. Reduce the heat to medium, cover and simmer until the lentils are tender, 20–25 minutes.

⚜ Meanwhile, remove the duck legs from the fat, scraping off as much of the excess fat as possible. Place the meat, skin side down, in a roasting pan. Place in the oven until the skin is crispy and the meat is hot throughout, about 15 minutes.

⚜ When the lentils are cooked, drain them in a fine-mesh sieve. Discard the bouquet garni and place the lentils in a saucepan. Add the stock and vinaigrette and bring to a boil. Stir in the parsley, then taste and adjust the seasoning.

⚜ Spoon a bed of lentils onto warmed individual plates and place the hot duck legs on top. Serve immediately.

Serves 4

Sautéed Breast of Duck with Wild Mushrooms

The magret *is the large, plumped breast of a mallard or Barbary duck. For especially moist and tender results, allow the cooked meat to rest for at least 5 minutes before slicing so the juices can redistribute through each breast. Use the wild mushrooms called for here, or replace them with your own favorites.*

2	boneless whole duck breasts, about 1 lb (500 g) each
	Salt and freshly ground pepper
¼	cup (2 oz/60 g) unsalted butter
2	tablespoons chopped shallots
2	cloves garlic, crushed and then finely chopped
6	oz (185 g) fresh chanterelle mushrooms, brushed clean, trimmed and coarsely chopped
6	oz (185 g) fresh oyster mushrooms, brushed clean, trimmed and coarsely chopped
5	oz (155 g) fresh shiitake mushrooms, brushed clean, trimmed and coarsely chopped
⅓	cup (3 fl oz/80 ml) dry white wine
1	cup (8 fl oz/250 ml) veal stock *(recipe on pages 224–225)* or purchased beef stock
1	tablespoon chopped fresh parsley

☙ Preheat an oven to 400°F (200°C).

☙ Using a sharp knife, trim off the excess fat from around the edges of the duck breasts. Score the remaining skin covering the breast in a cross-hatch pattern every 1 inch (2.5 cm). Rub salt and pepper to taste onto all sides of the breasts. Place them, skin side down, in an ovenproof sauté pan. Place the pan over high heat and heat until the breasts begin to sizzle loudly, 2–3 minutes. Then slip the sauté pan into the oven and cook for 10 minutes. Turn the breasts over and continue to cook in the oven until firm to the touch, about 5 minutes longer for medium-rare. Remove the duck breasts from the pan and keep warm.

☙ Pour off the fat from the sauté pan. Place the pan over medium-high heat. Add the butter and, when it melts, add the shallots and garlic and sauté just until the shallots are translucent, 1–2 minutes. Add all of the mushrooms and salt and pepper to taste and continue to sauté until the mushrooms begin to soften, 2–3 minutes.

☙ Add the wine and cook until reduced by one-third, about 2 minutes. Add the veal stock and bring to a boil. Reduce the heat to medium and simmer for 5 minutes. Stir in the parsley. Taste and adjust the seasoning.

☙ Meanwhile, cut the duck breasts crosswise on the diagonal into slices ½ inch (12 mm) thick.

☙ Spoon the mushrooms onto a warmed serving platter or individual plates. Arrange the sliced breasts on top. Serve immediately.

Serves 6–8

Roast Chicken Stuffed with Bread and Garlic

Some type of roast chicken is offered on the menu of nearly every traditional bistro. Here, it is stuffed with thick pieces of bread that have been liberally buttered and rubbed with garlic. The finished stuffing, saturated with the fragrant meat juices, can be served alongside the cooked meat.

1   roasting chicken, about 4 lb (2 kg)
    Salt and freshly ground pepper
6   whole cloves garlic, plus 2 cloves garlic, sliced paper-thin
1   day-old baguette, sliced into strips about 5 inches (13 cm) long and 1 inch (2.5 cm) thick
2   tablespoons unsalted butter, at room temperature
2   sprigs fresh thyme
1   lemon, cut in half
1   tablespoon olive oil
1   cup (8 fl oz/250 ml) water
¼   cup (2 fl oz/60 ml) veal stock or chicken stock *(recipes on pages 224–225)*

⚜ Preheat an oven to 450°F (230°C).

⚜ Rinse the chicken thoroughly with water and then pat dry with paper towels. Rub inside and out with salt and pepper to taste.

⚜ Cut one of the whole garlic cloves in half. Rub the cut sides of the clove over each baguette strip. Spread the strips on all sides with 1½ tablespoons of the butter.

⚜ Using the tip of a sharp knife, make at least 12 small incisions in the skin on all sides of the chicken. Slip 1 thin garlic slice into each incision, between the skin and the meat.

⚜ Rub the inside of the chicken with the remaining ½ tablespoon butter, and then press the remaining thin garlic slices against the cavity walls. Stuff the bread strips into the chicken cavity and, using kitchen string, truss the chicken by tying the legs together and then tying the legs and wings tight against the body. Tuck the 2 thyme sprigs between the chicken thighs and body.

⚜ Place the chicken in a roasting pan, breast side down, and place the lemon halves alongside. Drizzle the olive oil over the chicken and turn breast side up. Scatter the remaining 5 whole garlic cloves around the chicken.

⚜ Roast the chicken for 15 minutes. Turn breast side down and roast 10 minutes longer. Add the water to the roasting pan and continue to roast until the juices run clear when the thigh joint is pierced with a knife, 10–20 minutes longer.

⚜ Transfer the chicken from the roasting pan to a cutting board. Snip the strings and remove them. Remove the bread from the cavity; arrange it around the edge of a serving platter or place it in a separate dish. Carve the chicken into 8 serving pieces and arrange them in the center of the platter, or place the whole chicken on the platter to carve at the table.

⚜ Remove the lemons from the roasting pan. Place the pan over high heat, squeeze the lemons into the pan and deglaze by stirring to dislodge any browned bits from the pan bottom. Add the veal or chicken stock and bring to a boil. Pour the sauce through a fine-mesh sieve into a small serving pitcher.

⚜ Place the pitcher of sauce alongside the chicken and serve at once.

Serves 4

Rabbit with Mustard and Fava Beans

*Although most common to the Burgundy region, rabbit with mustard sauce is a
bistro favorite throughout France. The addition of fresh fava beans sets this particular
dish apart. Be sure to select beans that are young and tender or use fresh pasta
or peas in their place. This recipe is also delicious prepared with chicken.*

2 tablespoons olive oil
1 rabbit, about 2 lb (1 kg), cut into 8 serving pieces
1 small white onion, diced
4 cloves garlic, crushed
1 cup (8 fl oz/250 ml) dry white wine
1 teaspoon salt
½ teaspoon freshly ground pepper
   Bouquet garni *(see glossary, page 340)*
3 cups (24 fl oz/750 ml) veal or chicken stock *(recipes on pages 224–225)*
   Ice cubes
3 lbs (1.5 kg) fava (broad) beans
2 tablespoons Dijon-style mustard
2 tablespoons julienned fresh basil

❧ In a large sauté pan over high heat, warm the olive oil. Add the rabbit pieces and brown well, turning once, about 2 minutes on each side. Using tongs, transfer the rabbit to a plate and set aside.

❧ To the same sauté pan over medium heat, add the onion and the garlic and sauté until they begin to brown, about 2 minutes. Return the rabbit to the pan and add the wine, salt and pepper. Cook over medium heat until the liquid is reduced by half, about 10 minutes.

❧ Add the bouquet garni and stock to the pan and bring to a boil. Reduce the heat to medium and simmer, uncovered, until the meat falls easily away from the bone, 45–50 minutes.

❧ While the rabbit is simmering, fill a bowl with ice cubes and water and set aside. Remove the fava beans from their pods and discard the pods. Fill a saucepan three-fourths full with water and bring to a boil. Add the beans to the boiling water and boil for 2 minutes. Drain the beans, then plunge them immediately into the ice water. Remove from the water. Using a sharp knife, slit the skin on the edge of each bean and "pop" the bean free of its skin. Discard the skins and set the beans aside.

❧ Using tongs, remove the rabbit meat from the sauté pan and place it in the center of a serving platter.

❧ Strain the sauce remaining in the sauté pan through a fine-mesh sieve directly into a saucepan over medium heat. Add the fava beans and mustard and heat, stirring occasionally, until heated through.

❧ Pour the sauce over the meat, sprinkle the basil over the top and serve immediately.

Serves 4

New York Strip with French Fries

There are few dishes more frequently associated with classic bistro fare than the deliciously simple Steak Frites. To provide the best flavor and texture to pan-fried steak, the meat should be at room temperature at the start of cooking and the pan must be extremely hot when the meat is added.

RED WINE BUTTER
¼ cup (1 oz/30 g) chopped shallots
¾ cup (6 fl oz/180 ml) dry red wine
½ cup (4 oz/125 g) unsalted butter, cut into small pieces
½ teaspoon salt
¼ teaspoon freshly ground pepper

FRENCH FRIES
3 large russet potatoes
   Peanut oil for deep-frying

STEAKS
   Salt and freshly ground pepper
4 New York strip steaks or other tenderloin steaks, about 5 oz (155 g) each
2 tablespoons olive oil

🌿 To make the red wine butter, in a small saucepan over high heat, combine the shallots and red wine. Bring to a boil and boil until the liquid evaporates completely, about 10 minutes.

🌿 Place the butter pieces in a bowl, and pour the shallots over them. Add the salt and pepper and whisk until no lumps remain. Cover and refrigerate until the mixture is the consistency of butter, about 1 hour.

🌿 To make the french fries, peel the potatoes and slice lengthwise ¼ inch (6 mm) thick. Then cut each slice lengthwise into strips ¼ inch (6 mm) wide. Fill a bowl three-fourths full with water and add the potato strips. Let stand for 15–20 minutes, then drain, rinse, and drain again. Repeat the soaking process one more time.

🌿 In a deep-fat fryer or a large, heavy-bottomed saucepan, pour in peanut oil to a depth of 3 inches (7.5 cm). Heat to 350°F (180°C) on a deep-fat frying thermometer, or until a crust of bread becomes golden within moments of being dropped into the oil.

🌿 Drain the potatoes and pat dry with paper towels. When the oil is hot, working in 2 or 3 batches, slip the potatoes into the oil and fry until they are lightly cooked and soft throughout, 5–7 minutes.

🌿 Using a slotted spatula, transfer the potatoes to paper towels to drain. Let cool completely, 15–20 minutes.

🌿 Bring the oil back to 350°F (180°C). When it is ready, again working in 2 or 3 batches, slip the potatoes into the oil and fry, turning occasionally, until they are crisp and golden brown, about 6 minutes. Using a slotted spoon, transfer the potatoes to a tray lined with paper towels. Keep warm while you cook the remaining potatoes.

🌿 While the final batch of potatoes is frying, prepare the steaks. Rub salt and pepper to taste onto both sides of each steak. In a large sauté pan over high heat, warm the olive oil. When the pan is hot, add the steaks and cook, turning once, until done to your liking, 1½–2 minutes on each side for medium-rare.

🌿 Transfer the steaks to warmed individual plates. Spoon 1–2 tablespoons of the butter on top of each steak. Sprinkle the french fries with salt and pepper to taste and place a mound of the hot fries alongside each steak. Serve immediately.

Serves 4

186

Braised Veal Short Ribs with Parsnips

Hearty and comforting braises like this one are always a popular addition to menus during the winter months. The short ribs should be cooked with all the fat intact, as it adds flavor and body to the sauce. If you like, you can remove the fat and bones from the meat just before serving. If parsnips are unavailable, use potatoes instead. Accompany the dish with plenty of fresh bread to soak up any remaining sauce.

SHORT RIBS

3	tablespoons olive oil
3	lb (1.5 kg) veal short ribs
2	carrots, peeled and diced
1	large white onion, diced
1	celery stalk
6	cloves garlic
1	cup (8 fl oz/250 ml) dry white wine
5	cups (40 fl oz/1.25 l) veal stock *(recipe on pages 224–225)* or purchased beef stock
	Bouquet garni *(see glossary, page 340)*
1	tablespoon salt
1	teaspoon freshly ground pepper

PARSNIPS

4	parsnips, peeled and cut into thin strips 2 inches (5 cm) long and ¼ inch (6 mm) wide
¾	cup (6 fl oz/180 ml) water
	Salt and freshly ground pepper
¼	cup (2 oz/60 g) unsalted butter
2	tablespoons chopped fresh parsley

To make the short ribs, in a large saucepan over high heat, warm the olive oil. When the pan is hot, add the veal short ribs and brown well on each side, about 2 minutes per side. Using tongs, transfer the short ribs to a plate. Set aside.

To the same saucepan over medium heat, add the carrots, onion, celery and garlic and sauté until they begin to brown, about 5 minutes.

Pour the wine into the pan and deglaze by stirring to dislodge any browned bits from the pan bottom. Bring to a boil and return the short ribs to the pan. Add the stock, bouquet garni, salt and pepper and return to a boil. Reduce the heat to medium-low and simmer until the meat begins to fall from the bones, about 1 hour.

Meanwhile, make the parsnips. In a large sauté pan over high heat, combine the parsnips, water and salt and pepper to taste. Bring to a boil and boil until the liquid evaporates and the parsnips are tender, about 5 minutes. Add the butter and sauté until the parsnips are golden brown, 3–4 minutes.

Once the meat and vegetables are done, using the tongs, transfer the short ribs to a warmed platter. Strain the juice remaining in the saucepan through a fine-mesh sieve directly over the ribs.

Arrange the parsnips alongside the meat. Sprinkle the parsley over the ribs and parsnips and serve at once.

Serves 4

Cassoulet

Cassoulet originated in the Languedoc region of southwest France. The main ingredient is always white beans to which are added a variety of different meats according to region. This one, combining lamb with sausage and duck confit, is similar to the classic cassoulets of Toulouse.

Duck leg confit *(recipe on page 181)*

4½ cups (2 lb/1 kg) dried white beans

1 white onion

5 whole cloves

½ cup (4 oz/125 g) rendered duck fat, from preparing the confit

1 carrot, peeled and coarsely chopped

2 celery stalks, coarsely chopped

⅔ cup (3 oz/90 g) garlic cloves (about 2 heads)

1 piece pancetta, ½ lb (250 g), cut into 1-inch (2.5-cm) cubes

10½ cups (84 fl oz/2.6 l) veal stock *(recipe on pages 224–225)*

2 cups (16 fl oz/500 ml) water

½ lb (250 g) smoked ham hock

2 tomatoes, cut into quarters

Bouquet garni *(see glossary, page 340)*

½ teaspoon salt

1 tablespoon whole black peppercorns

2 lb (1 kg) boneless lamb shoulder

2 tablespoons olive oil

1 cup (8 fl oz/250 ml) dry white wine

1 lb (500 g) cooked pork sausage, cut in half lengthwise

½ cup (2 oz/60 g) fine dried bread crumbs

⚜ Prepare the duck leg confit; set aside.

⚜ Sort through the beans, discarding any misshapen beans or stones. Place in a large bowl, add water to cover generously and let soak overnight. Drain the beans, rinse well; set aside.

⚜ Cut the onion in half and chop half of it. Stud the other half with the 5 cloves.

⚜ In a large, heavy-bottomed saucepan or stockpot over high heat, warm the rendered fat. Add the carrot, celery, chopped onion, garlic and pancetta and sauté until the vegetables start to brown, about 5 minutes.

⚜ Add the white beans, 8 cups (64 fl oz/2 l) of the veal stock, water, clove-studded onion, ham hock, tomatoes, bouquet garni, salt and peppercorns and bring to a boil. Reduce the heat to medium, cover and simmer until the beans are tender but not mushy, about 1 hour.

⚜ Meanwhile, trim any excess fat from the lamb shoulder and cut into 1-inch (2.5-cm) cubes. In a large sauté pan over high heat, warm the olive oil. Working in batches, add the lamb and sauté until the meat begins to brown, about 5 minutes. Using a slotted spoon, transfer the meat to a plate and set aside.

⚜ Pour off the fat from the pan and return the pan to high heat. When the pan is hot, pour in the wine and deglaze by stirring to dislodge any browned bits from the pan bottom. Return the lamb to the pan, add the remaining 2½ cups (20 fl oz/600 ml) veal stock and bring to a boil. Reduce the heat to medium and simmer until the lamb is tender when pierced with a fork, about 45 minutes.

⚜ Remove and discard the clove-studded onion and bouquet garni from the bean mixture. Preheat an oven to 400°F (200°C).

⚜ Remove the duck legs from the fat and place on a rack in a baking pan; reserve the rendered fat for other uses. Heat in the oven for 2–3 minutes until the fat melts off.

⚜ Add the duck legs, lamb shoulder and sausage to the beans. Bring to a boil and boil for about 3 minutes, stirring gently, to blend the flavors.

⚜ Transfer the contents of the pot to a large, heavy-bottomed baking dish, distributing the meats evenly, and sprinkle the bread crumbs evenly over the top. Bake in the oven until browned on top, about 20 minutes. Serve immediately.

Serves 8–10

Drunken Pork Shoulder with Cabbage and Pears

*Because pork shoulder is less expensive than the leg or the tenderloin and becomes more
tender with long cooking, it is a popular ingredient in the flavorful stews of the French countryside.
This "drunken" version features pork marinated and cooked in plenty of robust red wine.*

Bouquet garni *(see glossary, page 340)*
2 white onions, diced
2 carrots, peeled and diced
2 celery stalks, diced
3 cloves garlic
30 whole black peppercorns
5 cups (40 fl oz/1.25 l) dry red wine, such as Cabernet or Merlot
Salt to taste, plus 1 tablespoon salt
3 lb (1.5 kg) boneless pork shoulder, cut into 1-inch (2.5-cm) cubes
6 tablespoons (3 fl oz/90 ml) olive oil
4 cups (32 fl oz/1 l) veal stock or chicken stock *(recipes on pages 224–225)*
1 head green cabbage, thinly sliced
3 tablespoons unsalted butter
¼ vanilla bean (pod), split in half lengthwise
3 ripe but firm pears, such as Comice, cored, peeled and cut into ¾-inch (2-cm) cubes
3 tablespoons chopped fresh parsley

🌱 In a large shallow nonaluminum dish, combine the bouquet garni, onions, carrots, celery, garlic, peppercorns, 4½ cups (36 fl oz/1.1 l) of the red wine and salt to taste. Stir to mix. Add the pork and turn to coat evenly. Cover and refrigerate for at least 5 hours or as long as overnight.

🌱 Drain the meat and vegetables in a sieve, capturing the marinade in a small saucepan. Bring the marinade to a boil, then remove it from the heat and set aside. Separate the meat from the vegetables; set aside separately.

🌱 In a sauté pan over high heat, warm 4 tablespoons (2 fl oz/60 ml) of the olive oil. Pat the meat dry with paper towels. Working in small batches, add the meat to the pan and brown on all sides, about 2 minutes. Transfer the meat to a large saucepan.

🌱 To the same sauté pan used for browning the meat, add the reserved vegetables and sauté over medium-high heat until they begin to brown, about 5 minutes.

🌱 Transfer the vegetables to the saucepan holding the meat. Add the reserved red wine marinade. Bring to a boil over high heat and boil until reduced by half, about 10 minutes. Add the veal or chicken stock and return to a boil. Reduce the heat to medium and simmer, uncovered, until the pork is tender, 50–60 minutes.

🌱 Meanwhile, fill another large saucepan two-thirds full with water, add the 1 tablespoon salt and bring to a boil. Add the cabbage, return to a boil and cook until wilted, about 2 minutes. Drain the cabbage, rinse with cold water and drain again.

🌱 In a frying pan over medium heat, melt the butter. Add the cabbage and sauté for 2 minutes. Remove from the heat and set aside.

🌱 In another small sauté pan, combine the remaining ½ cup (4 fl oz/ 125 ml) red wine, the vanilla bean and the pears and bring to a boil. Reduce the heat to medium and simmer, turning the fruit every few minutes, until tender, 5–10 minutes.

🌱 Drain the meat and vegetables in a sieve, capturing the juices in a bowl. Cover the juices to keep them warm. Separate the pork from the vegetables; discard the vegetables.

🌱 Arrange a bed of the cabbage on a warmed platter. Place the pork on top of the cabbage, and pour the juices over the top. Scatter the poached pear cubes around the meat. Garnish with the parsley and serve at once.

Serves 4–6

193

Roast Pork Tenderloin with Apple-Onion Marmalade

*When pork was introduced in France by the Gauls during the rule of the Roman Empire,
it was considered a meat fit primarily for the common people. These days, advanced farming
techniques produce meat that is far more tender and lean than the original. The best part
of the pork—the tenderloin—is now the basis for a myriad of sophisticated dishes.*

3 tablespoons plus ¼ cup (2 fl oz/ 60 ml) olive oil

1 white onion, thinly sliced

⅓ cup (3 fl oz/80 ml) balsamic vinegar

⅓ cup (3 fl oz/80 ml) sherry vinegar

1 cup (8 fl oz/250 ml) water
   Salt and freshly ground pepper

2 pork tenderloins, about ¾ lb (375 g) each

2 fresh thyme sprigs

2 tablespoons unsalted butter

1 small green apple, peeled, cored and cut into ½-inch (12-mm) cubes

3 pitted prunes, thinly sliced

1 cup (8 fl oz/250 ml) veal stock or chicken stock *(recipes on pages 224–225)*

2 tablespoons finely chopped fresh parsley

❧ In a sauté pan over medium heat, warm the 3 tablespoons olive oil. Add the onion and sauté until golden brown, about 5 minutes. Add the balsamic vinegar, sherry vinegar, water and salt and pepper to taste and cook until the liquid has evaporated and the onions are very soft, about 45 minutes. Set aside.

❧ Preheat an oven to 450°F (230°C).

❧ Rub salt and pepper to taste on all sides of the tenderloins. Place them in a roasting pan. Pour the ¼ cup (2 fl oz/ 60 ml) olive oil over the top. Place 1 thyme sprig on each tenderloin.

❧ Place the pan in the oven and roast the pork for 10 minutes. Turn the pork over and roast until firm and pale pink in the center when cut with a knife, about 10 minutes longer.

❧ While the pork is cooking, in a large sauté pan over medium heat, melt the butter. Add the apple and prunes and sauté until slightly soft and caramelized, 3–5 minutes. Add the onion marmalade mixture to the pan and continue to sauté until the flavors have blended, 2–3 minutes longer.

❧ Add the stock to the pan and bring to a boil. Immediately remove from the heat and cover to keep warm.

❧ When the pork is done, transfer it to a cutting board, cover with aluminum foil and let rest for 5 minutes. Then, using a sharp knife, cut the pork tenderloins into slices ½ inch (12 mm) thick. Arrange the pork slices on a warmed serving platter.

❧ Spoon the warm marmalade mixture over the pork. Sprinkle with the parsley and serve immediately.

Serves 4

Sautéed Lamb Shoulder with Garlic and Thyme

The combination of lamb with garlic and herbs is a classic European preparation. To vary the recipe, serve it with a variety of different side dishes, such as spicy couscous with garbanzo beans or ratatouille. A red Bordeaux or other hearty, slightly complex wine is always a nice accompaniment.

3	tablespoons olive oil
2	lb (1 kg) boneless lamb shoulder, trimmed of fat and cut into 1-inch (2.5-cm) cubes
½	cup (2 oz/60 g) chopped white onion
1	small carrot, peeled and diced
1	head garlic, separated into cloves and peeled
1	teaspoon salt, plus salt to taste
¼	teaspoon freshly ground pepper, plus ground pepper to taste
1	tomato, coarsely chopped
1	tablespoon finely chopped fresh thyme
1	cup (8 fl oz/250 ml) dry white wine
3	cups (24 fl oz/750 ml) veal stock *(recipe on pages 224–225)* or purchased beef stock

In a large sauté pan over high heat, warm 2 tablespoons of the olive oil. Working in batches, add the lamb and sauté until the meat begins to brown, about 5 minutes. Using a slotted spoon, transfer the meat to a plate and set aside.

Pour off the fat from the pan and place over medium-high heat. Add the remaining 1 tablespoon olive oil to the pan, and, when it is hot, add the onion, carrot and garlic and sauté until the vegetables begin to brown, 4–5 minutes.

Return the lamb to the pan and add the 1 teaspoon salt, the ¼ teaspoon pepper, tomato, thyme and wine. Reduce the heat to medium and cook until the liquid is reduced by half, about 5 minutes. Add the veal stock and bring to a boil over high heat. Reduce the heat to medium and simmer until the lamb is tender when pierced with a fork, about 45 minutes.

Pour the contents of the sauté pan through a fine-mesh sieve into a clean container. Remove the meat and vegetables from the sieve and separate them. Keep the meat warm.

Place the vegetables and all of the strained liquid into a food processor fitted with a metal blade or in a blender and process or blend on high speed until the sauce is smooth, about 30 seconds.

Pour the sauce into a saucepan and rewarm over medium heat. Season to taste with salt and pepper.

Place the lamb on a warmed serving platter or individual plates and pour the warmed sauce over the top. Serve immediately.

Serves 4

Desserts

A lthough some of the most sophisticated bistros, like the best French restaurants, feature a pastry cart from which diners may select their choice of the daily specialties, most bistro desserts tend toward more homespun fare. In fact, desserts are not a daily selection for most bistro habitués, who instead elect to finish their meals with a bit of cheese and fresh fruit, leaving the sweets for special occasions.

Therefore, when dessert is ordered, it is enjoyed with both great relish and some measure of abandon. In this chapter, you'll encounter several desserts that continue to appear on bistro menus year after year. Fresh fruit, an essential element of the French dessert repertoire, is well represented here by a crisp apple tart and a baked pudding known as clafouti. Even more evident is the generous use of eggs and cream, which show up most delectably in the dense crème brûlée, creamy lemon custard tart and delicate chocolate soufflé.

To cap the meal in truly French style, you might offer a glass of chilled Champagne or a small flute of sweet dessert wine to complement the delicate flavors of your final course.

Chocolate Soufflé

This featherlight soufflé contains no flour, so it is both more chocolatey and more delicate than most others and should be served immediately. Cook it in a large soufflé dish or individual ones; just take care not to fill the dishes more than two-thirds full and adjust the cooking time as necessary.

¼ cup (2 oz/60 g) unsalted butter, melted
2 tablespoons plus ½ cup (4 oz/ 120 g) granulated sugar
3 oz (90 g) unsweetened chocolate, finely chopped
3 egg yolks
5 egg whites
Confectioners' (icing) sugar, optional

🌿 Preheat an oven to 375°F (190°C). Brush the melted butter on the bottom and sides of a soufflé dish 7½ inches (19 cm) in diameter and 4 inches (10 cm) deep.

🌿 Place the prepared soufflé dish in a refrigerator for about 2 minutes, then sprinkle the bottom and sides with the 2 tablespoons granulated sugar, coating evenly.

🌿 Place the chocolate in the top pan of a double boiler or in a heatproof bowl over (not touching) barely simmering water in a pan. Stir just until the chocolate melts, then remove it from the heat. Add ¼ cup (2 oz/60 g) of the remaining granulated sugar, stir to combine, then whisk in the egg yolks. Remove from the heat and let cool.

🌿 Place the egg whites in a clean bowl and, using an electric mixer set on medium-high speed, beat the egg whites until they form stiff but moist peaks. Pour the remaining ¼ cup (2 oz/60 g) granulated sugar into the egg whites and continue to beat until the peaks are stiff and glossy.

🌿 Using a rubber spatula and working in several batches, carefully fold the egg whites into the melted chocolate until no streaks remain. Do not overmix. Pour the mixture into the prepared soufflé dish.

🌿 Bake until the top has risen and is firm to the touch, 20–25 minutes. Sift confectioners' sugar lightly over the top, if desired, then serve at once.

Serves 4–6

Mixed Fruit Clafouti

Clafouti, a classic pudding which originated in the Limousin region of France, is traditionally prepared with black cherries. In this recipe, a variety of fruits have been used, but you can incorporate nearly any of your favorites. Sift a dusting of confectioners' (icing) sugar over the top of the cooled cakes before serving, if you like.

½ cup (3 oz/90 g) whole blanched almonds or ⅔ cup (3 oz/90 g) purchased ground almonds

½ cup (4 fl oz/125 ml) milk

½ cup (4 fl oz/125 ml) heavy (double) cream

⅓ cup (3 oz/90 g) plus 1 tablespoon sugar

2 eggs

½ vanilla bean (pod), split in half lengthwise

1 tablespoon unsalted butter

¾ cup (3 oz/90 g) peeled, cored and diced firm green apple

1 mango, peeled, pitted and diced

½ cup (2 oz/60 g) blackberries

🌿 Preheat an oven to 400°F (200°C).

🌿 If you are using whole almonds, place the nuts in a nut grinder or in a food processor fitted with the metal blade. Grind or process until the nuts are a fine powder. (Do not overprocess.)

🌿 In a large bowl, combine the milk, cream, ground almonds, the ⅓ cup (3 oz/90 g) sugar and the eggs. Using the tip of a knife, scrape the seeds from the vanilla bean directly into the bowl. Using a wire whisk, mix until well combined; set aside.

🌿 In a sauté pan over medium heat, melt the butter. Add the apple and the 1 tablespoon sugar and sauté, stirring, until lightly caramelized, 3–4 minutes. Remove from the heat.

🌿 Scatter the apples, mango and blackberries in the bottom of 4 round gratin dishes 5½ inches (14 cm) in diameter. Pour the milk–cream mixture evenly over the fruit.

🌿 Bake until the pudding is set and a knife inserted into the center comes out clean, 20–25 minutes.

🌿 Transfer to a rack and let cool for at least 30 minutes before serving warm.

Serves 4

Chocolate Cream Puffs

The best cream puffs bake into perfect hollow balls ideal for filling with custard or whipped cream. The dough should be the consistency of thick mayonnaise. If it is too thick, add another egg yolk to achieve the correct consistency. If you like, substitute pastry cream (recipe on page 227) for the chocolate cream, and/or drizzle chocolate sauce over the puffs just before serving.

PASTRY PUFFS
1   cup (8 fl oz/250 ml) water
5   tablespoons (2½ oz/75 g) unsalted butter, cut into small pieces
¼   teaspoon salt
½   teaspoon sugar
1   cup (4 oz/125 g) sifted all-purpose (plain) flour
5   eggs

CHOCOLATE CREAM
13 oz (400 g) semisweet (plain) chocolate, finely chopped
2   cups (16 fl oz/500 ml) heavy (double) cream
¼   cup (2 oz/60 g) sugar

Preheat an oven to 400°F (200°C). Butter and flour a large baking sheet.

To make the pastry puffs, in a saucepan, combine the water, butter, salt and the ½ teaspoon sugar and bring to a boil. As soon as it boils, remove the pan from the heat and add the flour all at once. Using a rubber spatula or a wooden spoon, briskly beat in the flour. Place the saucepan over high heat and continue beating briskly for 2 minutes. Remove from the heat again and scrape the contents of the pan into a large bowl. Add 4 of the eggs, one at a time, beating vigorously after each addition until smooth.

Place the dough in a pastry (piping) bag with a ½-inch (12-mm) plain tip. Pipe mounds about 2 inches (5 cm) in diameter and 3 inches (7.5 cm) apart onto the prepared baking sheet. You should have 16–20 mounds in all.

In a small bowl, beat the remaining egg until well blended. Using a pastry brush, lightly brush each mound with the egg.

Bake until the puffs are golden brown, about 30 minutes. Transfer the puffs to a rack and let cool completely, about 30 minutes.

When the puffs are cool, slice off the top one-third of each puff. Set the bottoms and tops aside.

To make the chocolate cream, place the chocolate in the top pan of a double boiler or in a heatproof bowl over (not touching) barely simmering water in a pan. Stir just until the chocolate melts, then remove from the heat.

Pour the cream into a bowl. Using an electric mixer set on high speed, beat until soft peaks form. Add the ¼ cup (2 oz/60 g) sugar and beat until stiff peaks form, about 20 seconds.

Pour all of the melted chocolate into the whipped cream as quickly as possible, and continue to mix on high speed until evenly combined, about 1 minute.

Place the chocolate cream in a clean pastry (piping) bag fitted with a ½-inch (12-mm) plain tip. Pipe the cream into the bottoms of the cooled puffs so a little bit of the cream is exposed between the crusts. Replace the tops on the filled bottoms and serve immediately.

Serves 4–6

Crème Brûlée

Most bistro menus include some variety of this sugar-topped custard. To prevent the custard from melting while you caramelize the sugar, chill the custard well before you sprinkle it with the sugar, and broil it just until the sugar melts and browns.

4   cups (32 fl oz/1 l) heavy (double) cream
1   vanilla bean (pod), split in half lengthwise
7   egg yolks
½   cup (4 oz/125 g) plus 1½ tablespoons sugar for the custard, plus 7 teaspoons sugar for topping

⚓ Preheat an oven to 350°F (180°C).

⚓ In a large saucepan over high heat, combine the cream and vanilla bean and bring to a boil, stirring occasionally with a wire whisk to prevent sticking.

⚓ Meanwhile, in a bowl, using the whisk, stir together the egg yolks and the ½ cup (4 oz/125 g) plus 1½ tablespoons sugar until well blended.

⚓ As soon as the cream boils, immediately pour it in a slow, steady stream into the egg-sugar mixture, whisking constantly.

⚓ Strain the cream-egg mixture through a fine-mesh sieve into 7 ramekins each 3½ inches (9 cm) in diameter and 2¼ inches (5.5 cm) tall, dividing it evenly.

⚓ Place the ramekins in a shallow baking pan and pour in hot water to reach halfway up the sides of the ramekins. Bake until the custard is firm to the touch, about 1 hour and 10 minutes. Remove from the oven and remove the ramekins from the baking pan. Let cool completely, then cover and refrigerate until well chilled, 2–3 hours.

⚓ Preheat a broiler (griller).

⚓ Sprinkle 1 teaspoon of the sugar evenly over the top of each chilled ramekin. Place them on a baking sheet. Place the sheet in the broiler about 4 inches (10 cm) from the heat source and broil (grill) until the sugar caramelizes, about 5 minutes.

⚓ Remove from the broiler and serve immediately.

Serves 7

Basque Custard Torte

This simple custard-filled cake is native to the Basque region in southwest France. It is often filled with a creamy vanilla custard lightly spiked with the sweet anise flavor of Ricard liqueur, although some areas of the region prefer a filling of black cherries in syrup or cherry jam. To ease unmolding, make sure that the pastry cream is well sealed between the two layers of dough.

½ cup (3 oz/90 g) whole blanched almonds or ⅓ cup (1½ oz/45 g) purchased ground almonds

1 cup (8 oz/250 g) sugar

½ cup (4 oz/125 g) unsalted butter, at room temperature

2 egg yolks

1 tablespoon light or dark rum

1½ teaspoons almond extract (essence)

1½ teaspoons Ricard liqueur
Pinch of salt

½ vanilla bean (pod), split in half lengthwise

1½ cups (7½ oz/235 g) all-purpose (plain) flour

1 teaspoon baking powder

1 cup (8 fl oz/250 ml) pastry cream *(recipe on page 227),* cooled

🌿 If using whole almonds, place the nuts in a nut grinder or in a food processor fitted with the metal blade. Grind or process until the nuts are a fine powder. (Do not overprocess.) Set aside.

🌿 In a large bowl, using a whisk or an electric mixer set on medium speed, beat the sugar and butter until blended. Beat in the egg yolks one at a time, beating well after each addition. Add the rum, almond extract, liqueur and salt. Using the tip of a sharp knife, scrape the seeds from the vanilla bean directly into the bowl. Mix well.

🌿 Add the flour, ground almonds and baking powder. Using a wooden spoon or the paddle attachment of the electric mixer set on low speed, mix well until the ingredients come together to form a firm dough. Shape into a ball, wrap in plastic wrap and refrigerate for 2–3 hours.

🌿 Preheat an oven to 350°F (180°C). Butter and flour a cake pan 9 inches (23 cm) in diameter.

🌿 On a lightly floured work surface, roll out half of the dough into a round 11 inches (28 cm) in diameter

and ¼ inch (6 mm) thick. Drape the round over the rolling pin and transfer it to the prepared pan. Unwrap the round and press it gently into the pan. Using the rolling pin, roll over the top of the pan to trim away any uneven dough edges. Spread the pastry cream evenly over the bottom of the pastry-lined pan.

🌿 Roll out the remaining dough portion into a round about 9 inches (23 cm) in diameter and ¼ inch (6 mm) thick. Place the pan over the dough and, using the pan edge as a guide, cut out a round the size of the pan. Drape the round over the rolling pin and carefully transfer it to the pan, placing it atop the pastry cream, to form the top layer of the cake.

🌿 Bake until golden brown, 40–45 minutes. Transfer to a rack and let cool for 10 minutes. Invert onto the rack, turn right side up and let cool completely. Transfer to a serving plate and serve at room temperature.

Serves 8

French Apple Tart

French chefs have been perfecting the apple tart for centuries, creating numerous variations of this classic dessert. This recipe, combining a layer of custard under one of browned apple slices, is one of the most traditional. Brushing the fruit generously with butter before baking will ensure a beautiful golden brown top. Serve warm or at room temperature with crème fraîche or whipped cream, if you like.

Sweet pastry dough *(recipe on page 226)*

5 tart green apples, such as Granny Smith

1 cup (8 fl oz/250 ml) pastry cream *(recipe on page 227),* cooled

2 tablespoons unsalted butter, melted

1 tablespoon sugar

On a lightly floured work surface, roll out the dough into a round 12 inches (30 cm) in diameter and ⅛ inch (3 mm) thick. Drape the dough over a rolling pin and transfer it to a 10-inch (25-cm) tart pan with a removable bottom. Unwrap the dough from the pin and press it gently into the pan. Trim the pastry even with the pan rim and place the pastry-lined pan in the refrigerator.

Preheat an oven to 375°F (190°C).

Peel the apples, then cut them in half and core them. Slice the apples lengthwise as thinly as possible.

Remove the pastry shell from the refrigerator and spread the cooled pastry cream evenly over the bottom of the shell. It should be about ⅛ inch (3 mm) deep. Arrange the apple slices on top of the pastry cream in concentric circles. Brush the apple slices with the melted butter, coating them evenly, then sprinkle with the sugar.

Bake in the oven until golden brown and slightly caramelized, about 50 minutes.

Transfer to a rack and remove the pan sides. Place the tart on a serving plate and serve warm or at room temperature.

Serves 6–8

210

Goat Cheese Cake

Light and airy with a mild, sweet flavor, this simple cake is a popular choice when the meal does not include a cheese course, because it provides an ideal combination of cheese and dessert. Other fruits, such as quartered fresh figs or nectarines, can be used in place of the berries, if you prefer.

4   eggs, separated
5½   oz (170 g) fresh goat cheese
3   tablespoons sugar
½   cup (4 fl oz/125 ml) crème fraîche
½   cup (2 oz/60 g) fresh raspberries
½   cup (2 oz/60 g) fresh blackberries

✿ Preheat an oven to 375°F (190°C). Butter a cake pan 8 inches (20 cm) in diameter. Line the bottom with a circle of parchment (baking) paper cut to fit precisely; butter and flour the paper and the pan sides.

✿ Place the egg whites in a bowl. Using an electric mixer set on high speed, beat the whites until they form stiff but moist peaks.

✿ In another bowl, combine the goat cheese and sugar and, using a whisk, beat until well blended. Add the egg yolks, one at a time, beating well after each addition until smooth and creamy.

✿ Using a rubber spatula and working in several batches, carefully fold the beaten whites into the egg yolk mixture. (Do not overmix.) Pour the mixture into the prepared cake pan.

✿ Bake until the cake is golden, puffed and firm to the touch, about 25 minutes. Transfer to a rack to cool in the pan for 10 minutes, then invert onto the rack, lift off the pan and carefully peel off the paper. Transfer the cake to a serving plate, turn right side up and let cool completely.

✿ To serve, spread the crème fraîche evenly over the surface of the cake and then top with the berries. Alternatively, cut into wedges and serve warm, topping each piece with a swirl of crème fraîche and some berries just before serving.

Serves 4–6

Lemon Tart

Bistro dessert carts regularly feature at least one type of citrus tart. This recipe produces a creamy and tart lemon custard for filling a tender, flaky pastry shell. For a simple variation, lime or orange juice can be used in place of all or some of the lemon juice.

1   tablespoon plus ⅓ cup (3 fl oz/ 80 ml) unsalted butter, melted
    Sweet pastry dough *(recipe on page 226)*
4   lemons
4   eggs
1¾ cups (14 oz/440 g) sugar
½   cup (4 fl oz/125 ml) water

⚜ Preheat an oven to 400°F (200°C). Brush the bottom and sides of a 10-inch (25-cm) tart pan with a removable bottom with the 1 tablespoon melted butter.

⚜ On a lightly floured work surface, roll out the dough into a round 12 inches (30 cm) in diameter and ⅛ inch (3 mm) thick. Drape the dough over the rolling pin and transfer it to the prepared tart pan. Unwrap the dough from the pin and press it gently into the pan. Trim the pastry even with the pan rim.

⚜ Line the pastry-lined pan with waxed paper and add pie weights or dried beans. Bake until the pastry is half-cooked, about 15 minutes.

⚜ Meanwhile, cut 3 paper-thin slices from the center of 1 of the lemons and set aside. Into a bowl, grate the zest from the lemon halves and the remaining 3 whole lemons. Cut the whole lemons in half and squeeze the juice from the halves through a fine-mesh sieve into a measuring cup; you should have about ½ cup (4 fl oz/125 ml) juice.

⚜ Add the lemon juice and eggs to the zest and whisk until blended. Add 1¼ cups (10 oz/315 g) of the sugar and mix until well combined. Stir in the ⅓ cup (3 fl oz/80 ml) melted butter.

⚜ As soon as the crust is half-cooked, remove it from the oven and immediately remove the pie weights and waxed paper. Pour the citrus mixture into the warm tart shell and return it to the oven. Bake until the filling is set and the edges are golden brown, about 20 minutes.

⚜ Meanwhile, in a small saucepan over medium-high heat, combine the remaining ½ cup (4 oz/125 g) sugar and water. Bring to a boil, stirring constantly to dissolve the sugar. Add the reserved lemon slices, reduce the heat to low, and simmer until tender, about 10 minutes. Remove the pan from the heat and set aside. When the tart is done, transfer it to a rack and remove the pan sides. Let cool completely.

⚜ Remove the lemon slices from the sugar-water mixture, shaking briefly to remove any excess liquid, and arrange them in an overlapping pattern on the center of the tart. Transfer the tart to a serving plate and serve at room temperature.

Serves 6

Hazelnut and Roasted Almond Mousse Cake

For most French pastry chefs, a good génoise *(sponge cake) is the foundation for dozens of different desserts. This recipe marries the tender cake with a layer of rich hazelnut mousse.*

GÉNOISE
½ cup (4 oz/125 g) sugar
4 eggs
¾ cups (4 oz/125 g) all-purpose (plain) flour

MERINGUE
1 cup (8 oz/250 g) sugar
⅓ cup (3 fl oz/80 ml) water
4 egg whites

HAZELNUT MOUSSE
½ lb (250 g) unsalted butter
¼ lb (125 g) hazelnut (filbert) paste
4 egg yolks
1 cup (8 oz/250 g) sugar

SUGAR-ROASTED ALMONDS
8 teaspoons granulated sugar
½ cup (4 fl oz/120 ml) water
2 cups (9 oz/280 g) slivered blanched almonds

🌺 Preheat an oven to 400°F (200°C). Butter and flour a 10-inch (25-cm) cake pan. To make the *génoise,* in a large heatproof bowl, combine the sugar and eggs. Place over (not touching) gently simmering water in a pan. Whisk until it feels lukewarm. Remove from the pan and, using an electric mixer set on high speed, beat until cool and the batter falls in a thick ribbon, about 15 minutes. Sift the flour over the batter and, using a rubber spatula, fold it in. Pour into the prepared pan and smooth the top.

🌺 Bake just until the cake springs back to the touch, about 20 minutes. Invert onto a rack, carefully lift off the pan and let cool completely.

🌺 To make the meringue, in a small saucepan, bring the sugar and water to a boil. Meanwhile, in a bowl, using an electric mixer set on high speed, beat the egg whites until soft peaks form. Continue to boil the sugar-water mixture until it reaches the soft-ball stage, 240°F (115°C) on a candy thermometer.

With the mixer set on medium speed, beat the sugar mixture into the egg whites. Reduce the speed to low and continue beating until stiff, glossy peaks form, about 5 minutes. Spread the meringue in an even layer onto a baking sheet and chill.

🌺 To make the mousse, place the butter in a heatproof bowl set over a pan of gently simmering water. Let stand until very soft. Add the hazelnut paste and, using a wire whisk, beat until no lumps remain. Remove from the heat and beat in the egg yolks, one at a time, until creamy. Then gently fold in the meringue.

🌺 To assemble the cake, use a long, serrated knife to cut the *génoise* into 3 layers. Spoon one-third of the mousse over the bottom of a 10-inch (25-cm) springform cake pan. Top with a *génoise* layer. Repeat the mousse and *génoise* layers, ending with a *génoise* layer. Cover and refrigerate until set, about 2 hours.

🌺 To make the almonds, preheat an oven to 350°F (180°C). In a small saucepan, combine the sugar and water and bring to a boil, stirring to dissolve the sugar. Remove from the heat. Spread the almonds on a baking sheet. Drizzle with the sugar syrup and stir to coat. Roast, stirring every 5 minutes, until golden brown, about 5 minutes.

🌺 To unmold the cake, slide a knife blade between the mousse and pan sides. Invert onto a plate. Sprinkle the almonds on the top and sides and serve at once.

Serves 8–10

217

Pistachio and Chestnut Cream Mousse Cake

The pleasant green hue of pistachio paste has long made it a popular addition to mousses and ice creams. Look for pistachio paste and chestnut purée in specialty-food shops or prepare your own in a food processor.

Génoise layer, ½ inch (12 mm) thick *(recipe on page 217)*

CRÈME ANGLAISE

1	cup (8 fl oz/250 ml) milk
1	vanilla bean (pod), split in half lengthwise
4	egg yolks, at room temperature
½	cup (2 oz/60 g) granulated sugar
4	gelatin leaves
1	oz (30 g) pistachio paste
2	oz (60 g) chestnut purée
1½	cups (12 fl oz/375 ml) heavy (double) cream
½	cup (2 oz/60 g) finely chopped pistachio nuts
2	tablespoons confectioners' (icing) sugar

Make the *génoise* as directed and let cool completely.

To make the *crème anglaise,* in a saucepan, combine the milk and vanilla bean and bring to a boil. Meanwhile, in a large bowl, whisk together the egg yolks and granulated sugar. As soon as the milk boils, remove from the heat. Remove the vanilla bean and, using a knife tip, scrape the seeds into the milk; discard the bean.

Pour half of the boiling milk into the bowl holding the egg mixture, whisking vigorously. Return the pan to the heat, bring the milk to a boil and pour the egg mixture into the pan, whisking continuously. Stir over medium heat until the custard lightly coats the back of a wooden spoon, 2–3 minutes. You should have about 1 cup (8 fl oz/250 ml). Remove from the heat, press plastic wrap directly onto the surface and let cool.

Place 2 gelatin leaves in each of 2 small bowls. Add water to cover to both bowls; let stand until softened, about 5 minutes.

Combine ½ cup (4 fl oz/125 ml) of the cooled custard and the pistachio paste in a blender and mix on high speed until smooth, about 15 seconds. Transfer to a small saucepan over medium heat and heat until warm. Lift out 2 of the gelatin leaves and add to the warm custard. Whisk to mix well and set aside.

Put the remaining custard and the chestnut purée in a blender and mix on high speed until smooth, about 15 seconds. Transfer to another small saucepan over medium heat and heat until warm. Lift out the remaining 2 leaves, add to the chestnut custard and whisk well. Set aside.

In a bowl, place ¾ cup (6 fl oz/180 ml) of the cream. Using an electric mixer set on high speed, beat until soft peaks form. Add the pistachio custard and beat on low just until combined, about 30 seconds.

Place the *génoise* in a springform pan 10 inches (25 cm) in diameter and 2 inches (5 cm) deep. Pour the pistachio custard over the *génoise,* and refrigerate until set, about 10 minutes.

Whip the remaining cream and beat in the chestnut custard in the same way. Pour the chestnut custard over the set pistachio custard, cover and refrigerate for 4 hours.

To unmold, run hot water over a knife blade, wipe dry, and slide the blade between the mousse and the pan sides. Release the pan sides and slide the cake onto a plate. Sprinkle on the pistachio nuts and sift the confectioners' sugar over the top.

Serves 8

Coffee and Armagnac Parfait

This icy dessert combines the pleasure of strong coffee with a shot of good brandy. A base of heavy (double) cream provides a smooth texture, lasting body and stability. For an authentic presentation, serve it in traditional fluted parfait glasses. Cognac or another brandy may be substituted for the Armagnac, if you wish.

⅔ cup (5 oz/155 g) sugar
⅓ cup (3 fl oz/80 ml) water
4 egg yolks
2 cups (16 fl oz/500 ml) heavy (double) cream
2½ tablespoons coffee extract (essence)
⅓ cup (3 fl oz/80 ml) Armagnac
Unsweetened cocoa or roasted coffee beans, optional

❧ In a saucepan, combine the sugar and water. Stir until the sugar is dissolved; bring to a boil over high heat.

❧ Meanwhile, place the egg yolks in a heatproof bowl. As soon as the sugar-water syrup boils, remove from the heat and slowly pour the mixture into the egg yolks while whisking vigorously.

❧ Place the bowl over (not touching) barely simmering water in a pan. Continue to whisk vigorously until the mixture is frothy and stiff, 3–4 minutes.

❧ Remove the bowl from over the water and, using an electric mixer set on high speed or the whisk, continue to beat until the mixture cools down completely, about 5 minutes. Set aside.

❧ Place the cream in a large bowl. Using an electric mixer fitted with clean beaters, beat until soft peaks form. Add the coffee extract, Armagnac and cooled yolk mixture and, using a rubber spatula, fold together gently.

❧ Divide the mixture evenly among 4–6 individual parfait glasses. Cover and freeze for at least 5 hours or, preferably, overnight.

❧ Serve each parfait garnished with a dusting of cocoa or a few coffee beans, if desired.

Serves 4–6

Chardonnay Sorbet

This refreshing sorbet makes a pleasant finale to a summertime supper. The wine gives it a delicate texture that is at its best just after the sorbet is made. If you like, serve it in chilled glass dishes topped with fresh berries and accompanied with fine French butter cookies. Champagne or sparkling wine can be used in place of the Chardonnay.

1½ cups (12 fl oz/375 ml) water
1½ cups (12 oz/375 g) sugar
½ vanilla bean (pod), split in half lengthwise
½ lime
¼ lemon
¼ orange
4 cups (32 fl oz/1 l) Chardonnay

In a saucepan over high heat, combine the water, sugar, vanilla bean, lime, lemon and orange. Bring to a boil, stirring occasionally to dissolve the sugar. When the mixture begins to boil, reduce the heat to medium and simmer, uncovered, for 5 minutes, to infuse the syrup with flavor. Be sure not to reduce the liquid. Remove from the heat and, using a slotted spoon, scoop out the lime, lemon and orange. Let the citrus fruits cool slightly, then lightly squeeze them over the saucepan to release their juices.

Pour the syrup through a fine-mesh sieve into a bowl. Stir in the Chardonnay, cover and refrigerate for 2–3 hours until well chilled.

Pour the mixture into an ice cream maker and freeze following the manufacturer's directions until the sorbet becomes thick and smooth. The timing will depend upon the type of machine being used.

Remove from the ice cream maker, spoon into chilled serving dishes or glasses and serve immediately, or transfer to an airtight container and store in the freezer for up to 1 day.

Makes about 6 cups (1½ qt/1.5 l); serves 4–6

BASIC RECIPES

Bistro chefs keep a few staples on hand to draw upon in their cooking. Flavorful meat stocks are often left simmering on the stove top to use as needed. And, stored in the refrigerator, one may expect to find a good vinaigrette and fresh tomato sauce, as well as sweet fillings for desserts and tart shells ready for baking.

CHICKEN STOCK
FOND DE VOLAILLE

Homemade chicken stock provides a flavorful base for a range of soups, stews, sauces and braises. Enterprising home cooks can have fresh stock on hand simply by making the stock ahead and freezing it in small freezer bags to use as needed.

2	white onions
4	whole cloves
	Bouquet garni *(see glossary, page 340)*
6	lb (3 kg) chicken carcasses
2	large carrots, peeled and coarsely chopped
3	celery stalks, coarsely chopped
10	cloves garlic
1	tablespoon whole black peppercorns

⚜ Coarsely chop 1 of the onions. Stud the other whole onion with the 4 cloves.

⚜ In a stockpot, combine all the ingredients and add water just to cover (about 3¾ qt/3.75 l). Bring to a boil and, using a large spoon or wire skimmer, skim off any foam that forms on the surface. Reduce the heat to low and simmer, uncovered, for 1–1½ hours, reducing the liquid only slightly. Continue to skim off any foam that floats to the top during simmering.

⚜ Strain the stock through a fine-mesh sieve lined with cheesecloth (muslin) into a clean container. Discard the contents of the sieve. Use immediately, or let cool, cover and refrigerate for up to 1 week or freeze for up to 1 month. Lift off any solidified fat from the surface of the chilled stock before using.

Makes about 2½ qt (2.5 l)

VEAL STOCK
FOND DE VEAU

Stocks have a superior flavor when they are prepared in large quantities rather than in small amounts. Since you will probably not use all of this stock at once, however, you can freeze leftover stock in freezer bags or other containers for up to 1 month. For an even more intense flavor, add about 2 pounds (1 kg) oxtails with the veal bones.

8	lb (4 kg) large veal bones, such as leg bones
2	white onions
4	whole cloves
2	large carrots, peeled and coarsely chopped
3	celery stalks, coarsely chopped
10	cloves garlic
⅔	cup (5 fl oz/150 ml) tomato paste
	Bouquet garni *(see glossary, page 340)*
1	tablespoon whole black peppercorns
1	cup (8 fl oz/250 ml) water

Preheat an oven to 500°F (260°C). Place the veal bones in a roasting pan and roast for 20 minutes.

Meanwhile, coarsely chop 1 of the onions. Stud the other whole onion with the cloves.

Remove the pan from the oven and distribute the carrots, chopped and whole onion, celery, garlic and tomato paste evenly over the veal bones. Return to the oven and roast until the vegetables are lightly browned, about 15 minutes.

Using a slotted spoon, transfer all the contents of the roasting pan to a stockpot. Add the bouquet garni and peppercorns. Discard the fat from the roasting pan and place the pan over medium heat. When the pan is hot, add the water and deglaze the pan by stirring to dislodge any browned bits from the pan bottom. Pour the liquid into the stockpot.

Add water to the stockpot just to cover the ingredients (about 6 qt/6 l). Bring to a boil and, using a large spoon or a wire skimmer, skim off any foam that forms on top. Reduce the heat to low, cover and simmer for about 3 hours. Continue to skim off any foam that floats to the top during simmering.

Strain the stock through a fine-mesh sieve lined with cheesecloth (muslin) into a clean container. Discard the contents of the sieve.

Use immediately, or let cool, cover and refrigerate for up to 1 week or freeze for up to 1 month. Lift off any solidified fat from the surface of the chilled stock before using.

Makes about 3½ qt (3.5 l)

VINAIGRETTE
VINAIGRETTE

Many bistros provide oil and vinegar in separate cruets on the table for guests to mix together to taste. This recipe eliminates the guesswork, providing a good, basic vinaigrette that should suit any variety of uses.

2	tablespoons sherry vinegar
2	tablespoons balsamic vinegar
1	teaspoon salt
¼	teaspoon ground white pepper
⅔	cup (5 fl oz/150 ml) olive oil

In a small bowl, using a wire whisk, whisk together the sherry and balsamic vinegars, salt and white pepper.

Whisking continuously, add the olive oil in a slow, steady stream, whisking until well blended and emulsified, about 1 minute.

Makes about 1 cup (8 fl oz/250 ml)

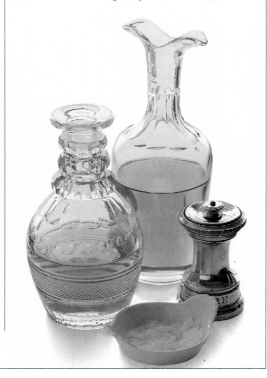

TOMATO AND RED PEPPER COULIS

COULIS DE TOMATES AUX POIVRONS ROUGE

The term coulis *refers to a liquid purée of cooked seasoned vegetables. Although delicious as a sauce on its own, a coulis can also be used to enhance other sauces and provide added flavor to an assortment of dishes. With the addition of a little olive oil and vinegar, it makes an excellent vinaigrette as well. If the coulis seems too thick, simply add water until you achieve the desired consistency.*

3   tablespoons olive oil
1   white onion, coarsely chopped
2   small red bell peppers (capsicums), seeded, deribbed and coarsely chopped
5   cloves garlic
3   tomatoes, coarsely chopped
    Bouquet garni *(see glossary, page 340)*
⅛   teaspoon cayenne pepper
1   teaspoon salt, plus salt to taste
¼   teaspoon ground white pepper, plus ground white pepper to taste
⅓   cup (3 fl oz/80 ml) water

☙ In a large saucepan over high heat, warm the olive oil. Add the onion, bell peppers and garlic and sauté until golden brown, about 10 minutes.

☙ Add the tomatoes, bouquet garni, cayenne, the 1 teaspoon salt, the ¼ teaspoon white pepper and the water and bring to a boil. Reduce the heat to medium, cover, and simmer gently until thickened, about 45 minutes.

☙ Working in batches, transfer the mixture to a blender or to a food processor fitted with the metal blade and purée until smooth, about 2 minutes. Taste and adjust the seasoning. Use immediately, or store in an airtight container in the refrigerator for up to 1 week or freeze for up to 1 month.

Makes 2½–3 cups (20–24 fl oz/ 625–750 ml)

SWEET PASTRY DOUGH

PÂTE SUCRÉE

Dense, buttery and rich, this sweet dough makes an ideal tart shell. If you like, you can prepare it ahead to use later; wrapped airtight in plastic wrap, it will keep in the refrigerator for up to 2 weeks.

½   cup (4 oz/125 g) plus 1 tablespoon unsalted butter, at room temperature, cut into pieces
½   cup (2 oz/60 g) confectioners' (icing) sugar, sifted
1   egg
2   cups (10 oz/315 g) all-purpose (plain) flour
⅛   teaspoon baking powder

☙ In a bowl, combine the butter and sugar. Using an electric mixer set on low speed, beat until smooth, about 3 minutes.

☙ Add the egg and beat until creamy. Using a rubber spatula, fold in the flour and baking powder just until incorporated. Then beat with the electric mixer set on low speed until the dough is evenly mixed and clings together, 2–3 minutes.

☙ Shape the dough into a ball, wrap tightly in plastic wrap and refrigerate for at least 2 hours or as long as 2 weeks. Bring to room temperature before using, then use as directed in individual recipes.

Makes enough dough for one 10-inch (25-cm) tart shell

PASTRY CREAM
CRÈME PÂTISSIÈRE

French pastry chefs use this cream as a filling for cakes and pastries, as a garnish and as an addition to hot and cold desserts. Because this recipe calls only for egg yolks, and no whites, it has an especially rich texture. You can make this pastry cream up to 1 day in advance and store it, covered, in the refrigerator.

4   egg yolks
½   cup (4 oz/125 g) sugar
⅓   cup (2 oz/60 g) plus 1 tablespoon all-purpose (plain) flour
2   cups (16 fl oz/500 ml) milk
½   vanilla bean (pod), split in half lengthwise

☙ In a large bowl, combine the egg yolks and sugar and whisk until thoroughly combined. Add the flour and stir until smooth; set aside.

☙ In a large saucepan over high heat, combine the milk and the vanilla bean and bring to a boil. As soon as the milk begins to boil, remove it from the heat. Remove the vanilla bean and, using the tip of a small, sharp knife, scrape the seeds directly into the milk. Discard the bean.

☙ Whisk half of the hot milk into the egg mixture. Return the saucepan to high heat and, as soon as the mixture comes to a boil, pour the contents of the bowl into the saucepan, whisking constantly.

☙ Using a wooden spoon, stir over high heat until the mixture is smooth. Return to a boil and boil, stirring, for 2 minutes longer.

☙ Remove the pan from the heat and press a piece of plastic wrap directly onto the surface of the hot cream to prevent a skin from forming. Let cool completely before using.

Makes 2¼ cups (18 fl oz/560 ml)

THE
MEDITERRANEAN

Appetizers

Whether you enter a Greek taverna, Turkish *lokanta,* Spanish *taberna,* or Portuguese *tasca,* your first sight will likely be of a table spread with an irresistible display of room-temperature dishes. In Greece and Turkey, these delectable appetizer offerings are known as *mezethes,* in Spain they are *tapas* and in Portugal *acepipes.* They will be brought to you one or two at a time, usually each on its own plate. A waiter will circulate through the room with the hot items, offering perhaps just a single fabulous taste with each visit to your table. Don't be shy, for among these dishes will be much-requested specialties that cannot be found elsewhere.

In fact, you may want to make a whole meal of these tempting plates, just as the locals often do. A few tastes will convince you: Dip your bread into a mound of cool roasted eggplant or serve it alongside a platter of sizzling garlic shrimp. Try a piping hot fritter of salt cod or zucchini, or lace a skewer of just-fried mussels with the nut-thickened sauce known as *tarator.*

These widely varied plates will introduce you to the wealth of savory flavors to follow in the rest of the taverna meal. Indeed, there is no better way to know the palate—the signature tastes of a country—than through these tantalizing appetizers.

Garlic Shrimp

*In Spanish tabernas, these shrimp—fragrant with garlic and olive oil—
are brought to the table sizzling in a little metal pan. Have plenty of bread on hand
to sop up the delicious pan juices. Serve with lemon wedges, if desired.*

¼ cup (2 fl oz/60 ml) olive oil
4 large cloves garlic, finely minced
1 teaspoon red pepper flakes
1 lb (500 g) medium shrimp (prawns), peeled and deveined
2 tablespoons fresh lemon juice
2 tablespoons dry sherry
1 teaspoon paprika
   Salt and freshly ground black pepper
   Chopped fresh flat-leaf (Italian) parsley for garnish

In a sauté pan over medium heat, warm the olive oil. Add the garlic and red pepper flakes and sauté for 1 minute. Raise the heat to high and add the shrimp, lemon juice, sherry and paprika. Stir well, then sauté, stirring briskly, until the shrimp turn pink and curl slightly, about 3 minutes. Season to taste with salt and pepper and sprinkle with parsley. Serve hot.

Serves 4

Zucchini Fritters

Although these fritters are at their best when hot, in many Turkish cafés they are served at room temperature accompanied by the yogurt-cucumber sauce called cacık *(recipe on page 337). Traditionally part of the* meze *course, they also make a nice side dish for seafood, poultry or lamb.*

1 lb (500 g) small zucchini (cour-gettes), coarsely grated
Salt
½ lb (250 g) feta cheese, or equal parts feta and kasseri or ricotta
6 green (spring) onions, minced
½ cup (½ oz/15 g) chopped fresh dill
¼ cup (⅓ oz/10 g) chopped fresh mint
¼ cup (⅓ oz/10 g) chopped fresh flat-leaf (Italian) parsley
3 eggs, lightly beaten
1 cup (5 oz/155 g) all-purpose (plain) flour
Freshly ground pepper
Peanut oil for frying

❊ Place the zucchini in a sieve or colander, salt it lightly and toss to mix. Let stand for 30 minutes to draw out the excess moisture. Using a kitchen towel, squeeze the zucchini dry and place it in a bowl. Crumble the cheese over the zucchini and add the green onions, dill, mint, parsley, eggs, flour and salt and pepper to taste. Stir to mix well.

❊ In a deep frying pan over medium-high heat, pour in the peanut oil to a depth of ¼ inch (6 mm). When the oil is hot, using a serving spoon, drop spoonfuls of the batter into the oil, being careful not to crowd the pan. Fry, turning once, until nicely browned on both sides, 2–3 minutes per side. Using a slotted spoon or spatula, transfer the fritters to paper towels to drain. Keep warm until all the fritters are cooked.

❊ Arrange the fritters on a warmed platter and serve hot.

Serves 8 as an appetizer, 4 as a side dish

Potato Omelet

Unlike most omelets, this classic Spanish tapa *is usually served at room temperature and, as the name* tortilla *suggests, it has a flat, cakelike shape. A large nonstick frying pan is ideal for cooking the omelet, which also makes a good main course for four at lunchtime.*

½ cup (4 fl oz/125 ml) plus 3 tablespoons olive oil

2 lb (1 kg) baking potatoes, peeled and sliced ¼ inch (6 mm) thick

  Salt and freshly ground pepper

2 onions, thinly sliced

6 eggs, lightly beaten

  Chopped fresh flat-leaf (Italian) parsley for garnish

※ In a large frying pan over medium heat, warm the ½ cup (4 fl oz/125 ml) olive oil. Add half of the potatoes and fry, turning as needed, until tender but not browned, 10–12 minutes. (Don't worry if the slices stick to one another a little.) Using a slotted spatula, transfer to a platter and season to taste with salt and pepper. Repeat with the remaining potatoes. Set the potatoes and the frying pan aside.

※ In a small sauté pan over medium heat, warm 2 tablespoons of the olive oil. Add the onions and sauté until soft and golden, 15–20 minutes. Transfer the onions to a large bowl and let cool slightly. Stir in the eggs and season to taste with salt and pepper. Fold in the fried potatoes.

※ Place the large frying pan over low heat and warm the oil that remains in it. When the oil is hot, pour in the potato-egg mixture and cook until the top of the omelet is set and the bottom is golden, 8–10 minutes. Invert a large plate on top of the frying pan and invert the plate and pan together, unmolding the omelet browned side up. Add the remaining 1 tablespoon olive oil to the pan and slide the omelet back into the pan, browned side up. Continue to cook until golden brown on the second side, about 4 minutes longer.

※ Turn the omelet out onto a serving plate, sprinkle with parsley and cut into wedges. Serve hot or at room temperature.

Serves 6–8

Salt Cod Fritters

These crispy fritters are among the most popular acepipes *in Portugal. Made from the preserved fish that has long been a staple of the Iberian peninsula and other Mediterranean countries, they are also a regular feature on the menus of Spanish tapas bars.*

½ lb (250 g) salt cod
2 boiling potatoes, about 10 oz (315 g) total weight, unpeeled
Milk, if needed
2 tablespoons olive oil, plus olive oil or vegetable oil for deep-frying
1 small onion, minced
2 cloves garlic, finely minced
2 eggs
3 tablespoons chopped fresh flat-leaf (Italian) parsley
3 tablespoons chopped fresh cilantro (fresh coriander)
Pinch of ground cayenne pepper
Freshly ground black pepper

❀ Place the salt cod in a bowl and add cold water to cover. Cover and refrigerate for 36–48 hours, changing the water 4 or 5 times. Drain the cod well, rinse in cold water and place in a saucepan. Add water to cover and slowly bring to a low boil. Reduce the heat to low and simmer gently until the cod is tender when pierced with a fork and flakes easily, 15–20 minutes.

❀ Meanwhile, place the potatoes in a saucepan with water to cover and bring to a boil over high heat. Boil until tender when pierced with a fork, 10–15 minutes. Drain well and when cool enough to handle, peel, place in a bowl and mash with a potato masher or a fork. Set aside.

❀ When the cod is done, drain and let cool. Using your fingers, break up the cod, removing any errant bones, skin or tough parts. Taste it. If it seems too salty, heat enough milk to cover the cod. Place the cod in a bowl, add the hot milk to cover and let stand for 30 minutes, then drain.

❀ Place the cod in a food processor fitted with the metal blade and, using on-off pulses, process until coarsely chopped. Transfer to a bowl.

❀ In a small sauté pan over medium heat, warm the 2 tablespoons olive oil. Add the onion and sauté until tender, about 8 minutes. Add the garlic and sauté for 2 minutes longer. Remove from the heat.

❀ Add the potatoes and onion to the cod and mix well. Beat in the eggs, parsley and cilantro. Season to taste with cayenne and black pepper. (The mixture should be just stiff enough to hold a shape. If it is too stiff, beat in a little milk.) Using a spoon, form into balls about 1 inch (2.5 cm) in diameter.

❀ In a deep, heavy frying pan, pour in oil to a depth of 3 inches (7.5 cm) and heat to 375°F (190°C) on a deep-frying thermometer (or until a little bit of the fritter mixture dropped into the oil sizzles immediately). Slip the balls into the oil, a few at a time, and fry, turning occasionally, until golden, about 4 minutes. Using a slotted spoon, transfer to paper towels to drain. Keep warm until all the fritters are cooked.

❀ Arrange the fritters on a warmed platter and serve hot.

Serves 6–8

DOLMADES

Stuffed Grape Leaves

No Greek meze *table is complete without dolmas, the family of stuffed vine or cabbage leaves and vegetables such as tomatoes, eggplants (aubergines) and zucchini (courgettes). These popular rice-filled grape leaves, known as* dolmades, *are usually served at room temperature with lemon wedges or yogurt. One 8-ounce (250-g) jar of grape leaves should provide enough for filling and lining the pan.*

1 cup (7 oz/220 g) long-grain white rice, preferably basmati
¼ cup (1½ oz/45 g) currants
¼ cup (1 oz/30 g) pine nuts, optional
¾ cup (6 fl oz/180 ml) olive oil
2 cups (10 oz/315 g) finely chopped yellow onion
1 teaspoon salt, plus salt to taste
1 cup (3 oz/90 g) finely chopped green (spring) onions
1 teaspoon ground allspice
1 teaspoon ground cinnamon
½ cup (3 oz/90 g) peeled, seeded, chopped and drained tomatoes (fresh or canned), optional
½ cup (¾ oz/20 g) chopped fresh flat-leaf (Italian) parsley
¼ cup (⅓ oz/10 g) chopped fresh mint or dill
¾ cup (6 fl oz/180 ml) hot water
Freshly ground pepper
36 grape leaves preserved in brine, plus grape leaves for lining pan, optional
2 cups (16 fl oz/500 ml) boiling water
Fresh lemon juice, plus lemon wedges for serving

Place the rice in a bowl, add cold water to cover and let stand for 30 minutes. At the same time, place the currants in a small bowl, add hot water to cover and let stand for 30 minutes until plumped. Drain the rice and currants and set aside.

Meanwhile, if using the pine nuts, preheat an oven to 350°F (180°C). Spread the nuts in a small pan and place in the oven until toasted and fragrant, 6–8 minutes. Set aside.

In a large sauté pan over medium heat, warm ½ cup (4 fl oz/120 ml) of the olive oil. Add the yellow onion and the 1 teaspoon salt and sauté until softened, about 5 minutes. Add the green onions and sauté until softened, about 5 minutes longer. Add the allspice, cinnamon and drained rice and cook, stirring, until the rice is opaque, about 4 minutes. Add the chopped tomatoes (if using), parsley, mint or dill, currants and hot water and cook, uncovered, until the water is absorbed and the rice is about half cooked, about 10 minutes. Stir in the pine nuts, if using. Season to taste with salt and pepper. Let cool.

Rinse the grape leaves in cool water and cut off the stems. Working in batches, lay them out on a table, shiny side down. Place a tablespoonful of the rice filling near the stem end of each leaf, fold the bottom end over the filling, then fold in the sides and roll up. Do not roll too tightly, as the rice will expand during cooking. Set aside, seam side down.

When all of the filling has been used, select a baking pan or large, deep frying pan that will hold the stuffed grape leaves in a single layer and line with more grape leaves, if using. Arrange the stuffed grape leaves in the pan, seam sides down. Place a heavy plate on top to keep the leaves from unrolling while cooking, then pour the boiling water and the remaining ¼ cup (2 fl oz/60 ml) olive oil around the leaves.

Cover and simmer gently over very low heat until the rice and leaves are tender, about 45 minutes. Remove from the heat and remove the plate. Sprinkle with a little lemon juice, let cool, then serve with lemon wedges. Or cover and refrigerate for up to 2 days; bring to room temperature before serving.

Makes 36 pieces

Fried Cheese

This taverna standby is named for the two-handled pan in which it is fried. Some cooks include the flourish of flambéing the cheese with brandy, but this dramatic touch adds little flavor and may toughen the cheese. Offer freshly cracked pepper and some crusty bread at the table, and pour a good ouzo.

½ lb (250 g) kefalotiri or kasseri cheese
About ¼ cup (1½ oz/45 g) all-purpose (plain) flour
1 teaspoon freshly ground pepper
Olive oil for frying
1 tablespoon dried oregano
2 tablespoons fresh lemon juice, plus lemon wedges for serving

❊ Cut the cheese into slices ½ inch (12 mm) thick, about 3 inches (7.5 cm) long and 2 inches (5 cm) wide. Rinse the cheese in cold water to remove excess salt, then pat dry with paper towels. Spread the flour on a plate and season it with the pepper. Dip the cheese pieces in the seasoned flour, turning to coat evenly on both sides.

❊ In a large, heavy sauté pan, pour in olive oil to a depth of ¼ inch (6 mm). Place over high heat until very hot but not smoking. Working with 2 or 3 cheese pieces at a time, carefully slip the pieces into the hot oil and fry, turning once, until golden brown on both sides, about 2 minutes per side. Using a slotted spoon, transfer the cheese to paper towels to drain. Keep warm until all the pieces are cooked.

❊ Arrange the cheese on a warmed platter and sprinkle with the oregano and lemon juice. Serve hot with lemon wedges on the side.

Serves 4

Fried Mussels with Nut Sauce

These crispy mussels are a popular menu item at the street stands that line busy wharves and open-air markets throughout Turkey. The accompanying nut sauce, known as tarator, *can be thickened with hazelnuts (filberts) or almonds in place of the walnuts; it is also good served with cooked vegetables and fish.*

NUT SAUCE

1	cup (4 oz/125 g) walnuts
1	tablespoon finely minced garlic
1½	cups (3 oz/90 g) fresh bread crumbs
⅓	cup (3 fl oz/80 ml) olive oil
3	tablespoons red or white wine vinegar or fresh lemon juice, or to taste
	Salt and freshly ground pepper

MUSSELS

40	large mussels in the shell
1	cup (8 fl oz/250 ml) water
1½	cups (7½ oz/235 g) all-purpose (plain) flour
	Peanut oil for deep-frying

❊ Soak 10 small wooden skewers in water to cover for at least 30 minutes.

❊ To make the nut sauce, preheat an oven to 350°F (180°C). Spread the walnuts on a baking sheet and place in the oven until toasted and fragrant, 8–10 minutes. Let cool, then place in a food processor fitted with the metal blade or in a blender. Add the garlic and bread crumbs and use rapid on-off pulses to combine. Add the olive oil and vinegar or lemon juice and purée until smooth; thin to a spoonable consistency with water, if necessary. Season to taste with salt, pepper and more vinegar or lemon juice, if needed; transfer to a bowl. Set aside.

❊ Discard any mussels that do not close to the touch, then scrub the mussels well under running water.

❊ Pour water to a depth of 1 inch (2.5 cm) in a large, wide sauté pan and add the mussels. Place over high heat, cover and cook until the mussels open, 3–4 minutes. Drain the mussels and discard any that have not opened. Remove the mussels from their shells, gently pulling off their beards. Drain the skewers and thread 4 mussels on each skewer.

❊ In a wide, shallow bowl, combine the water and flour and stir to make a thin batter. Set aside.

❊ In a deep frying pan or wok, pour in peanut oil to a depth of 2–3 inches (5–7.5 cm). Heat to 375°F (190°C) on a deep-frying thermometer (or until a tiny bit of the batter dropped into the oil sizzles immediately).

❊ Working in batches, dip the mussel-loaded skewers into the batter, then slip them into the oil. Fry, turning as needed, until golden on all sides, 2–3 minutes. Using tongs, transfer to paper towels to drain. Keep warm until all the mussels are cooked.

❊ To serve, arrange the skewers on a serving dish. Serve hot with the sauce on the side.

Serves 4–8

Grilled Eggplant Salad

Although technically termed a salad in Greece, this purée (called baba ghanoush *in the Middle East) is often served as a spread alongside tomato wedges, olives and bread. If you prefer a smoky flavor, grill or broil the eggplants; for a milder taste, roast them in a 400°F (200°C) oven, or cook them on a stove-top*

3   cups (24 oz/750 g) plain yogurt
3   large globe eggplants (auber-
    gines), 2½–3 lb (1.25–1.5 kg)
    total weight
3   tablespoons fresh lemon juice
3   cloves garlic
1   teaspoon salt, plus salt to taste
⅓   cup (3 fl oz/80 ml) olive oil
⅔   cup (2½ oz/75 g) finely chopped
    walnuts, optional
1   or 2 pinches ground cayenne
    pepper or minced fresh jalapeño
    chili pepper, optional
    Freshly ground black pepper
    Chopped fresh flat-leaf (Italian)
    parsley for garnish

❊ Line a large sieve with cheese-cloth (muslin), place it over a bowl and spoon the yogurt into the sieve. Refrigerate for 4–6 hours to drain off the excess water. You should have 1–1½ cups (8–12 oz/250–375 g) drained yogurt.

❊ Preheat a broiler (griller) or pre-pare a fire in a charcoal grill. Using a fork, pierce the skin on either side of each eggplant. Place on a broiler pan or a grill rack and broil or grill, turning as needed, until blistered, charred and soft throughout when pierced with a knife, about 20 min-utes. (If the eggplants are darkening quickly and are not softening, finish cooking them in an oven preheated to 400°F/200°C.) Set aside to cool.

❊ When the eggplants are cool enough to handle, cut them in half and scoop out the pulp, discarding as many seeds as possible.

❊ For a smooth purée, place the pulp in a food processor fitted with the metal blade and purée until free of lumps. For a chunkier purée, chop with a knife on a cutting board. Transfer the purée to a serving bowl. Add the lemon juice and mix well.

❊ In a mortar, combine the garlic with the 1 teaspoon salt and mash with a pestle until puréed. Add the purée to the eggplant along with the olive oil and, if using, the walnuts and the cayenne or jalapeño. Mix well and season to taste with salt and pepper. Garnish with parsley and serve.

Serves 4–6

LAHMACUN

Lamb Pizza

Open-faced meat pies like these are popular café food in Syria, Lebanon and Israel, as well
as in Turkey. The dough is a cross between that used for an Italian pizza and Turkish pide bread.
You can also shape it into smaller 4-inch (10-cm) pies. Add the chilies if you prefer a little heat.

SPONGE
1	envelope (2½ teaspoons) active dry yeast
1	teaspoon sugar
½	cup (4 fl oz/125 ml) lukewarm water (105°F/43°C)
½	cup (2½ oz/75 g) unbleached bread flour

DOUGH
4½	cups (22½ oz/700 g) unbleached bread flour
2	teaspoons salt
2	tablespoons olive oil
1½	cups (12 fl oz/375 ml) lukewarm water (105°F/43°C)

LAMB FILLING
2	tablespoons olive oil
1	large onion, finely chopped
4	cloves garlic, minced
1	lb (500 g) ground (minced) lamb
1½	cups (9 oz/280 g) peeled, seeded and chopped tomatoes
½	cup (2 oz/60 g) minced mild green chili peppers, optional
½	teaspoon ground allspice
1	teaspoon ground cinnamon
½	cup (¾ oz/20 g) chopped fresh flat-leaf (Italian) parsley
	Salt and ground black pepper
¼	cup (1 oz/30 g) pine nuts
	Olive oil for brushing on pizzas
¼	cup (⅓ oz/10 g) chopped fresh mint

※ To make the sponge, in a small bowl, dissolve the yeast and sugar in the lukewarm water. Stir in the flour and let stand in a warm place until bubbly, about 5 minutes.

※ *To make the dough in an electric stand mixer,* place the flour in the bowl of a mixer and add the sponge, salt, olive oil and lukewarm water. Using the paddle attachment, mix on low speed to combine. Then attach the dough hook and beat on medium speed until the dough is smooth, elastic and pulls cleanly from the bowl sides, 5–6 minutes.

※ *To make the dough by hand,* place the flour in a large bowl and add the sponge, salt, olive oil and lukewarm water. Stir until a soft dough forms, then turn out onto a lightly floured work surface and knead until smooth and elastic, about 10–12 minutes.

※ Shape the dough into a ball, place in an oiled bowl and turn to coat evenly. Cover the bowl with plastic wrap and let rise in a warm place until doubled, 45–60 minutes.

※ Meanwhile, make the lamb filling: In a large sauté pan over medium heat, warm the olive oil. Add the onion and sauté until tender, about 10 minutes. Add the garlic and lamb, raise the heat to high and sauté until

it begins to brown, 5–8 minutes. Add the tomatoes, chilies (if using), allspice and cinnamon and cook uncovered, stirring occasionally, for about 30 minutes. The mixture should be very thick. Stir in half of the parsley and season to taste with salt and pepper. Let cool.

※ Meanwhile, turn out the dough onto a lightly floured work surface and knead briefly. Divide into 12 equal portions and form each portion into a ball. Place the balls on the work surface, cover with a kitchen towel and let rest for 30 minutes.

※ Preheat an oven to 350°F (180°C). Spread the pine nuts in a small pan and toast in the oven until fragrant, 6–8 minutes. Let cool.

※ Raise the oven temperature to 500°F (260°C). Roll out each ball of dough into a round 6 inches (15 cm) in diameter. Place the rounds spaced well apart on baking sheets. Brush lightly with olive oil and then divide the filling evenly among them, leaving a ½-inch (12-mm) border uncovered. Sprinkle evenly with the pine nuts.

※ Bake until the crust is golden, about 6 minutes. Sprinkle with the remaining parsley and the mint and serve hot.

Makes twelve 6-inch (15-cm) pizzas

Cheese–Filled Pastries

Although these cheese-filled Turkish pastries are commonly shaped as triangles for the popular borek, *they are equally delicious in the form of plump, round cigars. They can be filled and shaped up to 2 days in advance and refrigerated, covered, in a single layer on a parchment-lined baking sheet; fry just before serving.*

6   oz (185 g) feta cheese, crumbled
6   oz (185 g) cottage cheese or shredded Monterey Jack cheese
2   eggs, lightly beaten
¼   cup (⅓ oz/10 g) chopped fresh flat-leaf (Italian) parsley
2   tablespoons chopped fresh dill
¼   teaspoon freshly grated nutmeg
    Salt and freshly ground pepper
9   sheets filo dough (about 6 oz/ 185 g), thawed in the refrigerator if frozen
¼   cup (2 oz/60 g) clarified unsalted butter, melted
    Peanut or olive oil for deep-frying

✣ In a bowl, combine the feta cheese, cottage cheese or jack cheese, eggs, parsley, dill and nutmeg. Mix well, then season to taste with salt and pepper.

✣ Remove the filo sheets from their package and lay the stacked sheets flat on a work surface. Cut the stack into quarters, forming squares measuring about 6 inches (15 cm) on a side. Cover the stack with a damp towel or plastic wrap to prevent the sheets from drying out. Working with 1 square at a time, place it on the work surface, brush it lightly with butter and then spoon a narrow strip of the cheese mixture (2–3 table-spoons) along one end, leaving a ¾-inch (2-cm) border on the bottom and sides. Fold in the sides, bring the bottom up over the filling and then roll up like a cigar. Seal the edge with a little water and repeat with the remaining squares and filling until all have been used.

✣ In a deep frying pan, pour in peanut or olive oil to a depth of 2½ inches (6 cm) and heat to 350°F (180°C) on a deep-frying thermometer (or until a tiny piece of filo dropped into the oil turns golden within moments). Working in batches, care-fully slip the rolls into the hot oil and fry, turning as needed, until golden on all sides, about 5 minutes. Do not crowd the pan. Using a slot-ted spoon or tongs, transfer to paper towels to drain.

✣ Arrange the rolls on a warmed platter and serve hot.

Makes 36 rolls

Spinach Filo Pie

One of Greece's best-known dishes, this pie can also be served as a side dish or in larger portions as a main dish. Tablespoons of the same mixture can be used to fill tiropetes, little triangles folded from 3-inch (7.5-cm) strips cut lengthwise from filo sheets and brushed with clarified butter; they bake in 10–15 minutes.

1½ lb (750 g) spinach

3 tablespoons olive oil

½ cup (1½ oz/45 g) chopped green (spring) onions

½ cup (¾ oz/20 g) chopped fresh flat-leaf (Italian) parsley

½ cup (¾ oz/20 g) chopped fresh dill

¾ lb (375 g) feta cheese, crumbled

1 cup (8 oz/250 g) cottage cheese, if needed

3 eggs, lightly beaten

1 teaspoon freshly grated nutmeg

Salt and freshly ground pepper

18 sheets filo dough (¾ lb/375 g), thawed in the refrigerator if frozen

½ cup (4 oz/125 g) clarified unsalted butter, melted

※ Remove the stems from the spinach, chop the leaves coarsely and rinse well in several changes of water. Drain and set aside.

※ In a large frying pan over medium heat, warm the olive oil. Add the green onions and sauté until tender, about 5 minutes. Transfer to a bowl.

※ Add the spinach to the same pan and place over high heat. Cook, turning the spinach with tongs or a fork, until wilted, about 4 minutes. (The leaves will wilt in their own moisture.) Transfer to a sieve and drain well, pressing out the excess moisture with the back of a spoon.

※ Chop the spinach coarsely. Add it to the green onions, then stir in the parsley, dill and feta cheese. If the feta is salty, add the cottage cheese to mellow the overall flavor. Add the eggs and nutmeg and stir well. Season to taste with salt and pepper. Set aside.

※ Butter an 11-by-16-by-2½-inch (28-by-40-by-6-cm) baking dish. Remove the filo sheets from their package, lay them flat on a work surface and cover with a damp towel or plastic wrap to prevent them from drying out. Lay a filo sheet in the prepared dish and brush it lightly with the butter. Top with 8 more filo sheets, brushing each one with butter. Spread the spinach mixture evenly over the filo layers. Then top with the remaining 9 filo sheets, again brushing each sheet lightly with the butter, including the top sheet. Cover and refrigerate the pie for 30 minutes so the butter will set.

※ Meanwhile, preheat an oven to 350°F (180°C).

※ Using a sharp knife, cut the pie into 16 equal pieces. Bake until golden brown, about 30 minutes. Remove from the oven and let stand for 5 minutes. Recut the pieces and serve hot.

Makes 16 pieces

Soups and Vegetables

When you order soups in the Mediterranean, rarely will they be refined light broths. More often they are hearty concoctions, given body by the addition of white beans or lentils, rice, pasta or stale bread, or they are studded with meatballs or pieces of chicken or fish. These robust bowls are meant to satisfy rather than titillate, and they can be a whole meal with just an appetizer to start and some good crusty bread alongside.

Fresh vegetables maintain an equally prominent place in the Mediterranean diet. In addition to their popularity in the region's soups and stews, they are equally at home served plain with just a drizzle of olive oil or in combination with any of an array of grains.

A delectable pilaf, enriched with eggplant and tomato, can serve as a main course. So, too, can stuffed tomatoes and sweet bell peppers, both glistening with olive oil and served right from the vessels in which they are baked. Side dishes of spinach or other cooked greens arrive on platters, with a garnish of lemon. Fried vegetables are delivered to the table at the last minute, sizzling hot and waiting to be dipped into a sprightly sauce. Even a simple Greek salad appears effortlessly delicious because, in every case, only the best seasonal vegetables have been used.

"Green" Soup with Kale and Potatoes

The dark green Galician cabbage used by Portuguese cooks for this winter soup
is not easily found outside of Portugal, but kale or collard greens can be substituted.
Bowls of the soup are often drizzled with chili pepper sauce (recipe on page 339).

¼ cup (2 fl oz/60 ml) plus
4 teaspoons olive oil

1 large yellow onion, chopped

2 cloves garlic, finely minced

3 baking potatoes, about 1 lb
(500 g) total weight, peeled and
sliced ¼ inch (6 mm) thick

6 cups (48 fl oz/1.5 l) water

2 teaspoons salt, plus salt to taste

¾ lb (375 g) kale or collard greens

¼ lb (125 g) *chouriço* or *linguiça*
sausage
Freshly ground pepper

❊ In a large saucepan over medium heat, warm the ¼ cup (2 fl oz/60 ml) olive oil. Add the onion and sauté until tender, about 8 minutes. Add the garlic and potatoes and sauté over medium-high heat for a few minutes longer. Add the water and the 2 teaspoons salt. Cover and simmer over medium heat until the potatoes are very soft when pierced with a fork, about 20 minutes.

❊ Meanwhile, rinse the greens well, drain and remove the tough stems. Working in batches, stack the leaves, roll them up like a cigar and cut crosswise into very thin strips. Set aside.

❊ In a sauté pan over medium heat, cook the sausage, turning to brown all sides, until firm and cooked through, about 10 minutes. Let cool, then cut into slices ½ inch (12 mm) thick. Set aside.

❊ When the potatoes are ready, remove from the heat and, using a wooden spoon or a potato masher, mash them to a purée in the water in the pan. Return the pan to low heat, add the sliced sausage and cook, stirring, for 5 minutes. Add the greens, stir well and simmer, uncovered, for 3–5 minutes. (Do not overcook; the greens should remain bright green and slightly crunchy.) Season to taste with salt and pepper.

❊ Ladle the soup into warmed bowls, drizzle each serving with 1 teaspoon olive oil and serve hot.

Serves 4

Bread Soup with Cilantro, Garlic and Poached Egg

*This Portuguese soup from the province of Alentejo is known as a sopa seca, or
"dry soup," because its primary ingredient is bread. Each serving is topped with a
poached egg that the diner must break with a spoon and swirl into the soup.*

1   tablespoon minced garlic
1   teaspoon salt
1   cup (1½ oz/40 g) chopped
     fresh cilantro (fresh coriander)
     Pinch of red pepper flakes,
     optional
½   cup (4 fl oz/120 ml) olive oil
3   thick slices coarse-textured
     peasant bread, crusts removed,
     cut into 1½-inch (4-cm) cubes
     (about 6 cups/12 oz/375 g)
4   eggs
3–4   cups (24–32 fl oz/750 ml–1 l)
     chicken stock, optional

※ In a mortar, combine the garlic, salt, ½ cup (¾ oz/20 g) of the cilantro and the red pepper flakes, if using. Mash with a pestle to form a paste. Add ¼ cup (2 fl oz/60 ml) of the olive oil, 1 tablespoon at a time, and mix until well blended. Evenly divide the garlic paste among 4 warmed soup bowls and keep warm.

※ Preheat an oven to 350°F (180°C). Brush the bread cubes with the remaining ¼ cup (2 fl oz/60 ml) olive oil and toast in the oven, turning a few times, until golden brown, 8–10 minutes.

※ Distribute the bread cubes evenly among the soup bowls and toss them with the garlic mixture.

※ In a deep frying pan, bring a generous amount of water to a rolling boil. Reduce the heat to medium-low so that the water barely simmers.

Crack each egg and gently release it just above the surface of the water. Simmer undisturbed until the whites are set but soft and the yolks are still runny, about 3 minutes. Using a slotted spoon, carefully remove the eggs and set aside on a plate.

※ You may use the egg-poaching water (you will need 3–4 cups/ 24–32 fl oz/750 ml–1 l) for finishing the soup or you may use stock. Bring the water or stock to a boil and pour it over the bread cubes in each soup bowl, using only as much as needed to cover the bread. Carefully slip a poached egg into the center of each bowl. Sprinkle with the remaining ½ cup (¾ oz/20 g) cilantro. Serve hot.

Serves 4

Fish Soup

This Greek soup takes its name from the kettle—kakavi—in which it is cooked. You can be as lavish as you like and use clams and scallops in place of the mussels and shrimp. Kakavia can be a rich first course or a meal in itself. Thick slices of grilled bread make a delicious accompaniment.

2 lb (1 kg) mussels

4 lb (2 kg) assorted thick fish fillets such as bass, flounder, halibut, haddock, snapper, cod and grouper
Salt

½ cup (4 fl oz/125 ml) olive oil

2 cups (7 oz/220 g) sliced yellow onions

1 cup (3 oz/90 g) sliced leeks, carefully washed

4 cloves garlic, finely minced

2 celery stalks, chopped

1½ cups (9 oz/280 g) peeled, seeded and chopped tomatoes (fresh or canned)

4 fresh thyme sprigs

1 bay leaf

½ cup (½ oz/20 g) chopped fresh flat-leaf (Italian) parsley

1 cup (8 fl oz/250 ml) dry white wine

7 cups (56 fl oz/1.75 ml) water

1 lb (500 g) shrimp (prawns), peeled and deveined
Fresh lemon juice
Freshly ground pepper

✹ Discard any mussels that do not close to the touch, then scrub the mussels under running water and remove their beards. Place in a bowl and refrigerate until needed.

✹ Cut the fish fillets into 1½-inch (4-cm) pieces. Place on a plate, sprinkle with salt and refrigerate until needed.

✹ In a large saucepan or kettle over medium heat, warm the olive oil. Add the onions and leeks and sauté until translucent, about 8 minutes. Add the garlic, celery, tomatoes, thyme, bay leaf and ¼ cup (¼ oz/ 10 g) of the parsley and sauté for about 2 minutes longer.

✹ Add the wine and water and bring to a boil over high heat. Reduce the heat to medium and simmer for 15 minutes. Add the fish pieces, cover and cook for 5 minutes. Add the shrimp and mussels, re-cover and cook until the mussels open, 3–4 minutes. Discard any mussels that have not opened.

✹ Season to taste with lemon juice, salt and pepper. Ladle into warmed bowls. Sprinkle with the remaining ¼ cup (¼ oz/10 g) parsley. Serve hot.

Serves 12 as a first course, 6 as a main course

Chilled Tomato Soup

This peasant soup from the Andalusia region of Spain was originally made with crumbled bread, water, oil and vinegar. After the Spanish conquistadores returned from the New World with tomatoes and peppers, gazpacho evolved into the refreshing summer soup we know today.

2 slices day-old, coarse-textured peasant bread, crusts removed
1 small onion, chopped
2 cloves garlic, minced
1 small cucumber, peeled, seeded and coarsely chopped
2 lb (1 kg) fresh, ripe tomatoes, peeled, seeded and coarsely chopped
2 small green bell peppers (capsicums), seeded, deribbed and coarsely chopped
6 tablespoons (3 fl oz/90 ml) virgin olive oil
3 tablespoons red wine vinegar
  Salt and freshly ground pepper
  Ice water or part ice water and part chilled tomato juice, if needed

GARLIC CROUTONS
2 slices coarse-textured peasant bread
¼ cup (2 fl oz/60 ml) olive oil
1 teaspoon chopped garlic

❊ Place the bread slices in a bowl, add water to cover and let stand until soft, 3–5 minutes. Remove the bread and squeeze it dry with your hands.

❊ In a blender or a food processor fitted with the metal blade, combine the soaked bread, onion, garlic, cucumber, most of the tomatoes and 1 of the bell peppers. Process until smooth or chunky, as you like. Pour into a bowl.

❊ Finely chop the remaining tomatoes and the bell pepper and stir them into the bowl. Then stir in the olive oil and vinegar and season to taste with salt and pepper. If the soup is too thick, add a little ice water or a mixture of ice water and tomato juice. Cover and refrigerate until well chilled, or for up to 3 days.

❊ To make the garlic croutons, cut the bread slices into ½-inch (12-mm) cubes. In a large sauté pan over medium-high heat, warm the olive oil. Add the garlic and sauté, stirring, for 1 minute. Add the bread cubes and sauté until golden brown on all sides, 4–5 minutes. Using a slotted spoon, transfer the croutons to paper towels to drain.

❊ Ladle the soup into chilled bowls, top with the croutons and serve.

Serves 4

Meatball Soup with Egg and Lemon

Avgolemono is the Greek term for the classic Mediterranean egg-and-lemon mixture used as a thickener for soups or stews. In Turkey, the same blend is called terbiyeli. While simple versions of this soup include just rice, and others call for chicken and rice, leeks and celery and even fish, the most interesting and filling interpretations feature these little meatballs.

1 lb (500 g) ground (minced) lean beef or lamb

1 cup (5 oz/155 g) grated or finely minced onion

6 tablespoons (2½ oz/75 g) long-grain white rice or ½ cup (2 oz/60 g) fine dried bread crumbs

½ cup (½ oz/20 g) chopped fresh flat-leaf (Italian) parsley

2 tablespoons chopped fresh mint or dill

3 eggs
   Salt and freshly ground pepper

6 cups (48 fl oz/1.5 l) chicken stock

¼ cup (2 fl oz/60 ml) fresh lemon juice

In a bowl, combine the meat, onion, rice or bread crumbs, ¼ cup (¼ oz/10 g) of the parsley, the mint or dill and 1 of the eggs. Season to taste with salt and pepper. Using your hands, knead the mixture until well mixed. Form the mixture into tiny meatballs about ½ inch (12 mm) in diameter.

In a large saucepan over medium-high heat, bring the stock to a boil. Add the meatballs, reduce the heat to low, cover and simmer gently until the meatballs are cooked, 25–30 minutes.

In a bowl, beat the remaining 2 eggs until very frothy. Gradually beat in the lemon juice. Then gradually beat in about 1½ cups (12 fl oz/375 ml) of the hot soup, beating constantly to prevent curdling. (This step tempers the eggs so that they won't scramble when added to the soup.) Continue to beat until thickened, then slowly stir the egg mixture into the hot soup. Heat through, but do not allow the soup to boil.

Ladle into warmed bowls, sprinkle with the remaining ¼ cup (¼ oz/10 g) parsley and serve hot.

Serves 6

Greek Salad

*The simple Greek salad that appears on every taverna table is no culinary groundbreaker.
What makes it so special in Greece is the intense flavor of the local tomatoes and cucumbers,
so use the best-quality produce you can find. In most instances, the salad is dressed simply
with virgin olive oil, but fresh lemon juice or vinegar can also be added.*

DRESSING
½   cup (4 fl oz/125 ml) virgin olive oil

2–3   tablespoons fresh lemon juice

3   tablespoons dried oregano
Freshly cracked pepper

1   clove garlic, finely minced (optional)

2–3   cups (2–3 oz/60–90 g) torn assorted salad greens such as romaine (cos), escarole (Batavian endive) or frisée

4   small ripe tomatoes, cored and cut into wedges

1   large cucumber, peeled, seeded and cut into wedges

1   red (Spanish) onion, thinly sliced into rings

2   small green bell peppers (capsicums), seeded, deribbed and thinly sliced crosswise into rings

½   lb (250 g) feta cheese, coarsely crumbled

20   Kalamata olives

☒ To make the dressing, in a bowl, stir together the olive oil, lemon juice, oregano, cracked pepper to taste, and the garlic, if using. Set aside.

☒ In a large salad bowl, combine the greens, tomatoes, cucumber, onion and bell peppers. Drizzle the dressing over the top and toss gently to mix. Sprinkle the feta cheese and olives over the top and serve.

Serves 4

Spinach with Raisins and Pine Nuts

Although this particular recipe has a Spanish name, you can find similar dishes prepared in Italy, Greece and Turkey. The combination of nuts and dried fruits suggests its Arabic origins. If the spinach leaves are especially large, you may tear or cut them into smaller pieces for faster cooking and easier eating.

¼ cup (1½ oz/45 g) raisins
¼ cup (1 oz/30 g) pine nuts
3 tablespoons olive oil
1 small onion, chopped
2 lb (1 kg) spinach, stems removed and carefully washed
Salt and freshly ground pepper

❈ Place the raisins in a bowl, add hot water to cover and let stand until plumped, about 20 minutes.

❈ Meanwhile, preheat an oven to 350°F (180°C). Spread the pine nuts in a small pan and place in the oven until toasted and fragrant, 8–10 minutes. Set aside.

❈ In a wide sauté pan over medium heat, warm the olive oil. Add the onion and sauté until tender, about 10 minutes. Add the spinach to the pan and stir constantly until it is wilted, about 4 minutes.

❈ Drain the raisins and add them to the pan along with the pine nuts. Season to taste with salt and pepper, stir well and serve hot.

Serves 4

Sautéed Mushrooms with Garlic

*Savor these garlicky sautéed mushrooms hot from the pan. Spoon them over grilled bread as
a snack or alongside grilled lamb, beef or chicken as a flavorful side dish. For a particularly delicious
variation, combine chanterelles, portobellos and cremini with the more common white mushrooms.*

5   tablespoons (2½ fl oz/75 ml)
    olive oil or equal parts unsalted
    butter and olive oil
2   tablespoons minced garlic
¼   cup (1½ oz/45 g) diced bacon
    or cooked diced ham
1   lb (500 g) fresh mushrooms *(see
    note above),* brushed clean and
    halved if small or sliced ¼ inch
    (6 mm) thick
¼   cup (2 fl oz/60 ml) dry white
    wine or dry sherry, if needed
⅓   cup (½ oz/15 g) chopped fresh
    flat–leaf (Italian) parsley, or
    ¼ cup (⅓ oz/10 g) chopped
    fresh flat–leaf (Italian) parsley
    and 2 tablespoons chopped
    fresh thyme
Salt and freshly ground pepper

※ In a large sauté pan over medium heat, warm the olive oil or melt the butter with the olive oil. Add the garlic and bacon or ham and sauté for 2 minutes. Raise the heat to high, add the mushrooms and continue to sauté, stirring briskly, until they release their juices and the liquid evaporates, 5–8 minutes.

If the mushrooms do not release much liquid, add the wine or sherry and cook until the liquid evaporates.

※ Add the parsley or the parsley and thyme and stir well. Season to taste with salt and pepper and serve hot.

Serves 4

Stuffed Eggplant

The name of this famous Turkish eggplant dish means "the imam (priest) fainted," a condition probably brought on by how delicious it is. If possible, prepare this dish from 24–48 hours in advance so the flavors can mellow. If you cannot find Asian or small globe eggplants, you can substitute large globe eggplants by cutting them in half lengthwise and making the slits for stuffing in the cut side.

8   Asian (slender) eggplants or 4 very small globe eggplants (aubergines), about 2 lb (1 kg) total weight

½   cup (4 fl oz/125 ml) olive oil

3   large onions, halved and thinly sliced

2   cups (12 oz/375 g) peeled, seeded and diced tomatoes (fresh or canned)

12   cloves garlic, finely minced
Salt and freshly ground pepper
Pinch of sugar

½   cup (¾ oz/20 g) chopped fresh flat-leaf (Italian) parsley

1   cup (8 fl oz/250 ml) hot water

❊ Cut off and discard the stems from the eggplants. Using a sharp knife, peel the eggplants to form a striped pattern that resembles a barber pole.

❊ In a large sauté pan over medium heat, warm the olive oil. Add the eggplants and sauté until tender and softened on all sides, 5–8 minutes for the Asian variety and 15 minutes for the globe variety. Using a slotted spatula or tongs, carefully transfer the eggplants to a baking dish, arranging them side by side.

❊ Add the onions to the oil remaining in the pan and sauté over medium heat until tender, about 8 minutes. Add the tomatoes and garlic and continue to sauté for 2 minutes longer. Season to taste with salt and pepper and add the sugar. Stir in the parsley and set aside.

❊ Preheat an oven to 350°F (180°C).

❊ Cut a lengthwise slit about halfway through each eggplant and to within 1 inch (2.5 cm) of both ends. Carefully pull the slit open to make a pocket. Stuff each slit with an equal amount of the tomato-onion mixture. Add the hot water to the pan, cover with aluminum foil and bake until the eggplants are very tender when pierced with a fork, 15–20 minutes for the Asian variety and 30–45 minutes for the globe variety.

❊ Transfer the eggplants to a platter. Let cool. Serve at room temperature.

Serves 4

City–Style Braised Artichokes

Despite its Greek name, this delicious ragout is believed to have originated in Istanbul, and both the Turks and Greeks claim it as their own. Peas or favas may be added to the mixture. If adding favas, immerse the shelled beans in boiling water for 1 minute, then drain and peel off their skins.

Juice of 2 lemons, plus fresh lemon juice to taste, optional

3 tablespoons all-purpose (plain) flour

6 large artichokes with 1–2 inches (2.5–5 cm) of stem intact

½ cup (4 fl oz/125 ml) olive oil

1 yellow onion, chopped

8 green (spring) onions, coarsely chopped

3 carrots, peeled and diced

2 large white boiling potatoes, cut into 1-inch (2.5-cm) dice, or 6–8 tiny new potatoes, halved

1 cup (5 oz/155 g) shelled peas or shelled and peeled fava (broad) beans (optional; *see note above*)

Salt and freshly ground pepper

½ cup (¾ oz/20 g) chopped fresh dill

※ Fill a large bowl with cold water and add the juice of 2 lemons and the flour. Snap off the tough outer leaves from the artichokes. Using a paring knife, trim the dark green parts from the base and stem. Cut the artichokes lengthwise into quarters and scoop out and discard the prickly chokes. As they are cut, drop the artichoke quarters into the bowl of lemon water to prevent discoloring until they are needed.

※ In a large sauté pan over medium heat, warm the olive oil. Add the onion and sauté until softened, about 2 minutes. Add the green onions and carrots and sauté until tender, about 5 minutes longer.

※ Drain the artichokes and add to the pan along with the unpeeled potatoes and enough hot water to cover the vegetables. Cover and cook over low heat until the potatoes and artichokes are tender, about 25 minutes. If using peas or favas, add them during the last 10–15 minutes of cooking.

※ Season to taste with salt and pepper and some lemon juice, if desired. Transfer to a serving dish and let cool. Sprinkle with the dill and serve at room temperature.

Serves 4–6

Rice Pilaf with Pine Nuts and Currants

Simple rice pilafs like this one often accompany kebabs or vegetarian dishes in tavernas throughout the Mediterranean. Fragrant basmati rice is a particularly good choice for this dish, as each grain holds its shape and resists gumminess. If sautéed chicken livers are added, the dish is known as ic pilav.

2 cups (14 oz/440 g) long-grain white rice, preferably basmati

2 teaspoons salt, plus salt to taste

4 cups (32 fl oz/1 l) boiling water

4 chicken livers, optional

2 tablespoons plus ¼ cup (2 oz/60 g) unsalted butter

1 onion, chopped

3 tablespoons pine nuts

½ teaspoon ground cinnamon or ground allspice

3 cups (24 fl oz/750 ml) chicken stock or equal parts chicken stock and water

¼ cup (1½ oz/45 g) dried currants
   Freshly ground pepper

3 tablespoons chopped fresh flat-leaf (Italian) parsley or dill

※ In a bowl, combine the rice with the 2 teaspoons salt and pour in the boiling water. Stir well and let stand until the water is cold.

※ Meanwhile, if using the chicken livers, in a small sauté pan over medium-high heat, melt the 2 table-spoons butter. Add the livers and sauté until browned and firm but still pink in the center, about 5 minutes. Let cool, then chop coarsely. Set aside.

※ Drain the rice and rinse well under cool running water. Drain again and set aside.

※ In a saucepan over medium heat, melt the ¼ cup (2 oz/60 g) butter. Add the onion and pine nuts and sauté until pale golden brown, about 8 minutes. Add the rice and cook, stirring, until opaque, about 5 min-utes. Add the cinnamon or allspice,

the stock or stock and water, currants and chicken livers, if using. Season to taste with salt and pepper. Cover and cook over medium-low heat until the liquid is absorbed, about 15 minutes.

※ Uncover the pan, drape a folded kitchen towel over the pan and re-place the lid. Cook over very low heat for 10 minutes longer. Turn off the heat and let stand for 15 minutes before serving. Sprinkle with the parsley or dill and serve.

Serves 4

Eggplant and Tomato Pilaf

This flavorful pilaf can become the centerpiece of a meal as easily as it can be a side dish. The tomatoes lend a lovely pink to the rice. Accompany the pilaf with cooked greens and yogurt-cucumber sauce (recipe on page 337) or plain yogurt.

2 eggplants (aubergines), about 3 lb (1.5 kg) total weight

2 cups (14 oz/440 g) long-grain white rice, preferably basmati

2 teaspoons salt, plus salt to taste

4 cups (32 fl oz/1 l) boiling water

1 cup (8 fl oz/250 ml) olive oil, or as needed

1 onion, chopped

2 large tomatoes, peeled, seeded and chopped

½ teaspoon ground cinnamon

½ teaspoon ground allspice

1 teaspoon freshly ground pepper

2 cups (16 fl oz/500 ml) hot water or tomato juice
  Chopped fresh mint

❊ Peel the eggplants and cut into ½-inch (12-mm) cubes. Place the cubes in a colander, salt lightly and toss gently to mix. Let stand for about 1 hour to drain off the bitter juices.

❊ Meanwhile, in a bowl, combine the rice with the 2 teaspoons salt and pour in the boiling water. Stir well and let stand until the water is cold. Drain the rice and rinse well under cool running water. Drain again and set aside.

❊ Rinse the eggplant cubes with cool water, drain well and pat dry with paper towels.

❊ In a large sauté pan over medium-high heat, warm 3 tablespoons of the olive oil. Working in 3 batches and adding 3 tablespoons olive oil with each batch, add the eggplant cubes and sauté until golden brown on all sides, about 5 minutes. Using a slotted spoon, transfer the cubes to paper towels to drain and set aside.

❊ In a saucepan over medium heat, warm the remaining 3 tablespoons olive oil. Add the onion and sauté until tender, about 8 minutes. Add the rice and cook, stirring, until opaque, about 3 minutes. Add the tomatoes and cook, stirring, for 5 minutes longer. Add the sautéed eggplant, cinnamon, allspice, salt to taste and pepper and stir well. Pour in the hot water or tomato juice, cover and cook over low heat until the liquid is absorbed, 15–20 minutes.

❊ Uncover the pan, drape a folded kitchen towel over the rim and replace the lid. Let stand for 15–20 minutes before serving. Sprinkle with mint and serve.

Serves 4

Fish and Shellfish

No matter where you are in the Mediterranean, the sea or a freshwater stream is never far away. So it comes as no surprise that fish and shellfish appear in abundance on the taverna table. Invariably they are served fresh from the waters, and they are usually grilled or fried and occasionally baked, braised or poached.

Because freshness is a given, lengthy marinades and complex sauces are seldom part of the preparation. Lemon wedges are the most common garnish, serving to heighten the scent of the sea, and most sauces—*romesco, tarator, skordalia, piri-piri*—are placed on the side, to be used as an accent and not a disguise.

Fish may be wrapped in grape leaves or a thin slice of cured ham before grilling, or threaded onto skewers with fresh bay leaves and slivers of onion. If fish is marinated at all, it is for a short time in an understated mixture of olive oil, lemon juice and and one or two carefully chosen herbs or spices. And if cooked in a sauce, it is always a simple one, perhaps combining just tomato, garlic, onion and a splash of wine.

Stewed Clams with Sausage, Ham and Tomatoes

The name for this dish from the Algarve province of Portugal comes from the clam-shaped copper cooking vessel, known as a cataplana, *in which it is classically cooked. Serve this popular* tasca *dish as a light supper or lunch, with lots of bread for soaking up any extra juices, or spoon it over rice or alongside boiled potatoes for a more substantial main course. Serve chili pepper sauce (recipe on page 339) on the side.*

2½ lb (1.25 kg) small clams in the shell such as Manilas

2 tablespoons olive oil

3 yellow or red (Spanish) onions, thinly sliced

4 cloves garlic, finely minced

1½ tablespoons red pepper flakes or 2 fresh small hot chili peppers, seeded and finely chopped (optional)

1 bay leaf, crumbled

¼ lb (125 g) smoked ham or prosciutto, diced

¼ lb (125 g) *chouriço* sausage, casing removed and crumbled

½ cup (4 fl oz/125 ml) dry white wine

2 cups (12 oz/375 g) diced canned tomatoes and their juices

½ cup (¾ oz/20 g) chopped fresh flat-leaf (Italian) parsley
Freshly ground black pepper
Lemon wedges

❈ Discard any clams that do not close to the touch. Scrub the clams well under running water, place in a bowl of water, and refrigerate until needed.

❈ In a large sauté pan over medium heat, warm the olive oil. Add the onions and sauté until tender, about 8 minutes. Add the garlic and the red pepper flakes, if using, and sauté for 3 minutes longer. Add the fresh chilies (if using), the bay leaf, ham or prosciutto, sausage, wine and tomatoes. Stir well and simmer over low heat, uncovered, for 25 minutes.

❈ Add the clams, hinge sides down, and cover the pan. Raise the heat to high and cook until the clams open, 3–5 minutes. Discard any clams that have not opened.

❈ Ladle into warmed soup bowls, sprinkle with parsley and top with a liberal grinding of black pepper. Serve hot with lemon wedges.

Serves 4

Shrimp with Tomatoes, Oregano and Feta

This dish is served at seaside tavernas all over Greece. The shrimp can be sautéed and dressed with the tomato sauce up to 4 hours in advance. At serving time, sprinkle on the feta cheese and slip under a broiler or into an oven. Serve with plenty of crusty bread for capturing the delicious juices.

1½ lb (750 g) large shrimp (prawns), peeled and deveined
    Salt and freshly ground black pepper
4   tablespoons (2 fl oz/60 ml) olive oil
1   small yellow onion, chopped, or 6 green (spring) onions, chopped
4   cloves garlic, finely minced
    Pinch of ground cayenne pepper, optional
2   tablespoons dried oregano
1½ cups (12 fl oz/375 ml) tomato sauce or 4 large tomatoes, peeled, seeded and diced
    Pinch of sugar, if needed
½   lb (250 g) feta cheese, crumbled
¼   cup (⅓ oz/10 g) chopped fresh flat-leaf (Italian) parsley

❊ Preheat an oven to 450°F (230°C) or preheat a broiler (griller).

❊ Sprinkle the shrimp with salt and black pepper. In a large sauté pan over medium-high heat, warm 2 tablespoons of the olive oil. Add the shrimp and sauté, stirring briskly, until pink and beginning to curl, 2–3 minutes. Using a slotted spoon, transfer the shrimp to 4 flameproof ramekins or small gratin dishes, distributing them evenly.

❊ In the same pan over medium heat, warm the remaining 2 tablespoons olive oil. Add the yellow onion or green onions and sauté until tender, about 8 minutes. Add the garlic, cayenne (if using), and oregano and sauté for 2 minutes longer. Add the tomato sauce or diced tomatoes and simmer until thickened slightly, about 2 minutes longer. Add the sugar if the tomatoes are not sweet and season to taste with salt and black pepper.

❊ Pour the sauce over the shrimp, dividing it evenly. Then sprinkle the feta over the tops. Bake or broil until the cheese melts, 5–8 minutes if baking or 3–5 minutes if broiling.

❊ Sprinkle the shrimp with the parsley and serve hot.

Serves 4

Fish in Grape Leaves

Cooking fish in grape leaves is an ancient Mediterranean tradition. Whole large sardines and tiny red mullets are among the most popular choices, although fish fillets can also be adapted to this method of cooking. In place of the lemon wedges, you can make a simple dressing of 5 tablespoons olive oil, 2–3 tablespoons fresh lemon juice and a complementary herb of your choice.

¼ cup (2 fl oz/60 ml) olive oil

2 tablespoons chopped fresh flat-leaf (Italian) parsley or fennel fronds

2 teaspoons chopped fresh thyme or dried oregano

Juice of 1 lemon

Salt and freshly ground pepper

2 lb (1 kg) fresh large sardines, cleaned with heads left on, or 4 fish fillets such as sea bass, cod or sole, about 6 oz (185 g) each

Bottled grape leaves, rinsed of brine and stems removed

Lemon wedges

※ In a large, shallow nonaluminum dish, whisk together the olive oil, parsley or fennel, thyme or oregano, lemon juice and season to taste with salt and pepper. Add the fish and turn to coat well. Let marinate at room temperature for about 1 hour.

※ Preheat a broiler (griller) or prepare a fire in a charcoal grill. Using 1 or 2 grape leaves per whole fish or fillet, wrap the leaves around the center, leaving exposed the head and tail of each fish or both ends of each fillet; secure the leaves with toothpicks, if needed.

※ Place the fish packets on a broiler pan or an oiled grill rack and broil or grill, turning once, until opaque throughout, 7–10 minutes per side for whole fish and 5–6 minutes per side for fish fillets.

※ Transfer to a warmed platter and serve hot with lemon wedges.

Serves 4

Gratin of Salt Cod and Potatoes

Gomes de Sá was a well-regarded restaurateur from the city of Porto, and this dish, one of his specialties, has become a permanent part of the sizable Portuguese repertoire of salt cod recipes. This bacalhau *classic can be assembled up to 8 hours in advance and then reheated in the oven just before serving time.*

1   lb (500 g) skinless salt cod fillets
Hot milk, if needed

1½ lb (750 g) boiling potatoes (about 3 large), peeled

6   tablespoons (3 fl oz/90 ml) olive oil

2   onions, thinly sliced

2   cloves garlic, minced (optional)

½   cup (¾ oz/20 g) chopped fresh flat-leaf (Italian) parsley

1   teaspoon freshly ground pepper

20 oil-cured black olives

2   eggs, hard-cooked and sliced

※ Place the salt cod in a bowl and add cold water to cover. Cover and refrigerate for 24–48 hours, changing the water often.

※ Drain the cod well, rinse in cold water and place in a saucepan. Add water to cover and slowly bring to a gentle boil. Reduce the heat to low and simmer gently until the cod is tender when pierced with a fork and flakes easily, 15–20 minutes.

※ Drain the cod and let cool. Using your fingers, break up the cod, removing any errant bones, skin or tough parts. Taste it. If it seems too salty, place in a bowl, add hot milk to cover and let stand for 30 minutes, then drain.

※ Place the potatoes in a saucepan and add water to cover. Bring to a boil over high heat and boil until cooked through but still firm when pierced with a fork, 10–15 minutes. Drain well and when cool enough to handle, cut into slices ¼ inch (6 mm) thick. Set aside.

※ In a large sauté pan over medium heat, warm 2 tablespoons of the olive oil. Add the onions and sauté until tender but not browned, about 8 minutes.

Add the garlic, if using, and sauté for 2 minutes longer. Using a slotted spoon, transfer to a plate and set aside.

※ In the same pan over medium heat, warm 3 tablespoons of the olive oil. Add the potatoes and sauté, stirring briskly, until golden, 5–8 minutes. Remove from the heat.

※ Preheat an oven to 400°F (200°C). Oil an 11-by-7-by-1½-inch (28-by-18-by-4-cm) oval gratin dish or 4 individual gratin dishes. Layer half of the potatoes in the dish or dishes. Top with half of the cod, then half of the onions and parsley. Sprinkle with the pepper. Repeat the layering with the remaining potatoes, cod and onions. Drizzle with the remaining 1 tablespoon olive oil.

※ Bake until golden, about 25 minutes. Garnish with the olives and hard-cooked eggs, sprinkle with the remaining parsley and serve.

Serves 4

Grilled Swordfish Kebabs

One of the simplest and best fish recipes of the Turkish Aegean, these flavorful kebabs are equally popular in Greece. If the cherry tomatoes are not firm, skewer them separately and remove them from the heat as soon as they are done. Dress the brochettes with a vinaigrette of olive oil and lemon juice or serve with nut sauce (recipe on page 244). Rice pilaf (page 274) is the classic accompaniment.

6   tablespoons (3 fl oz/90 ml) fresh lemon juice

1   teaspoon paprika

2   bay leaves, crushed, plus 12 whole bay leaves

2   lb (1 kg) swordfish fillets, cut into 1¼-inch (3-cm) cubes

2   lemons, thinly sliced, plus lemon wedges for serving

2   green bell peppers (capsicums), seeded, deribbed and cut into 1¼-inch (3-cm) squares

16   ripe but firm cherry tomatoes
Salt and freshly ground pepper

In a shallow nonaluminum bowl, whisk together the olive oil, lemon juice, paprika and crushed bay leaves. Add the swordfish cubes, turning to coat well. Cover and let marinate in the refrigerator for about 4 hours.

Prepare a fire in a charcoal grill or preheat a broiler (griller).

Remove the fish cubes from the marinade, reserving the marinade. Thread the cubes onto metal skewers, alternating them with the whole bay leaves, lemon slices, bell peppers and cherry tomatoes. Sprinkle with salt and pepper.

Place the skewers on an oiled grill rack or a broiler pan and grill or broil, turning as needed and basting a few times with the reserved marinade, until the fish is opaque throughout, about 10 minutes.

Transfer the skewers to a warmed platter and serve hot with lemon wedges.

Serves 4

Fish in Almond Sauce

This simple taberna *dish features the classic Catalan nut sauce known as* picada. *With its heady mixture of nuts, bread and garlic,* picada *is evidence of the Arabic influence in Spanish cooking.* Merluza *(hake) is traditionally used in this dish, but you may substitute cod, sea bass, flounder or other firm white fish.*

ALMOND SAUCE

½	cup (2½ oz/75 g) slivered blanched almonds
2	tablespoons olive oil
1	large onion, finely chopped
1	teaspoon paprika
1	tablespoon finely minced garlic
¼	cup (½ oz/15 g) fresh bread crumbs
	Pinch of saffron threads, crushed (optional)
1½	cups (9 oz/280 g) peeled, seeded and diced tomatoes (fresh or canned)
1	cup (8 fl oz/250 ml) fish stock or dry white wine
	Salt and freshly ground pepper
1	cup (5 oz/155 g) shelled peas, optional
4	firm white fish fillets, each about 5 oz (155 g) *(see note above)*
	Salt and freshly ground pepper
¼	cup (⅓ oz/10 g) chopped fresh flat-leaf (Italian) parsley or mint

❊ To make the almond sauce, preheat an oven to 350°F (180°C). Spread the almonds on a baking sheet and place in the oven until toasted and fragrant, 8–10 minutes. Let cool.

❊ Place ¼ cup (1¼ oz/37 g) of the almonds aside to use for garnish. Using a food processor fitted with the metal blade or a nut grinder, finely grind the remaining almonds, being careful not to overgrind to a paste. Set the ground nuts aside.

❊ In a sauté pan over medium heat, warm the olive oil. Add the onion and sauté until tender but not browned, about 8 minutes. Add the paprika, garlic, ground almonds, bread crumbs and the saffron, if using, and sauté for 3 minutes longer. Add the tomatoes and stock or wine and cook over medium heat, stirring occasionally, until slightly thickened, 5–8 minutes. Season to taste with salt and pepper. Remove from the heat and set aside.

❊ If using the peas, bring a saucepan three-fourths full of water to a boil. Add the peas and boil until barely tender, 3–6 minutes.

❊ Raise the oven temperature to 450°F (230°C). Sprinkle the fillets on both sides with salt and pepper and place in a single layer in a baking dish. Spoon the sauce over the fish, add the peas, if using, and bake in the oven until the fish is opaque throughout, 10–12 minutes. Garnish with the reserved toasted almonds and the parsley or mint. Serve at once.

Serves 4

Stuffed Squid

Different variations on stuffed squid are found on taverna tables in Greece and Portugal as well as Spain. The squid are sometimes served atop a bed of wilted assorted greens, such as dandelion, escarole (Batavian endive), kale, arugula (rocket) and chicory (curly endive).

12	medium or 16 small squid

BREAD CRUMB FILLING

3	tablespoons olive oil
1½	cups (6 oz/185 g) chopped onion
4	cloves garlic, minced
½	cup (3 oz/90 g) chopped serrano, prosciutto or similar cured ham (optional)
1–1½	cups (2–3 oz/60–90 g) fresh bread crumbs
¼	cup (2 fl oz/60 ml) fresh lemon juice
6	tablespoons (⅓ oz/10 g) chopped fresh flat-leaf (Italian) parsley
	Salt and freshly ground pepper
	Olive oil for brushing
	Salt and freshly ground pepper

OLIVE OIL DRESSING

⅓	cup (3 fl oz/80 ml) virgin olive oil
3–4	tablespoons fresh lemon juice
3	tablespoons dried oregano

To clean each squid, grip the head and pull it and the attached innards gently but firmly from the body. Using your fingertips, squeeze out the small, round beak from the mouth at the base of the tentacles. Using a sharp knife, cut away the eyes, reserving the tentacles. Using your fingers, clean out the body pouch under running water, being careful not to tear it. Remove and discard the transparent quill-like cartilage from along one side of the pouch. Rub off the filmy brownish skin from the body and rinse the tentacles and body well. Chop the tentacles and set the bodies and tentacles aside.

Preheat a broiler (griller) or prepare a fire in a charcoal grill.

To make the bread crumb filling, in a sauté pan over medium heat, warm the olive oil. Add the onion and sauté until tender, 8–10 minutes.

Add the garlic, ham (if using), chopped tentacles and enough of the bread crumbs to bind the mixture together. Sauté over medium heat for 2 minutes. Stir in the lemon juice and parsley and season to taste with salt and pepper. Let cool.

Carefully stuff the bread crumb mixture into the squid bodies and skewer the ends closed with toothpicks. Thread the squid crosswise onto long metal skewers. Brush them with olive oil and sprinkle with salt and pepper. Place on a broiler pan or a grill rack and broil or grill, turning once, until the squid are tender and opaque, about 3 minutes per side.

Meanwhile, make the dressing: In a small bowl, whisk together the virgin olive oil, lemon juice and oregano.

Slide the squid off the skewers onto a warmed platter, drizzle the dressing evenly over the top and serve hot.

Serves 4

Trout Wrapped in Ham

*This savory fish dish, from the region of Navarra in the northeast, is one of the best-known preparations
for trout in all of Spain. Although often accompanied with just boiled potatoes and a squeeze of lemon,
the trout is also frequently served with a topping of sautéed mushrooms, given as an option below.*

4 freshwater trout, cleaned with heads intact, each about ¾ lb (375 g)
  Salt and freshly ground pepper
8 thin slices serrano, prosciutto or similar cured ham
  About 1 cup (5 oz/155 g) all-purpose (plain) flour
⅓ cup (3 fl oz/80 ml) olive oil

MUSHROOM TOPPING (OPTIONAL)
¼ cup (2 fl oz/60 ml) dry white wine
2 tablespoons unsalted butter
1½ cups (4½ oz/140 g) sliced fresh mushrooms

  Lemon wedges

※ Sprinkle the trout inside and out with salt and pepper. Slip 1 slice of ham inside each trout. Wrap a second ham slice around the center of each trout, leaving the head and tail exposed. Skewer the cavity closed with toothpicks or tie with kitchen string. Spread the flour on a large plate.

※ In a large sauté pan or frying pan over medium heat, warm the olive oil. Dip the trout in the flour, coating it evenly, and fry, turning once, until golden on both sides, about 4 minutes per side. Transfer to a warmed platter or individual plates.

※ If a mushroom topping is desired, raise the heat to high, pour the wine into the pan and deglaze the pan by stirring to dislodge any browned bits from the pan bottom. Reduce the heat to medium, add the butter and when it melts, add the mushrooms. Sauté until tender, about 8 minutes.

※ Remove the toothpicks or string from the trout and spoon the mushrooms over them, if using. Serve hot with lemon wedges.

Serves 4

Paella

*Taking its name from the shallow, two-handled metal pan in which it is traditionally
cooked, paella can be as simple or as extravagant as time and money permit. Paella originated
in Valencia, although many regions of Spain have their own special variations.*

24   small clams in the shell
24   mussels in the shell
1   chicken, 3 lb (1.5 kg), cut into serving pieces
   Salt and freshly ground pepper
   Olive oil
½   lb (250 g) chorizo sausages
1   lb (500 g) medium shrimp (prawns), peeled and deveined
2   onions, chopped
6   cloves garlic, finely minced
2   red or green bell peppers (capsicums), seeded, deribbed and diced
1½   cups (9 oz/280 g) peeled, seeded and diced tomatoes (fresh or canned)
3   cups (21 oz/655 g) short-grain white rice
6   cups (48 fl oz/1.5 l) chicken stock
¼   teaspoon saffron threads, crushed with a mortar and pestle
1   cup (5 oz/155 g) shelled peas, shelled and peeled fava (broad) beans, or lima beans
   Lemon wedges
   Strips of roasted and peeled pimiento pepper (capsicum), optional

❈ Discard any clams or mussels that do not close to the touch. Scrub them well under running water and pull the beards from the mussels. Place the clams in a bowl of water and the mussels in a dry bowl and store in the refrigerator until needed.

❈ Rinse the chicken pieces and pat dry. Sprinkle with salt and pepper to taste. Place a large, deep sauté pan over high heat and pour in enough olive oil to film the pan bottom lightly. Add the chicken and brown well on all sides, 8–10 minutes. Using tongs or a slotted spoon, transfer the chicken to a plate; set aside.

❈ If needed, pour a little more olive oil into the oil remaining in the pan and place over medium-high heat. Add the sausages and cook, turning, until firm and browned on all sides, about 5–8 minutes. Using the tongs or slotted spoon, transfer the sausages to the plate with the chicken. Cut the sausages into chunks and set aside.

❈ Add the shrimp to the same pan and sauté over medium-high heat, stirring briskly, until pink and beginning to curl, 2–3 minutes. Again, transfer with the tongs or slotted spoon to the plate holding the other ingredients.

❈ Add the onions to the oil remaining in the pan and sauté over medium heat until softened, 5–6 minutes, adding a little more olive oil if needed to prevent scorching. Add the garlic and bell peppers and sauté until beginning to soften, about 5 minutes longer. Add the tomatoes and cook, stirring, for 3 minutes longer. Stir in the rice, pour in the chicken stock and add the saffron. Bring to a boil, then reduce the heat to low and simmer, uncovered, for 10 minutes.

❈ Add the browned chicken and sausages and the peas or beans, pushing them into the rice slightly, and simmer, uncovered, for 10 minutes.

❈ Drain the clams. Scatter the clams, mussels and the reserved shrimp over the top, cover and cook until the clams and mussels open, 4–5 minutes. Discard any clams and mussels that have not opened.

❈ Remove from the heat and let stand for a few minutes until most of the liquid is absorbed and the rice is tender. Serve directly from the pan or spoon onto individual plates. Garnish with lemon wedges and strips of pimiento, if using.

Serves 4–6

Poultry and Meat

Fresh meat and poultry have not always been a daily feature on Mediterranean menus. In the past, meat was used sparingly, usually offered in small portions or to enhance the flavor of a soup, pilaf or bean ragout. But, as the prosperity of the region has grown, meat and poultry dishes have become more common menu items.

Stews make up a large part of the repertoire, as do meats and small birds cooked over an open flame. The aromas rising from a kitchen grill or rotisserie frequently offer the first tantalizing greeting to customers as they pass through the doors of a taverna. Portions are often smaller than those customarily served in America or Europe. A skewer with just a few pieces of meat is a typical serving, and diners are expected to round out their meals with vegetables, a pilaf or potatoes and bread.

Lamb and pork are the most popular meats, and the animals are routinely eaten when very young. Although a lamb chop may be just a bite or two and the leg but a few pounds, the meat is exceptionally sweet and uncommonly tender. Both meat and poultry, which is generally free-range, often require only a few fresh herb sprigs or a simple marinade and a squeeze or two of lemon to highlight their full, natural flavors.

Grilled Chicken Kebabs

The yogurt in this classic marinade tenderizes the chicken, yielding succulent results. If you like, grill vegetables on separate skewers so their cooking can be easily monitored. Serve the kebabs with pita bread or pilaf and spoon some yogurt-cucumber sauce (recipe on page 337) over the grilled vegetables.

4   cloves garlic, minced
¼   cup (2 fl oz/60 ml) fresh lemon juice
1   tablespoon paprika
½   teaspoon ground cayenne pepper
½   teaspoon freshly ground black pepper, plus pepper to taste
1   tablespoon chopped fresh thyme
1   cup (8 oz/250 g) plain yogurt
1½   lb (750 g) boneless, skinless chicken breasts or thighs
     Olive oil for brushing
     Salt

⊠ In a food processor fitted with the metal blade or in a blender, combine the onion, garlic, lemon juice, paprika, cayenne, the ½ teaspoon black pepper and the thyme. Use rapid on-off pulses to combine well. Add the yogurt and pulse to mix.

⊠ Rinse the chicken and pat dry. Cut into 1-inch (2.5-cm) cubes and place in a nonaluminum container. Pour the yogurt mixture over the chicken and turn to coat. Cover and let marinate in the refrigerator for 8 hours.

⊠ Prepare a fire in a charcoal grill or preheat a broiler (griller).

⊠ Remove the chicken pieces from the marinade, reserving the marinade, and thread them onto metal skewers.

Brush the chicken with olive oil and then sprinkle with salt and pepper.

⊠ Place the skewers on an oiled grill rack or a broiler pan and grill or broil, turning and basting once with the reserved marinade, until no longer pink in the center when cut into with a knife, 4–5 minutes per side for breast meat and 5–6 minutes per side for thigh meat.

⊠ Transfer the skewers to warmed individual plates or a platter. Serve hot.

Serves 4

Chicken with Eggplant, Peppers and Tomatoes

Like ratatouille, samfaina is a mixture of onions, garlic, eggplant, peppers and tomatoes cooked down to a fragrant and unctuous stew. It makes a wonderful addition to a tortilla (recipe on page 236) and is a good sauce for fish. Serve with rice, mashed potatoes or slices of grilled bread.

1   frying chicken, about 4 lb (2 kg), cut into serving pieces
     Salt and freshly ground pepper
¼   cup (2 fl oz/60 ml) olive oil
¼   lb (125 g) diced cooked ham or cured ham such as serrano or prosciutto, optional
2   large onions, sliced or coarsely chopped
1   lb (500 g) Asian (slender) eggplants (aubergines), unpeeled, or 1 globe eggplant, about 1 lb (500 g), peeled
3   cloves garlic, minced
¾   lb (375 g) zucchini (courgettes), cut into ½-inch (12-mm) chunks
2   green or red bell peppers (capsicums), seeded, deribbed and cut lengthwise into strips ½ inch (12 mm) wide
1½   lb (750 g) tomatoes, peeled, seeded and chopped (fresh or canned)
1   bay leaf
2   tablespoons chopped fresh thyme, oregano or marjoram
½   cup (4 fl oz/125 ml) dry white wine

❂ Rinse the chicken pieces and pat dry. Sprinkle with salt and pepper.

❂ In a large sauté pan over medium-high heat, warm the olive oil. Add the chicken and brown on all sides, about 8 minutes. Using tongs or a slotted spoon, transfer to a plate.

❂ To the oil remaining in the pan, add the ham, if using, and sauté over medium heat for 1 minute. Add the onions and sauté until tender and translucent, about 10 minutes.

❂ Cut the eggplant(s) into 1-inch (2.5-cm) cubes and add to the onions along with the garlic, zucchini and bell peppers. Sauté until beginning to soften, about 5 minutes longer.

❂ Add the tomatoes, bay leaf, thyme or other herb and wine and stir well. Return the chicken to the pan and turn the pieces to mix evenly with the *samfaina*. Cover and simmer over low heat until the chicken is tender and opaque throughout, 25–35 minutes. Discard the bay leaf and season to taste with salt and pepper.

❂ Transfer to a warmed serving dish and serve hot.

Serves 4

Roast Chicken with Oregano and Lemon

When Greek cooks roast chicken, more likely than not they will produce this venerable taverna dish, in which the accompanying potatoes become especially tender, juicy and lemony. Serve with white wine and a zesty Greek salad (recipe on page 265), if you like.

1   roasting chicken, about 5 lb (2.5 kg)

1   lemon, quartered

½   cup (4 fl oz/125 ml) olive oil
Salt to taste, plus 1 teaspoon salt
Freshly ground pepper

12   cloves garlic, crushed

2   teaspoons plus 3 tablespoons dried oregano

⅓   cup (3 fl oz/80 ml) fresh lemon juice

2   teaspoons coarsely cracked pepper

6   white boiling potatoes, peeled and cut into large wedges

1   cup (8 fl oz/250 ml) water or chicken stock, or as needed

¼   cup (⅓ oz/10 g) chopped fresh flat-leaf (Italian) parsley

❈ Preheat an oven to 400°F (200°C).

❈ Rinse the chicken and pat dry. Rub the chicken inside and out with the cut lemon quarters, 1–2 table-spoons of the olive oil and sprinkle with salt and ground pepper. Place the lemon quarters, 4 of the garlic cloves and the 2 teaspoons oregano in the chicken cavity. Place the chicken on a rack in a roasting pan.

❈ In a small saucepan, combine the remaining olive oil, the lemon juice, 2 tablespoons of the oregano, the coarsely cracked pepper and the 1 teaspoon salt and bring to a sim-mer over medium heat. Simmer for 3 minutes to blend the flavors. Re-move from the heat and set aside.

❈ Place the potatoes around the chicken and sprinkle them with the remaining 1 tablespoon oregano and the remaining 8 garlic cloves. Spoon a little of the simmered lemon-oil mixture over the chicken. Pour 1 cup (8 fl oz/250 ml) water or stock evenly over the potatoes and place in the oven. Roast for 15 min-utes. Baste the chicken with some of the lemon-oil mixture and reduce the heat to 350°F (180°C). Roast the chicken, basting with the lemon-oil mixture every 10–15 minutes, until the juices run clear when the thigh joint is pierced or an instant-read thermometer inserted in the thickest portion of the thigh away from the bone registers 165°F (74°C), about 1 hour.

❈ Transfer the chicken to a warmed platter. If the potatoes aren't golden brown, raise the heat to 450°F (230°C) and cook for 15–20 minutes longer, adding more water or stock if needed to prevent sticking.

❈ Arrange the potatoes alongside the chicken. Using a large spoon, skim off the fat from the roasting pan, then pour the pan juices into a serving container. Sprinkle the chicken and potatoes with the pars-ley. Carve the chicken and pass the pan juices at the table.

Serves 4

Sausage and Green Pepper Ragout

This rustic stew of sausages and sweet green peppers is a specialty of the villages on Mount Pelion in central Greece. The traditional loukanika *sausage is subtly seasoned with orange zest, marjoram, coriander and allspice. You may want to add a bit of these aromatics to the stew if you can find only Italian sausage. Serve with simmered white beans or crusty bread.*

4   tablespoons (2 fl oz/60 ml) olive oil

1   lb (500 g) Greek *loukanika* or Italian sweet sausages, sliced ¾ inch (2 cm) thick

1   lb (500 g) long sweet green peppers (capsicums), seeded, deribbed and cut lengthwise into strips 1 inch (2.5 cm) wide

1   lb (500 g) tomatoes, peeled, seeded and chopped (fresh or canned)

1   tablespoon dried oregano

¼   teaspoon ground allspice, optional

½   teaspoon ground coriander, optional

2   teaspoons grated orange zest, optional

  Salt and freshly ground pepper

❊ In a large sauté pan over high heat, warm 2 tablespoons of the olive oil. Add the sausages and brown on all sides, about 5 minutes. Using a slotted spoon, transfer the sausages to a plate and set aside.

❊ Add the remaining 2 tablespoons oil to the pan. Then add the sweet peppers and sauté over medium heat until softened, 5–8 minutes.

❊ Return the sausages to the pan and add the tomatoes, oregano and, if using Italian sausage, add the allspice, coriander and orange zest. Cover and simmer over low heat until the flavors have blended and the sauce has thickened, 15–20 minutes.

❊ Season the ragout to taste with salt and pepper. Transfer to a warmed serving dish and serve hot.

Serves 4

SIS KOFTE

Grilled Meatballs

Quintessential taverna fare, these flavorful meatballs—Turkey's answer to American hamburgers—are grilled quickly over charcoal, then served tucked into warm pita bread with sliced tomatoes and onions and a garlicky yogurt sauce. The onions are traditionally flavored with sumac, a slightly sour, peppery ground spice used in many Middle Eastern cuisines.

YOGURT SAUCE
4   cups (32 oz/1 kg) plain yogurt
3   large cloves garlic, finely minced
3   tablespoons olive oil
1   tablespoon red wine vinegar or fresh lemon juice, or to taste
¼   cup (⅓ oz/10 g) chopped fresh mint
    Salt and freshly ground pepper

ONION SALAD
1   lb (500 g) red (Spanish) or white onions
1   tablespoon salt
½   cup (¾ oz/20 g) chopped fresh flat–leaf (Italian) parsley
1   teaspoon sumac, optional

MEATBALLS
2   lb (1 kg) ground (minced) lean lamb or beef
2   yellow or red (Spanish) onions, grated (about 1½ cups/7½ oz/ 235 g)
2   cloves garlic, finely minced
2   eggs
1   tablespoon chopped fresh thyme
1   teaspoon freshly ground pepper
½   teaspoon salt, plus salt to taste
    Olive oil for brushing

6 pita breads, warmed

�֎ To make the yogurt sauce, line a large sieve with cheesecloth (muslin), place it over a bowl and spoon the yogurt into the sieve. Refrigerate for 4–6 hours to drain off the excess water. You should have 1½–2 cups (12–16 oz/375–500 g) drained yogurt. Add the garlic, olive oil and vinegar or lemon juice to the drained yogurt. Stir well and fold in the mint. Season to taste with salt and pepper. Cover and refrigerate until needed.

✖ Prepare a fire in a charcoal grill or preheat a broiler (griller).

✖ To make the onion salad, cut any large onions in half and then thinly slice all of the onions. Place the onion slices in a large sieve or colander, add the salt and toss well. Let stand for 15 minutes. Rinse the onion slices with cool water and pat dry with paper towels. Place in a bowl and add the parsley and the sumac, if using. Toss well and set aside.

✖ To make the meatballs, in a bowl, combine the lamb or beef, grated onions, garlic, eggs, thyme, pepper and the ½ teaspoon salt. Mix with your hands until the mixture holds together well. Form into 12 ovals about 3 inches (7.5 cm) long and 1½ inches (4 cm) wide and thread them onto metal skewers.

✖ Brush the meatballs with olive oil and sprinkle with salt. Place the skewers on an oiled grill rack or a broiler pan and grill or broil, turning to brown on all sides, until cooked through, about 8 minutes.

✖ Remove the skewers from the grill or broiler and slip the meatballs off the skewers. Cut the pita breads into halves and tuck a meatball into the each half. Serve at once. Offer the yogurt sauce and onion salad at the table for guests to add to taste.

Serves 6

Braised Pork with Quinces

Quinces are prized in Greece and Turkey during the fall months, when their unique scent perfumes every kitchen. If you cannot find quinces, substitute apples or pears and reduce the sugar to 2 tablespoons. Although pork is naturally sweet and a wonderful foil for quince, this stew can also be made with beef or lamb.

2½ lb (1.25 kg) boneless pork shoulder, trimmed of excess fat and cut into 2-inch (5-cm) cubes

2 teaspoons ground cinnamon

2 teaspoons ground cumin
   Juice of 1 lemon

3 lb (1.5 kg) quinces

2 tablespoons unsalted butter

½ cup (4 oz/125 g) sugar

1 cup (8 fl oz/250 ml) pomegranate juice or water

¼ cup (2 fl oz/60 ml) olive oil

2 onions, chopped
   Pinch of ground cayenne pepper, optional

1 cup (8 fl oz/250 ml) chicken stock or water
   Salt and freshly ground black pepper

❈ Rub the meat with 1 teaspoon each of the cinnamon and cumin. Place the spice-coated meat in a non-aluminum bowl, cover and let marinate for 2 hours at room temperature or overnight in the refrigerator.

❈ Fill a large bowl three-fourths full with water and add the lemon juice. Peel the quinces, core them and then slice thickly. As they are cut, drop them into the bowl of lemon water to prevent discoloring until all are cut.

❈ Drain the quince slices and pat dry. In a sauté pan over high heat, melt the butter. Add the quinces and sauté until softened, about 10 minutes. Sprinkle with the sugar and continue to sauté until golden, 15–20 minutes longer. Add the pomegranate juice or water and simmer over medium heat until tender, 15–20 minutes. Remove from the heat and let stand for 1 hour.

❈ Return the quinces to a simmer over medium heat and simmer for 15 minutes longer. Remove from the heat and let stand for 1 hour longer; or let cool, cover and let stand overnight.

❈ In a large, heavy sauté pan over medium heat, warm the olive oil. Add the pork and brown on all sides, about 10 minutes. Using a slotted spoon, transfer the pork to a plate and set aside.

❈ To the fat remaining in the pan, add the onions. Sauté over medium heat until tender, about 8 minutes. Add the remaining 1 teaspoon each cinnamon and cumin and the cayenne, if using. Sauté a few minutes longer to blend the flavors and then return the meat to the pan. Add the 1 cup (8 fl oz/250 ml) stock or water and stir well. Reduce the heat to low, cover and simmer for 1 hour.

❈ Place the pan holding the quinces over medium heat and bring to a simmer. Simmer for 15 minutes. Add the quinces and their juices to the meat and continue to simmer over low heat until the meat is tender and the flavors have blended, about 30 minutes longer. Season to taste with salt and pepper.

❈ Spoon the stew into a warmed serving dish and serve hot.

Serves 6

Lamb Stew with Artichokes

While artichokes are the classic choice for this dill-scented Greek stew, you could replace them with celery, fennel or carrots. The last-minute avgolemono *thickening of egg and lemon is an added flourish that truly pulls the dish together. The stew can be prepared a day or two ahead; add the* avgolemono *during reheating.*

3–4 tablespoons olive oil

2½ lb (1.25 kg) boneless lamb shoulder, trimmed of excess fat and cut into 2-inch (5-cm) pieces

3 onions, chopped

3 cloves garlic, minced

1½ cups (12 fl oz/375 ml) water or chicken stock, or as needed

½ cup (4 fl oz/120 ml) fresh lemon juice

6 medium-sized artichokes

2 lb (1 kg) assorted greens such as romaine (cos), dandelion greens or Swiss chard (silverbeet), stemmed, well rinsed, drained and torn into bite-sized pieces (optional)

Salt

½ cup (¾ oz/20 g) chopped fresh dill

Freshly ground pepper

2 eggs, at room temperature

In a large sauté pan over high heat, warm 2 tablespoons of the olive oil. Working in batches, add the lamb and brown on all sides, about 10 minutes. Using a slotted spoon, transfer the browned lamb to a large, heavy pot.

Add more olive oil if needed to the sauté pan and then add the onions. Sauté over medium heat until softened, about 5 minutes. Add the garlic and sauté for 3 minutes longer. Transfer the contents of the sauté pan to the pot containing the lamb. Raise the heat to high, pour ½ cup (4 fl oz/125 ml) of the water or stock into the sauté pan, and deglaze the pan by stirring to dislodge any browned bits from the pan bottom. Then add the pan juices to the lamb.

Add the remaining 1 cup (8 fl oz/250 ml) water or stock to the pot, or as needed to cover the meat. Bring to a boil, reduce the heat to low, cover and simmer for 45 minutes.

Meanwhile, fill a large bowl three-fourths full with water and add ¼ cup (2 fl oz/60 ml) of the lemon juice. Snap off the tough outer leaves from the artichokes. Using a paring knife, trim the dark green parts from the base and stem. Cut the artichokes lengthwise into quarters, then scoop out and discard the prickly chokes. As they are cut, drop the artichokes into the bowl of lemon water to prevent discoloring until needed.

If using the greens, fill a large saucepan three-fourths full with water and bring to a boil. Add salt to taste and then the greens. Boil until tender, about 10 minutes, then drain well.

When the lamb has simmered for 45 minutes, drain the artichokes and add them to the pot along with the greens. Continue to simmer until the lamb and artichokes are tender, about 20 minutes longer.

Add the dill and season to taste with salt and pepper. Simmer for 5 minutes. At the last minute, in a bowl, beat the eggs until very frothy. Gradually beat in the remaining ¼ cup (2 fl oz/60 ml) lemon juice. Then gradually beat in about 1 cup (8 fl oz/250 ml) of the hot lamb juices, beating constantly to prevent curdling. Slowly stir the egg mixture into the hot stew. Heat through but do not allow the stew to boil.

Transfer to a warmed serving dish and serve hot.

Serves 4

Baked Lamb and Eggplant

This famous Greek dish is believed to have been carried to Greece by the Arabs in the Middle Ages. Moussaka *can be prepared in advance and gently reheated before serving.*

3 lb (1.5 kg) eggplants (aubergines)
Salt

MEAT SAUCE
2 tablespoons olive oil
3 large yellow onions, chopped
2 lb (1 kg) ground (minced) lean lamb
3 cups (18 oz/560 g) canned chopped plum (Roma) tomatoes
3 tablespoons tomato paste
4 cloves garlic, finely minced
½ cup (4 fl oz/125 ml) red wine
1 tablespoon dried oregano
¾ cup (1 oz/30 g) chopped fresh flat-leaf (Italian) parsley
1 tablespoon ground cinnamon
Pinch of ground cloves or allspice
Salt and freshly ground pepper

Olive oil for brushing

BÉCHAMEL SAUCE
3 tablespoons unsalted butter
3 tablespoons all-purpose (plain) flour
3 cups (24 fl oz/750 ml) hot milk
½ teaspoon freshly grated nutmeg
Salt and freshly ground pepper
3 eggs, lightly beaten
1 cup (8 oz/250 g) whole-milk ricotta cheese

½ cup (2 oz/60 g) fine dried bread crumbs
1 cup (4 oz/125 g) freshly grated kefalotiri or Parmesan cheese

※ Peel the eggplants and cut into slices ½ inch (12 mm) thick. Place the eggplant slices in a colander, sprinkle with salt and let stand for 1 hour to drain off the bitter juices.

※ Meanwhile, make the meat sauce: In a large frying pan over medium heat, warm the olive oil. Add the onions and sauté until tender, about 8 minutes. Add the lamb and cook until the meat loses its redness and starts to brown, 5–7 minutes. Add the tomatoes, tomato paste, garlic, wine, oregano, parsley, cinnamon and ground cloves or allspice and simmer over low heat until thickened and most of the liquid is absorbed, about 45 minutes. If it begins to look too dry, add a little water. Taste and adjust the seasonings with salt, pepper and the spices. Set aside.

※ Preheat an oven to 400°F (200°C). Rinse the eggplant slices with cool water, drain well and pat dry with paper towels. Place on baking sheets, brush the tops with olive oil and bake in the oven, turning once and brushing on the second side with oil, until tender, golden and translucent, 15–20 minutes. Transfer to paper towels to drain.

※ To make the béchamel sauce, in a small saucepan over low heat, melt the butter. Whisk in the flour and raise the heat to medium. Cook, stirring, for 2 minutes. (Do not brown.) Gradually whisk in the hot milk and bring to a boil over high heat. Reduce the heat to medium and simmer until thickened, 2–3 minutes. Add the nutmeg, season to taste with salt and pepper and remove from the heat. In a small bowl, whisk the eggs and ricotta until well blended, then whisk into the hot sauce.

※ Reduce the oven temperature to 350°F (180°C).

※ To assemble the *moussaka,* oil an 11-by-15-inch (28-by-37.5-cm) baking dish. Sprinkle ¼ cup (1 oz/30 g) of the bread crumbs on the bottom of the dish. Arrange half of the eggplant slices in the dish and spoon the meat sauce over them. Layer the remaining eggplant slices on top and pour the béchamel evenly over the surface. Sprinkle with the remaining ¼ cup (1 oz/30 g) bread crumbs and then with the cheese.

※ Bake until heated through and the top is golden brown, about 45 minutes. Remove from the oven and let stand for 15 minutes before cutting into squares to serve.

Serves 8–10

Grilled Lamb on Skewers

*The tantalizing aroma of grilling lamb pervades the cities of the eastern Mediterranean. In Greece,
this same preparation is called* arni souvlakia. *The marinade also works well on lamb chops and on butterflied
leg of lamb. Serve atop eggplant and tomato pilaf (recipe on page 277) or with pita bread.*

2 small onions, grated

1 cup (8 fl oz/250 ml) olive oil

1 teaspoon freshly ground black pepper, plus ground black pepper to taste

1 teaspoon dried oregano or 2 teaspoons fresh thyme

1 teaspoon ground cinnamon

1 teaspoon ground cumin

Pinch of ground cayenne pepper, optional

2 lb (1 kg) tender lamb from the leg, trimmed of fat and cut across the grain into 1½-inch (4-cm) cubes

1 red (Spanish) onion, cut into 1-inch (2.5-cm) squares

Salt

2 ripe but firm tomatoes, cored and halved

2 green bell peppers (capsicums), seeded, deribbed and cut into 1½-inch (4-cm) squares

Yogurt-cucumber sauce *(recipe on page 337)*

※ In a nonaluminum bowl, combine the onions, ¾ cup (6 fl oz/190 ml) of the olive oil, the 1 teaspoon black pepper, oregano or thyme, cinnamon, cumin and the cayenne, if using. Stir to mix well, then add the lamb cubes, turning to coat evenly. Cover and let marinate overnight in the refrigerator.

※ Prepare a fire in a charcoal grill or preheat a broiler (griller).

※ Remove the lamb cubes from the marinade, reserving the marinade, and thread them onto metal skewers, alternating them with the onion pieces. (Do not pack the lamb and onion pieces too tightly or they will not cook evenly.) Brush the lamb and onions with some of the remaining ¼ cup (2 fl oz/60 ml) olive oil and sprinkle with salt and black pepper. Thread the tomatoes and bell peppers on separate skewers, brushing them with oil and sprinkling with salt and pepper as well.

※ Place the lamb-filled skewers on an oiled grill rack or a broiler pan and grill or broil, turning once and basting occasionally with the reserved marinade, until the meat is done to your liking, 8–10 minutes total for medium-rare. About 5 minutes before the lamb is ready, add the tomato and pepper skewers to the grill rack or broiler pan. Grill or broil, turning as needed, until tender when pierced with a knife, about 5 minutes.

※ Transfer the skewers to a warmed serving dish or individual plates. Serve hot with the yogurt-cucumber sauce in a bowl on the side.

Serves 4–6

Roast Leg of Lamb with Yogurt

*While yogurt is more commonly used as a tenderizing marinade for lamb kebabs, in this
recipe from Crete it is mixed with cinnamon and spread on a leg of lamb during only the last
15 minutes of roasting. Surprisingly, the yogurt forms a wonderful savory crust.*

1	leg of lamb on the bone, 5–6 lb (2.5–3 kg)
6	cloves garlic plus 2 teaspoons minced garlic
2	teaspoons plus 3 tablespoons chopped fresh rosemary
5	tablespoons (2½ fl oz/75 ml) olive oil
4	tablespoons (2 fl oz/60 ml) fresh lemon juice
	Salt and freshly ground pepper
1½	cups (12 oz/375 g) whole or lowfat plain yogurt
1	teaspoon ground cinnamon
½	teaspoon all-purpose (plain) flour

❊ Using a small, sharp knife, cut about 12 slits, each about ½ inch (12 mm) deep, in the leg of lamb, spacing them evenly. Cut 3 of the garlic cloves into thin slivers and place in a small bowl with the 2 teaspoons rosemary. Mix well and insert the garlic mixture in the slits.

❊ Finely chop the remaining 3 garlic cloves and place in a small bowl. Add 2 tablespoons of the rosemary, 2 tablespoons of the olive oil and 2 tablespoons of the lemon juice and mix well. Rub this mixture all over the leg of lamb. Cover and let marinate for 2 hours at room temperature or overnight in the refrigerator.

❊ Preheat an oven to 350°F (180°C).

❊ Place the lamb in a roasting pan and sprinkle with salt and pepper. In a small bowl, whisk together the remaining 3 tablespoons olive oil, the remaining 2 tablespoons lemon juice, the remaining 1 tablespoon rosemary and the 2 teaspoons minced garlic. Roast the lamb, basting every 20 minutes with the oil-lemon mixture, for 1¼ hours.

❊ In another bowl, whisk together the yogurt, cinnamon and flour. Spoon the mixture over the lamb and continue to roast until the yogurt sauce sets up and the lamb is done to your liking, about 15 minutes longer for medium-rare. To test, insert an instant-read thermometer into the thickest part of the leg away from the bone; it should register 125°F (52°C) for medium-rare.

❊ Transfer the lamb to a warmed serving platter and let rest for 8–10 minutes, then carve and serve hot.

Serves 6

Pork Ragout with Sweet Red Peppers and Lemon

This recipe combines the best of two classic Portuguese dishes. One sautés and then braises pork slices with sweet red peppers and white wine; the other stews cumin-and-garlic-scented pork in white wine. The aromatic result is perfectly accented with slices of lemon and chopped cilantro.

3 tablespoons cumin seeds

2 tablespoons minced garlic

1 teaspoon kosher salt

1 teaspoon freshly ground pepper

1 tablespoon paprika

2 lb (1 kg) boneless pork shoulder, cut into 1-inch (2.5-cm) cubes

¼ cup (2 oz/60 g) lard or (2 fl oz/60 ml) olive oil

4 red bell peppers (capsicums), seeded, deribbed and cut lengthwise into strips ½ inch (12 mm) wide

1 cup (8 fl oz/250 ml) dry white wine

½ cup (4 fl oz/125 ml) chicken stock

6 paper-thin lemon slices, cut into half rounds

½ cup (¾ oz/20 g) chopped fresh cilantro (fresh coriander)

※ Put the cumin seeds in a small, dry frying pan and place over medium heat, swirling the pan occasionally, until toasted and fragrant, 2–3 minutes. Transfer to a spice grinder or peppermill and grind finely.

※ In a mortar, combine the ground cumin, garlic, salt, pepper and paprika and mash with a pestle to form a paste. Place the pork in a nonaluminum bowl and rub the paste evenly over the meat. Cover and let marinate overnight in the refrigerator.

※ Bring the meat to room temperature. In a large sauté pan over high heat, warm the lard or olive oil. Working in batches, add the pork and brown quickly on all sides, 5–8 minutes. Using tongs or a slotted spoon, transfer the pork to a large, heavy pot. Add the pepper strips to the fat remaining in the pan and sauté until softened, about 5 minutes.

※ Transfer the pepper strips to the pot containing the pork. Return the sauté pan to high heat, pour the wine into the pan and deglaze the pan by stirring to dislodge any browned bits from the pan bottom. Add the pan juices to the pork and peppers. Add the stock and lemon slices and bring to a boil. Quickly reduce the heat to low, cover and simmer until the pork is very tender, about 25 minutes.

※ Stir in the cilantro, then taste and adjust the seasonings. Spoon into a warmed serving dish and serve hot.

Serves 4–6

Desserts

If dessert is eaten in a taverna, it may consists of little more than a wedge of cheese or a piece of perfectly ripe fruit. Because the taverna and its Mediterranean counterparts often have only the most rudimentary kitchens, any pastries that might be served are usually bought at a local shop, where the baker may make just one or two sweets along with loaves of country-style bread.

The desserts that are made at a taverna are both simple and homey—vanilla-scented rice pudding and orange-flavored baked custard are just two of the favorites one can expect to find. Cheese- or fruit-filled tartlets or cookies are also baked on occasion, but only if space and time allow.

Dried fruits and nuts are an important part of the taverna dessert repertoire, and they are used with abundance in a variety of sweets and bite-sized treats. Dried figs stuffed with almonds and chocolate make tantalizing tidbits, perfect for savoring alongside a glass of port or sweet sherry. Whole Turkish apricots are also served stuffed, but with a filling of sweet cream and a coating of thick sugar syrup. Nuts are the featured ingredient in baklava, the Greek and Turkish pastry favorite in which delicate layers of filo and chopped nuts are enveloped by a subtle lemony syrup.

Cream–Filled Apricots

Whole dried Turkish apricots work well in this dessert. When cooked, they plump up to reveal a seam where the pit was removed, which becomes a pocket for stuffing. In Turkey, a thick, clotted cream made from water buffalo's milk and known as kaymak *is the prized stuffing ingredient. Italian mascarpone or French crème fraîche may be substituted.*

½ lb (250 g) whole dried Turkish apricots or dried apricot halves

1½ cups (12 oz/375 g) sugar

2 cups (16 fl oz/500 ml) water

2 teaspoons fresh lemon juice

1 cup (8 fl oz/250 ml) *kaymak,* mascarpone or crème fraîche

½ cup (2 oz/60 g) chopped unsalted pistachio nuts

❋ Place the apricots in a bowl, add water to cover and let stand overnight. Drain.

❋ In a saucepan over medium heat, combine the sugar and water. Bring to a simmer, stirring to dissolve the sugar. Simmer until thickened, about 10 minutes. Add the apricots and cook until tender, about 20 minutes. Stir in the lemon juice and continue to simmer for 1 minute longer.

❋ Using a slotted spoon, transfer the apricots to a baking sheet or large plate, reserving the syrup in the pan. Let cool enough to thicken slightly. If the syrup isn't thick, reduce it a bit over medium heat.

❋ *If using whole apricots,* carefully cut each apricot along the seam with a small, sharp knife to create a pocket. Using a small spoon or a pastry bag fitted with a plain tip, spoon or pipe the *kaymak* or other filling into each pocket.

❋ *If using apricot halves,* spoon the *kaymak* or other filling onto the centers of half of them. Top with the remaining apricot halves.

❋ Arrange the apricots side by side on a serving platter. Spoon the thickened syrup over the stuffed apricots and refrigerate until the syrup is set, about 30 minutes.

❋ To serve, bring the stuffed apricots to room temperature and sprinkle with the pistachios.

Serves 4–6

Rice Pudding

Rice pudding is a popular dessert in Spain, Turkey and Greece, as well as Portugal. It is commonly made with milk, and sometimes with water. For extra tenderness, Portuguese cooks first simmer the rice in water and then add it to the milk; in Greece, the rice is cooked directly in the milk. Garnishes range from nuts and raisins to pomegranate seeds and cinnamon.

4   cups (32 fl oz/1 l) milk
⅔   cup (5 oz/155 g) sugar
1   tablespoon unsalted butter
1   lemon zest strip, about 3 inches (7.5 cm) long
1   cinnamon stick
6   cups (48 fl oz/1.5 l) water
    Pinch of salt
½   cup (3½ oz/105 g) short-grain white rice
3   egg yolks
    Ground cinnamon for garnish
    Toasted sliced (flaked) or slivered almonds for garnish, optional

In a saucepan over medium-high heat, combine the milk, sugar, butter, lemon zest and cinnamon stick. Heat until small bubbles appear along the edge of the pan, then remove from the heat. Let stand for 30 minutes to develop the flavors.

Meanwhile, in another saucepan, bring the water to a boil. Add the salt and rice, reduce the heat to low and cook slowly until the rice kernels have swelled and are tender, 15–20 minutes. Drain.

Place the saucepan holding the milk mixture over medium heat and bring to a simmer. Add the rice and simmer uncovered, stirring often, until thickened, 15–20 minutes. Remove the lemon zest and cinnamon stick and discard.

In a bowl, using a fork or whisk, beat the egg yolks until lightly frothy. Gradually add about 1 cup (8 fl oz/250 ml) of the hot pudding to the yolks, beating constantly. Gradually pour the warmed yolks into the remaining pudding, stirring constantly. Cook over very, very low heat, stirring constantly, for 5 minutes.

Spoon the pudding into individual dessert bowls or one large serving bowl. Sprinkle with cinnamon and top with toasted almonds, if using. Serve at room temperature.

Serves 6–8

MELITINIA SANTORINIS

Sweet Cheese Tarts from Santorini

Cheese tarts are enjoyed all over the Mediterranean, but are especially popular in Greece and Portugal. This particular recipe, traditionally found in the tavernas on the sun-splashed island of Santorini, produces small, delicate tartlets.

PASTRY

- 2 cups (8 oz/250 g) sifted all-purpose (plain) flour
- ¼ teaspoon salt
- 1 teaspoon baking powder
- 2 tablespoons sugar
- 3 tablespoons unsalted butter, at room temperature
- ¼ cup (2 oz/60 g) vegetable shortening
- 1 egg, lightly beaten
- 1 tablespoon water, or as needed

CHEESE FILLING

- 1 lb (500 g) fresh soft cheese such as mizithra, ricotta or farmer or equal parts ricotta and cream cheese
- 1 cup (8 oz/250 g) sugar
- 2 tablespoons all-purpose (plain) flour
- 2 egg yolks
- 1 teaspoon ground cinnamon, plus cinnamon for garnish, optional
- Grated orange or lemon zest, optional

To make the pastry in a food processor fitted with the metal blade, combine the flour, salt, baking powder and sugar and process briefly to mix. Add the butter and shortening and process with rapid on-off pulses until the mixture resembles coarse meal. Add the egg and the 1 tablespoon water and process to form a soft dough, adding a little more water if needed. Gather the dough together and place it on a lightly floured work surface. Knead until the dough is smooth and holds together, 5–10 minutes. Wrap in plastic wrap; refrigerate until needed.

To make the pastry by hand, combine the flour, salt, baking powder and sugar in a bowl and stir to mix. Add the butter and shortening and, using a pastry blender or 2 knives, cut them into the dry ingredients until the mixture resembles coarse meal. Add the egg and the 1 tablespoon water and, using a fork, stir together until the mixture forms a soft dough, adding a little more water if needed. Gather the dough together, then knead, shape and refrigerate as directed for the processor method.

To make the cheese filling, in a bowl, combine the cheese(s), sugar, flour, egg yolks, the 1 teaspoon cinnamon and the orange or lemon zest, if using. Stir to mix thoroughly.

Preheat an oven to 350°F (180°C).

Divide the dough into 12 equal balls. On a lightly floured work surface, roll out each ball into a round 4 inches (10 cm) in diameter. Carefully transfer each round to a tartlet tin 2½ inches (6 cm) in diameter, pressing the dough firmly but gently into the tin and fluting the edges. Place the pastry-lined tins on a large baking sheet. Alternatively, butter a large baking sheet. Form the 4-inch (10-cm) rounds into free-form tart shells, pinching the edges to make a fluted rim, and place on the prepared baking sheet.

Carefully spoon the cheese filling into the tart shells, gently smoothing the tops with a rubber spatula. Bake until the tops are a pale golden brown, 20–25 minutes.

Transfer to wire racks and let cool. Sprinkle with cinnamon, if using, and serve at room temperature.

Makes 12 tartlets

Figs Stuffed with Chocolate and Almonds

Although the combination might not seem obvious at first glance, one taste of these confections shows how well suited dried figs are to the rich tastes and textures of chocolate and almonds. Serve this after-dinner sweet with a glass of good Portuguese port or Madeira.

½ cup (2½ oz/75 g) slivered blanched almonds, plus 12 whole blanched almonds

¼ cup (2 oz/60 g) sugar

2 oz (60 g) semisweet chocolate, chopped

12 large dried figs

❊ Preheat an oven to 350°F (180°C).

❊ Spread the slivered and whole almonds on a baking sheet, keeping them separate. Bake until toasted and fragrant, 8–10 minutes. Let cool. Set aside the 12 whole almonds. Leave the oven set at 350°F (180°C).

❊ In a food processor fitted with the metal blade, combine the sugar, slivered almonds and chocolate. Use rapid on-off pulses to form a coarse paste.

❊ Cut off the stems from the figs. Using a small, sharp knife, cut a small slit 1 inch (2.5 cm) deep in the top of each fig. Using a small spoon, stuff each slit with about 1 teaspoon of the almond-chocolate mixture. Pinch the openings closed. As the figs are stuffed, place them on a baking sheet, stem sides up.

❊ Bake for 5 minutes. Turn the figs over and continue to bake until softened, about 5 minutes longer.

❊ Remove from the oven and press a whole almond into the slit. Serve warm or at room temperature.

Serves 6

Baklava

Both the Greeks and the Turks lay claim to this masterpiece of the Middle Eastern sweets repertoire. Baklava can be made with walnuts, almonds, hazelnuts (filberts) or pistachios or a combination of walnuts and almonds. Sticky honey syrups are never used by Greek and Turkish bakers; instead, they prepare a simple sugar syrup flavored with lemon juice and zest.

4 cups (1 lb/500 g) almonds, walnuts or equal parts almonds and walnuts, coarsely chopped
¾ cup (6 oz/185 g) sugar
1 tablespoon ground cinnamon
¼ teaspoon ground cloves
½ lb (250 g) clarified unsalted butter, melted
1 lb (500 g) filo dough, thawed in the refrigerator if frozen

LEMON SYRUP
2 cups (16 fl oz/500 ml) water
2 cups (1 lb/500 g) sugar
2 lemon zest strips, each 3 inches (7.5 cm) long
2 tablespoons fresh lemon juice

❋ Preheat an oven to 350°F (180°C).

❋ In a bowl, combine the nuts, sugar, cinnamon and cloves.

❋ Lightly brush a 9-by-14-by-2-inch (23-by-35-by-5-cm) baking pan with some of the melted butter. Remove the filo sheets from their package, lay them flat on a work surface and cover with a damp towel or plastic wrap to prevent them from drying out. Lay a filo sheet in the prepared pan and brush it lightly with butter. Working with 1 sheet at a time, top with half of the remaining filo sheets (10–12 sheets), brushing each sheet with butter after it is placed in the pan. Spread the nut mixture evenly over the stacked filo sheets. Then top with the remaining filo sheets, again brushing each sheet lightly with butter, including the top sheet. Cover and refrigerate for about 30 minutes so the butter will set. (This step makes the baklava easier to cut.)

❋ Using a sharp knife, cut the baklava all the way through into diamond shapes, forming about 36 pieces in all. Bake until golden, 35–40 minutes.

❋ While the baklava is baking, make the syrup: In a deep saucepan, combine the water, sugar and lemon zest. Bring to a boil, reduce the heat to low and simmer until thickened, about 15 minutes. Remove the lemon zest and discard. Stir in the lemon juice.

❋ When the baklava is done, remove it from the oven. Pour the hot syrup evenly over the hot pastry. Let stand for 30 minutes to cool slightly, then recut the diamonds. Serve warm or at room temperature. Store leftover pieces covered at room temperature.

Makes about 36 pieces

FLAN DE NARANJA

Caramelized Orange Custard

Flan is the most popular dessert in almost every Spanish taberna, *as well as in Portuguese* tascas, *where a little port or orange zest is sometimes added to flavor the custard base. Usually the custard is caramelized—that is, baked in ramekins or custard cups that have been lined with caramel to create a sweet, golden sauce.*

Zest of 3 oranges, in long strips
2 cups (16 fl oz/500 ml) milk
2 cups (16 fl oz/500 ml) heavy (double) cream
1 cinnamon stick
2 cups (1 lb/500 g) sugar
¼ cup (2 fl oz/60 ml) water
6 whole eggs plus 3 egg yolks
1 teaspoon vanilla extract (essence)
3 tablespoons port wine, optional

In a saucepan over medium-high heat, combine the orange zest, milk, cream and cinnamon stick. Heat until small bubbles appear at the edge of the pan, then remove from the heat. Let stand for 1 hour to develop the flavors.

In a small, heavy saucepan over low heat, combine 1 cup (8 oz/250 g) of the sugar and the water. Stir until the sugar dissolves. Bring to a boil over high heat. Boil, without stirring, until the liquid is golden brown, 6–8 minutes. Carefully pour the hot syrup into the bottoms of eight 1-cup (8-fl oz/250-ml) ramekins or custard cups, immediately tilting and swirling the dishes to coat the bottoms and sides with the caramel. Place the dishes in a large baking pan. Set aside.

Preheat an oven to 325°F (165°C).

Strain the cream mixture through a sieve into a clean saucepan. Warm over medium-high heat until tiny bubbles appear along the edge of the pan. (Do not allow to boil.)

Meanwhile, in a bowl, whisk together the whole eggs, egg yolks and the remaining 1 cup (8 oz/250 g) sugar until frothy. Gradually beat in the hot cream mixture, a little at a time. Stir in the vanilla, and then the wine, if using. Strain the mixture through a sieve into the caramel-lined dishes, dividing it evenly.

Pour hot water into the baking pan to reach halfway up the sides of the custard cups. Cover the pan with foil and place in the oven. Bake until a knife inserted in the center of a custard comes out clean, about 30 minutes.

Remove the baking pan from the oven and remove the dishes from the pan. Let cool for 30 minutes, then cover and refrigerate until well chilled.

Just before serving, carefully run a knife around the inside edge of each custard and invert into individual shallow dessert bowls. Pour any extra caramel in the dishes over the custards and serve.

Serves 8

BASIC RECIPES

In tavernas and similarly rustic Mediterranean establishments, most dishes are composed of little else than a few simple ingredients that have been either grilled, roasted or stewed. Such dishes might seem quite plain if not for the redolent sauces with which they are customarily served. These sauces, some of which follow here, can transform anything from a small plate of roasted vegetables to a single skewer of grilled shrimp into a superb creation all its own.

GARLIC-POTATO SAUCE

SKORDALIA

Skordalia takes its name from skordo, or "garlic." Different versions of the sauce are thickened with potato or with bread and nuts or with all three. Some recipes call for only vinegar, while others, such as this one, also add lemon juice. Serve as an accompaniment to fried fresh fish or salt cod, cooked beets, fried zucchini (courgette) or eggplant (aubergine), and greens.

¾ cup (4 oz/125 g) blanched almonds or walnuts, optional

1 lb (500 g) baking potatoes or new potatoes, peeled and cut into 2-inch (5-cm) pieces

8 cloves garlic
  Coarse salt

3 tablespoons red wine vinegar, or to taste

¼ cup (2 fl oz/60 ml) fresh lemon juice

¾ cup (6 fl oz/180 ml) virgin olive oil
  Salt and freshly ground pepper

※ If using the nuts, preheat an oven to 350°F (180°C). Spread the almonds or walnuts on a baking sheet and place in the oven until toasted and fragrant, 8–10 minutes. Remove from the oven, let cool and chop. Set aside.

※ Meanwhile, bring a saucepan three-fourths full of water to a boil over high heat. Add the potato pieces and boil until tender when pierced with a fork, about 15 minutes. Drain well, return the potatoes to the pan and place over high heat for 1–2 minutes to evaporate the moisture, turning them to prevent scorching. Remove from the heat and, using a potato masher, mash the potatoes until smooth. Set aside.

※ In a mortar, combine the garlic with a little coarse salt and mash with a pestle until puréed. You should have about 2 tablespoons puréed garlic.

※ Stir the garlic into the potatoes and, using a whisk or fork, beat in 1 tablespoon of the vinegar, half of the lemon juice and half of the olive oil. Transfer to a food processor fitted with the metal blade. With the motor running, gradually add the remaining 2 tablespoons vinegar, the remaining lemon juice and olive oil, and the nuts, if using. Season to taste with more vinegar, if needed, and the salt and pepper. Transfer to a bowl and serve, or cover and refrigerate overnight. Bring to room temperature before serving.

Makes about 2¼ cups (18 fl oz/560 ml)

YOGURT-CUCUMBER SAUCE

TZATZIKI

Made from thick, rich sheep's milk yogurt, this tangy sauce is part of the meze *table in every Greek taverna. It can also be found in Turkey, where it is called* cacık. *For a similar consistency with cow's milk yogurt, you must first drain it of excess water. The sauce is delicious served with fried eggplant (aubergine) and zucchini (courgette), lamb chops or meatballs, or as a dip for pita bread.*

- 4 cups (32 oz/1 kg) plain yogurt
- 1 English (hothouse) cucumber, seeded and coarsely grated, or 2 small regular cucumbers, peeled, seeded and coarsely grated
- Salt
- 3 large cloves garlic, finely minced
- 1 tablespoon red wine vinegar or fresh lemon juice, or to taste
- 3 tablespoons olive oil
- ¼ cup (⅓ oz/10 g) chopped fresh mint or equal amounts chopped fresh mint and flat-leaf (Italian) parsley
- Freshly ground pepper

Line a large sieve with cheesecloth (muslin), place it over a bowl and spoon the yogurt into the sieve. Refrigerate for 4–6 hours to drain the excess water from the yogurt. You should have 1½–2 cups (12–16 oz/375–500 g) drained yogurt. Refrigerate until needed.

Place the grated cucumber in a sieve or colander, salt it lightly and toss to mix. Let stand for 30 minutes to draw out the excess moisture.

In a bowl, combine the drained yogurt, garlic, vinegar or lemon juice and olive oil and stir to mix well. Using a kitchen towel, squeeze the drained cucumber dry. Fold the cucumber into the yogurt mixture and then stir in the mint or mint and parsley. Season to taste with salt and pepper. Serve immediately, or cover and refrigerate overnight. Bring to room temperature before serving.

Makes about 2½ cups (20 fl oz/625 ml)

TOMATO-NUT SAUCE

SALSA ROMESCO

This Catalan sauce takes its name from a variety of mild dried pepper. For more spice, add some minced fresh jalapeño or more cayenne. In Catalonia, romesco is served with grilled shellfish and green onions. It is also wonderful on grilled fish, lamb, pork or leeks and asparagus or beets, and is addictive as a dipping sauce for fried potatoes.

2   dried ancho chili peppers
1   large red bell pepper (capsicum)
½   cup (2½ oz/75 g) blanched almonds
½   cup (2½ oz/75 g) hazelnuts (filberts)
2   tablespoons plus ⅔ cup (5 fl oz/ 160 ml) virgin olive oil
1   slice coarse-textured peasant bread, ½ inch (12 mm) thick, crust removed
3   large cloves garlic, minced
1   cup (6 oz/185 g) peeled, seeded, diced and well-drained tomatoes (fresh or canned)
1   tablespoon paprika
½   teaspoon ground cayenne pepper, or to taste
3   tablespoons red wine vinegar, or to taste
     Salt and freshly ground black pepper

❋ Place the ancho chilies in a bowl, add hot water to cover and let stand for 1 hour.

❋ Meanwhile, preheat a broiler (griller). Cut the bell pepper in half lengthwise and remove the stem, seeds and ribs. Place the pepper halves, cut sides down, on a baking sheet. Broil (grill) until the skins are blackened and blistered. Transfer the pepper halves to a plastic container, cover and let stand for 20 minutes. Peel off the skins, then chop the pepper. Set aside.

❋ Preheat an oven to 350°F (180°C). Spread the almonds and hazelnuts on a baking sheet, keeping them separate. Toast in the oven until fragrant and the skins of the hazelnuts begin to loosen, 8–10 minutes. Spread the hazelnuts on a kitchen towel. Cover with a second towel and rub the towels against the nuts to remove the skins. Set the almonds and hazelnuts aside.

❋ Drain the ancho chilies and remove the stems, seeds and ribs. Chop the chilies and set aside.

❋ In a small sauté pan over medium heat, warm the 2 tablespoons olive oil. Add the bread and fry, turning once, until golden on both sides, about 5 minutes. Transfer the bread to a food processor fitted with the metal blade or to a blender. Add the ancho chilies, almonds and hazelnuts, bell pepper, garlic, tomatoes, paprika, the ½ teaspoon cayenne and the 3 tablespoons vinegar. Purée until smooth. With the motor running, gradually add the ⅔ cup (5 fl oz/160 ml) olive oil. The mixture should be the consistency of sour cream. Season to taste with salt and pepper. Let stand for 15 minutes to blend the flavors, then taste and adjust the seasoning with cayenne pepper or vinegar, if needed. Transfer to a bowl and serve, or cover and refrigerate for up to 1 month. Bring to room temperature before serving.

Makes about 2½ cups (20 fl oz/625 ml)

CHILI PEPPER SAUCE
MOLHO DE PIRI-PIRI

Piri-piri is the Portuguese name for an extremely hot variety of pepper that traveled to Portugal via Angola. Much of the pepper's heat comes from the seeds, so use all or part of them, depending upon how hot you want your sauce. Serve this fiery condiment as a marinade or sauce for grilled marinated shrimp (prawns), lobster or chicken.

½ cup (2 oz/60 g) coarsely chopped fresh hot red chili peppers
3 cloves garlic, finely minced
1 teaspoon kosher salt
1 cup (8 fl oz/250 ml) olive oil
¼ cup (2 fl oz/60 ml) red wine vinegar, optional

※ Combine all of the ingredients in a jar. Cover and let stand in a cool, dark place for at least 1 week or for up to 1 month. Shake well before using.

Makes about 1½ cups (12 fl oz/375 ml)

MARINATED OLIVES
AZEITONAS

Whichever of these two different preparations you choose, be sure to marinate the olives for at least 2 days before setting them out with drinks as part of a meze or tapas table. They will keep very well for up to a week in the refrigerator.

FOR BLACK OLIVES
1 lb (500 g) brine-cured black olives, rinsed of brine
3 cloves garlic, crushed
1 teaspoon ground cumin
1 teaspoon red pepper flakes
  Olive oil

FOR GREEN OLIVES
1 lb (500 g) brine-cured green olives, rinsed of brine
4 cloves garlic, crushed
2 tablespoons dried oregano
2 thin orange or lemon zest strips
  Olive oil

※ Select either the black or green olives to prepare, or prepare both. Combine all the ingredients in a bowl, adding olive oil as needed to cover. Toss well to combine. Cover and refrigerate for at least 2 days. Bring to room temperature before serving.

Makes 1 or 2 lb (500 g or 1 kg)

Glossary

The following glossary defines common ingredients and cooking procedures, as well as special equipment, used in French, Italian and Mediterranean cooking.

Artichokes

These large flower buds of a variety of thistle, also known as globe artichokes, are native to the Mediterranean. When large, the tight cluster of tough, pointed leaves covers pale green inner leaves and a gray-green base—together comprising the heart, which conceals the prickly choke. In spring and early summer, Europeans prize small, baby artichokes (below) just 1 –2 inches (4–5 cm) in diameter. These immature specimens require only light trimming of their bases and tougher outer leaves before they are steamed whole or sliced to serve raw in salads.

TO TRIM ARTICHOKES

Cut off the stem and top half of each large artichoke. Remove the tough outer leaves and, using a small sharp knife, trim away the fibrous green layer at the base of the artichoke. Cut large artichokes lengthwise into quarters and cut away the prickly choke; leave small artichokes whole.

TO STEAM ARTICHOKES

Place the trimmed artichokes on a steamer rack over (not touching) boiling water. Cover and steam until tender when pierced with a fork, 5–7 minutes. Remove the artichokes from the rack and let cool.

Arugula

Also known as rocket, this green leaf vegetable has slender, multiple-lobed leaves and a peppery, slightly bitter flavor. Used raw in salads and cooked in pasta sauces.

Beans

Beans are popular rustic fare throughout the Mediterranean. Before using, dried beans should be carefully picked over to remove small stones or fibers or any discolored or misshapen beans. Soaking them in cold water for several hours rehydrates them and shortens their cooking time. Some popular varieties used in this book are:

Borlotti Medium-sized dried beans, shaped like kidney beans, with speckled pink or beige skins. Substitute pink kidney beans or pinto beans.

Cannellini Small, white, thin-skinned oval beans. Great northern or white (navy) beans may be substituted.

Cranberry Small, full-flavored, mealy-textured beans with mottled cranberry-and-tan skins. Pinto beans may be substituted.

Fava Also known as broad bean and resembling an over-sized lima bean, this variety spread northward from ancient Egypt into the Mediterranean. Fresh fava beans are sold in their long pods and are easily shelled. Some cooks also remove the tough but edible skin that encases each bean.

TO PREPARE FAVA BEANS

With your fingers, pop open the bean pods along their seams and pull out the individual beans. Use a thumbnail to split open the tough outer skin of each bean, then peel it off with your fingers.

Belgian Endive

A white to pale yellow-green leaf vegetable characterized by refreshing, slightly bitter, spear-shaped leaves, which are tightly packed in cylindrical heads 4-6 inches (10-15 cm) long. Also known as chicory or witloof.

Bell Peppers

These sweet, bell-shaped red, yellow or green peppers, also known as capsicums, were already making their way into French kitchens by the 16th century. The seeds of bell peppers are indigestible and should be removed before the peppers are added to dishes. Often the peppers are roasted, which loosens their skins for peeling and enhances their natural sweetness.

TO SEED A BELL PEPPER

Cut the pepper in half lengthwise and cut or pull out its stem and seeds, along with the white veins, or ribs, to which the seeds are attached.

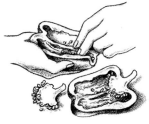

TO ROAST AND PEEL A BELL PEPPER

Seed the pepper as directed and place the halves, cut sides down, on a baking sheet. Place under a preheated broiler until the skins blister and turn a deep brown. Place the peppers in a plastic or paper bag. Seal and let steam for 10 minutes. Remove from the bag and peel off the skins.

Bouquet Garni

A standard seasoning in simmered savory French dishes, a bouquet garni is any small bundle of fresh or dried herbs tied together to keep them from dispersing in the liquid as they impart their flavor.

TO MAKE A BOUQUET GARNI

Place a sprig of parsley, a thyme sprig and a bay leaf on

a square of cheesecloth (muslin). Bring the corners of the cloth together and tie them securely with kitchen string.

Breads

To serve with Italian-style meals, or for bread crumbs, choose a good rustic loaf made from unbleached wheat flour, with a firm, coarse crumb.

Found in bistros and bakeries throughout France, the baguette (below) is a traditional white bread loaf, notable for its soft, flavorful crumb, crisp brown crust and long, narrow shape—usually about 2 feet (60 cm) in length and no more than 4 inches (10 cm) or so in diameter.

For Greek and Turkish specialties, also look for Greek pita (below) or Turkish *pide,* round or oval flat pocket breads.

TO MAKE BREAD CRUMBS
When a recipe calls for fresh bread crumbs, cut off the crusts from a good-quality loaf with a firm, coarse crumb. Crumble the bread into a food processor fitted with the metal blade. Process until small crumbs form. Store in an airtight container in the freezer .

Butter

While olive oil predominates in Mediterranean cuisines, unsalted butter is also used for cooking. To prevent butter from burning at high baking temperatures, it should be clarified—that is, its milk solids and water content removed from the fat—before use.

TO CLARIFY BUTTER
Melt the butter in a small saucepan over very low heat. Remove from the heat and let stand briefly. Using a spoon, skim off and discard the foam from the surface. Pour off the clear yellow oil, leaving the milky solids and water behind. The clarified butter can be refrigerated for up to 1 month or frozen for 2 months.

Capers

Capers, the buds of a common Mediterranean bush, grow wild all over Europe. For use as a savory flavoring ingredient, they are first preserved in salt, or more commonly, pickled in salt and vinegar.

Cheeses

FRENCH
There are hundreds of cheeses produced in France each year, with local versions on display in regional bistros everywhere.

Goat Generally soft, fresh and creamy, goat's milk cheeses, referred to in France as *chèvre,* are notable for their mild tang.

Sold in small rounds or logs (below, left), they are sometimes coated with pepper, ash or herbs, which add subtle flavor.

Roquefort This blue-veined ewe's milk cheese (below, center) comes exclusively from the Aveyron commune of Roquefort-sur-Soulzon. It is prized for its creamy texture and tangy flavor. Substitute any high-quality blue cheese.

Swiss This generic term describes any version of Swiss Emmenthaler (below, right), a firm whole-milk cheese with a yellow color; a mild, nutlike flavor; and distinctive holes that grow larger and more numerous with age.

ITALIAN
Scores of different cheeses are produced in Italy. Among the most popular varieties used in this book are:

Caciotta A creamy, semihard cheese ranging from mild to slightly tangy when aged. Made from all sheep's milk or a blend of sheep and cow's milk. Some varieties include *dolce sardo* from Sardinia, *caciotta toscana* from Tuscany and *pientino* from Pienza.

Emmenthaler This common variety of Swiss cheese has a firm, smooth texture, large holes, and a mellow, slightly sweet and nutty flavor.

Gorgonzola A specialty of Lombardy, Gorgonzola is named for a town just outside of Milan. This mild, creamy, pale yellow blue-veined cheese is made from fresh cow's milk. Some Gorgonzola tends to be salty. Milder varieties are labeled *dolcelatte,* literally "sweet milk." Other blue cheeses may be substituted.

Mascarpone A thick, fresh cream cheese. Similar to French crème fraîche, it is used to enrich sauces or desserts; it may also be sweetened and flavored to be eaten alone.

Mozzarella Mild, rindless white cheese, traditionally made from water buffalo's milk and sold fresh. Commercially produced and packaged cow's milk mozzarella is now much more common, although it has less flavor. Look for fresh mozzarella sold immersed in water. Small, bite-sized balls of the cheese are known as *bocconcini*. It may also be flavored and preserved by smoking.

Parmesan With a sharp, salty, full flavor acquired during at least two years of aging, the best examples of this hard, thick-crusted cow's milk cheese are prized among cooks and diners alike. Although it takes its name from the city of Parma, Parmesan originated midway between that city and Reggio, where the finest variety, *Parmigiano Reggiano*®, is produced. Buy in block form, to grate fresh as needed.

Pecorino Italian sheep's milk cheese, sold either fresh or aged. Among its most popular aged forms is *pecorino romano* from Rome and its vicinity.

Provolone Fairly firm cheese made either from cow's or water buffalo's milk. It is pale yellow and its flavor ranges from mild and slightly sweet to strong and tangy.

Ricotta A light, mild and soft fresh cheese made from twice-cooked milk—traditionally sheep's milk, although cow's milk ricotta is far more common today.

MEDITERRANEAN
Records trace the consumption of cheese in the Mediterranean as far back as the Bronze Age. Today, scores of cheeses may be found on the tables of casual restaurants everywhere in the region.

Farmer Similar in appearance to ricotta, this small-curd, cow's milk cheese is low in fat and has a fairly dry consistency.

Feta Traditional brine-cured Greek sheep's or goat's milk cheese (below, left).

Kasseri Greek sheep's or goat's milk cheese (below, right) with a semi-hard consistency similar to cheddar, punctuated by a few tiny holes, and a taste similar to feta.

Kaymak This Turkish thickened cream is used mostly in desserts. English-style clotted cream or French crème fraîche may be substituted.

Kefalotiri A hard, yellow common Greek grating cheese (center), made from the unpasteurized milk of a sheep or goat.

Mizithra A fresh cheese made from the whey produced in the making of feta or Kefalotiri cheese. Often fresh sheep's or cow's milk is added to enrich the final result.

Chestnut Purée
Often referred to by the French as *marrons*, chestnuts are grown in Corsica, the Ardèche, the Dordogne and Lozère. Sweetened chestnut purée, also known as chestnut cream, is a popular ingredient in French desserts. The purée is available in both its sweetened and unsweetened forms in cans or jars in specialty-food shops.

Chili Peppers
The New World's varied chili peppers, fresh and dried, were introduced to Mediterranean kitchens not long after the first voyage of Columbus. Those featured in this book include *ancho chilies,* the dried form of the ripened mild to hot *poblano chili;* the *jalapeño,* a small, thick-fleshed, fiery-hot green or red chili; mild to moderately hot chilies such as the blackish green *pasilla,* also known as the Chilaca chili; the long green *Anaheim,* also known as the New Mexico or simply the long green chili; and a variety of small, hot red chilies such as the *serrano* and *cayenne.*

Crème Fraîche
This lightly soured and thickened fresh cream is used by cooks throughout France as a sauce enrichment, topping or garnish for both savory and sweet dishes. To make a similar product at home, lightly whip ½ cup (4 fl oz/125 ml) heavy (double) cream; stir in 1 teaspoon sour cream. Then cover and let stand at room temperature until thickened, about 12 hours.

Currants, Dried
Produced from a small variety of grapes, these dried fruits resemble tiny raisins; but they have a stronger, tarter flavor than their larger cousins, which may be substituted for them in recipes.

Eggplant
Tender, mildly earthy, sweet vegetable-fruit covered with tough, shiny skin, which may be peeled or left on in long-cooked dishes. Eggplants vary in color from the familiar purple to red and from yellow to white. The most common variety is the large, purple globe eggplant, but many markets also carry the slender, purple Asian variety, which is more tender and has fewer, smaller seeds. Also known as aubergine.

Eggs
For the recipes in this book, use large eggs.

TO SEPARATE AN EGG
Tap the shell on the edge of a bowl and break it in half. Hold the shell halves over the bowl and gently transfer the whole yolk back and forth between them, taking care not to break the yolk; the clear white will drip into the bowl. Transfer the yolk to another bowl.

Fennel
This crisp, refreshing, anise-flavored bulb vegetable is sometimes sold under its Italian name, *finocchio.* The bulb, with its fine, feathery leaves and stems, is sold separately from the small yellowish-brown fennel seeds.

Filo Dough
Taking its name from the Greek word for leaf, this pastry dough consists of paper-thin sheets that are used to enfold a variety of savory and sweet dishes from the eastern Mediterranean. Also spelled *phyllo,* it may be found fresh or frozen in ethnic food stores and well-stocked markets; thaw frozen filo in the refrigerator before use. When working with filo, keep sheets you are not handling at the moment well covered to prevent drying out.

Foie Gras

The pale, rich, creamy liver—a specialty of Toulouse and Strasbourg—results from force-feeding geese or ducks with corn until their livers swell to a weight of as much as 2 pounds (1 kg) or more. In France, the liver is sold in several forms: raw; freshly cooked; partially cooked and canned; preserved in its own fat; and puréed and canned. For the recipes in this book, use fresh or vacuum-packed foie gras found in some specialty-food stores.

Garlic

Since the time of the Crusades, which spread the use of garlic throughout the Mediterranean, this intensely aromatic bulb has been a favorite flavoring in European kitchens. To ensure the best flavor, buy whole heads of dry garlic, separating individual cloves from the head as needed, and do not purchase more than you will use in 1 or 2 weeks.

TO PEEL A GARLIC CLOVE
Place it on a work surface and cover it with the side of a large knife. Press down firmly but carefully on the side of the knife to crush it slightly; the skin will slip off easily.

Grape Leaves

In Greek and Turkish dishes, grapevine leaves are commonly used as edible wrappers. If fresh leaves are available, rinse them thoroughly, then blanch in boiling water for about 30 seconds before use. Bottled leaves, available in ethnic delicatessens and the specialty-food section of well-stocked food markets, should be gently rinsed of their brine before use.

Ham

Cured pork products are hallmarks of the casual country cuisines of the Mediterranean. Three types of ham used in this book are:

Pancetta This unsmoked bacon is cured simply with salt and pepper. Available in Italian delicatessens and specialty-food stores, it may be sold flat, although it is commonly available sliced from a large sausage-shaped roll.

Prosciutto A specialty of Parma, Italy, this raw ham is cured by dry-salting for 1 month, then air-drying in cool curing sheds for 6 months or longer. Prosciutto has a distinctively intense, savory-sweet flavor. Used as an ingredient, it is also served as an antipasto, cut into tissue-thin slices that highlight its deep pink color.

Serrano Spain's answer to prosciutto, serrano ham has a somewhat tougher, chewier texture, which reflects the less-pampered pigs from which it is produced.

Herbs

A wide variety of fresh and dried herbs add complex aromatic character to foods. Some popular herbs include:

Basil A sweet, spicy herb used both dried and fresh.

Bay Leaf The dried leaves of the bay laurel tree give their pungent, spicy flavor to sauces and other simmered dishes.

Chervil With small leaves resembling flat-leaf (Italian) parsley, this herb possesses a subtle flavor reminiscent of both parsley and anise.

Chives Long, thin, fresh green shoots of the chive plant have a mild flavor that recalls the onion, a related plant.

Cilantro Green, leafy herb resembling flat-leaf (Italian) parsley, with a sharp, aromatic, somewhat astringent flavor. Also called fresh coriander and commonly referred to as Chinese parsley.

Dill Herb with fine, feathery leaves and sweet, aromatic flavor well suited to pickling brines, vegetables, seafood, and light meats. Sold fresh or dried.

Marjoram Pungent and aromatic, this herb may be used dried or fresh to season lamb and other meats, poultry, seafood, vegetables or eggs.

Mint Refreshing herb available in many varieties, with spearmint the most common. Used fresh to flavor a variety of dishes.

Oregano Noted for its aromatic, spicy flavor, which intensifies with drying. Also known as wild marjoram.

Parsley Although this popular fresh herb is available in two varieties, Italian flat-leaf parsley has a more pronounced flavor that makes it generally preferably to the common curly-leaf type.

Rosemary Used either fresh or dried, strong-flavored rosemary frequently scents meat dishes, as well as seafood and vegetables. Use it sparingly, except when grilling.

Sage Fresh or dried, this pungent herb goes well with pork, lamb, veal or poultry.

Tarragon Fresh or dried, this sweet, fragrant herb seasons salads, seafood, chicken, light meats, eggs and vegetables.

Thyme Delicately fragrant and clean tasting, this small-leaved herb is used fresh or dried to flavor savory dishes.

Julienne

French cooking term used to describe both the act of cutting ingredients into long, thin strips and the resulting strips themselves. To julienne an ingredient, cut it lengthwise into thin slices; then, stacking several slices together, slice again into julienne strips. A mandoline or the julienne-cutting disk of a food processor may also be used.

Juniper Berries
The aromatic dried berries of the juniper tree. Commonly used in pickling mixtures and to season poultry and game.

Kale
This rustic member of the cabbage family has long, dark green, crinkly leaves with a strong taste and sturdy texture.

Leeks
These sweet, moderately flavored members of the onion family are long and cylindrical, with a pale white root end and dark green leaves.

Mandoline
This common French cutting tool—available outside of France in well-stocked kitchen-supply stores—consists of straight and forked cutting blades firmly set at either end of a plastic, metal or wooden frame; some models include a folding stand that holds the frame at roughly a 45-degree angle. To slice vegetables quickly, repeatedly slide them down and up the frame across the blade of choice—a flat edge for slices or a forked edge for julienne.

Mortar and Pestle
Bowl-shaped mortars—stone, marble, earthenware, metal or wood—and rod-shaped pestles are the original rustic food processors of the Mediterranean. Together they are used to grind, pulverize, crush or purée all kinds of foods, from spice seeds to cooked vegetables.

Mushrooms
With their rich, earthy flavors and meaty textures, mushrooms inspire passion in Mediterranean cooks and diners alike. Most are available either fresh or dried; rehydrate dried mushrooms before using. Some types used here:

Chanterelles In season in France from early summer to early autumn, these subtly flavored, trumpet-shaped, generally pale yellow wild mushrooms are usually rapidly sautéed and served in omelets or with light meats. They are also known by the French *girolles*.

Cremini Similar in size and shape to common cultivated white mushrooms, this variety has a more pronounced flavor and a rich brown skin concealing creamy tan flesh.

Oyster These white, gray or pinkish wild or cultivated mushrooms have a tender tex-ture and mild flavor faintly reminiscent of oysters.

Porcini Rich, meaty wild mushrooms, also known by the French term *cèpe*.

Portobello Fully mature cremini mushrooms, portobellos (below, left) are noted for their wide, flat, deep brown caps and rich, mildly meaty taste.

Shiitake Meaty in flavor and texture, these Asian mushrooms (below, right) have flat, dark brown caps 2–3 inches (5–7.5 cm) wide.

White These common cultivated mushrooms come in three sizes, from the smallest, or button (below, center), to cup, to the largest, or flat mushrooms.

Nuts
European cooks make use of a wide variety of nuts in savory and sweet dishes. Some featured in this book include:

Almonds Mellow, sweet-flavored, widely popular oval nuts.

Hazelnuts Also known as filberts, these spherical nuts, are used whole, chopped, coarsely ground into a powder or finely ground into a paste. They have a special affinity with chocolate, and are teamed with it in many Italian sweets. Look for the paste in most specialty-food stores.

Pine Nuts These small, ivory-colored nuts are the seeds of a species of Mediterranean pine tree, and have a rich, delicately resinous flavor.

Pistachios These mildly sweet, full-flavored, crunchy green nuts are native to Asia Minor.

Walnuts Mentioned in Homer's epic poems, walnuts have a rich flavor and a crisp texture. English walnuts are the most common variety.

TO TOAST NUTS
Toasting brings out the full flavor and aroma of nuts. To toast any kind of nut, preheat an oven to 325°f (165°c). Spread out the nuts in a single layer on a baking sheet and toast until they just begin to change color, 8–10 minutes for most nuts and about 5 minutes for pine nuts. Let cool to room temperature before chopping or grinding.

Oils
Although olive oil is usually the first choice of cooks throughout the Mediterranean for sautéing, frying, and making sauces and dressings, other oils are also used. Store in air-tight containers, away from heat and light.

Olive Oil Extra-virgin olive oil is extracted from olives on the first pressing without use of heat or chemicals. It is valued for its distinctive fruity flavor. Virgin olive oil has a less refined flavor but is just as pure. Products which are labeled pure olive oil are less aromatic and flavorful and may be used for general cooking purposes.

Peanut Oil This pale gold oil, subtly flavored with the peanut's richness, can be heated to fairly high temperatures for deep-frying, and may also be used for sautéing as well as in dressings.

Vegetable Oil The term may be applied to any of several refined pure or blended oils pressed or otherwise extracted from any of a number of different sources—corn, cottonseed, peanuts, safflower seeds, soybeans, sunflower seeds. Such oils are selected for their pale color, neutral flavor and high cooking temperature.

Olives
The olive tree was a sacred symbol of ancient Athens, and olives are still prominently featured in the foods of Greece as well as in other Mediterranean countries. In Italy, particularly in the more southerly regions with harsher soil, olive trees thrive. Ripe black and underripe green olives are cured in combinations of salt, seasonings, brines, oils and vinegars to produce a wide range of piquant and pungent results, including the Kalamata olive. If Italian varieties called for in the recipes are unavailable, you can substitute similar Italian or Greek cured olives.

Onions, White
These white-skinned, white-fleshed onions tend to be sweet and mild in flavor. If unavailable, substitute with mild yellow onions.

Pasta Machine
The classic Italian device for making pasta at home is a hand-cranked stainless-steel machine that passes fresh pasta dough between a pair of adjustable rollers. Set at their widest distance, the rollers knead the dough; then the distance between them is progressively narrowed as the dough is passed through at each setting until the desired degree of thinness is reached. For flat cuts, the dough is then cranked through a cutting attachment to make strands.

Polenta
Soldiers of Imperial Rome ate *pulmentum*, a mush of millet, chickpea (garbanzo) flour or spelt. Over time, this gruel—its name evolved to the Italian polenta—incorporated other grains, eventually settling on corn, which began to gain popularity in the late 17th century. Today, the term refers to the mush and to the cornmeal from which it is made.

Puff Pastry
This light, flaky pastry—also known as *pâte feuilletée* or *feuilletage*—is made by repeatedly layering pastry dough and butter or another solid fat to form a thin dough that puffs in the oven. Although many types of puff pastry have been made by hand in France for centuries,

commercially manufactured frozen varieties are now also available.

Quince
The yellowish green fruit of a tree originating in Asia but grown throughout the Mediterranean. Resembling a lumpy pear, the quince has a hard, harshly acidic flesh that becomes delicate and sweet when cooked.

Radicchio
The most common variety has small reddish purple leaves with creamy white ribs, formed into an elongated sphere. Radicchio may be served raw in salads, or cooked, usually by grilling. Also called red chicory.

Rice
Originating in Asia, rice first reached Europe when Alexander the Great introduced it to the markets of Greece following his invasion of India in 327 B.C. Arab merchants later popularized it on the Iberian

Peninsula. The best Italian rice is grown in the Piedmont and Lombardy, with short, round grains such as *Arborio*, *Vialone Nano* and *Carnaroli* prized for the creamy consistency and chewy texture they give to risotto.

Long-Grain White The most popular type, with long, slender grains that steam to a fluffy consistency. The basmati variety, in particular, is prized for its aroma and flavor.

Short-Grain White Any of several varieties of milled rice whose grains cook up to a more starchy, sticky consistency—characteristics prized in, for example, the paella of Spain.

Salt
Coarse-grained salt is used primarily in marinades and seasonings. Kosher salt is a flaked variety of coarse-grained salt that is free of additives and often preferred for cooking.

Salt Cod
Throughout the Mediterranean, and particularly in Portugal, Spain and France, codfish that has been preserved by salting and drying has been a basic food for centuries. Before cooking, salt cod must be reconstituted and rid of some of its saltiness by soaking.

Sausages

Fresh and dried sausages may be served as simple appetizers or used as an ingredient in robust dishes. The sausages called for in this book include:

Chorizo The cured pork sausage of Spain, mildly spiced but still robustly flavored with paprika and garlic.

Chouriço The cured pork sausage of Portugal, flavored with a combination of garlic, paprika, salt, and other spices.

Italian Sweet Sausages The fresh pork sausages of northern Italy are generally sweet and mild in flavor, and sometimes flavored with fennel seed.

Linguiça A type of *chouriço,* this Portuguese dried sausage has a distinctive garlicky flavor.

Loukanika Fresh Greek pork sausage traditionally flavored with orange zest, marjoram, coriander and allspice.

Mortadella A specialty of Bologna, this wide, air-cured, mottled pork sausage has a mildly spicy flavor and fine texture.

Shallots

These small cousins of the onion have a papery brown skin, purple-tinged flesh and a flavor resembling both sweet onion and garlic.

Shellfish

Popular in Mediterranean dishes, some varieties include:

Clams These grayish tan bivalves are much used in the dishes of Spain and Portugal. When making appetizers and dishes such as paella, seek out small, sweet clams such as the Manila variety.

Mussels These common bivalves must be cleaned before cooking to remove any dirt caked on their bluish black shells and to remove their "beards," the fibrous threads by which they connect to rocks or piers in the coastal waters where they live.

TO CLEAN MUSSELS
First, holding the mussel under running water, scrub it thoroughly with a firm-bristled brush. Then grasp the beard and pull it off. Be sure to discard any mussels whose shells do not close to the touch.

Scallops Bivalve mollusks with rich, slightly sweet flesh. Sea scallops are shaped like plump discs about 1½ inches (4 cm) in diameter, while bay scallops are considerably smaller. Usually sold already shelled. Remove the tough muscle, or foot, from sea scallops.

Shrimp Raw shrimp (prawns) are generally sold with the heads already removed but the shells still intact. Before cooking, they are usually peeled and their thin, veinlike intestinal tracts removed.

TO PEEL AND DEVEIN FRESH SHRIMP
Use your thumbs to split open the thin shell along the concave side, between the legs, then carefully peel it away (below). Using a small, sharp knife, make a shallow slit along the shrimp's back to expose the veinlike, usually dark intestinal tract. Using the tip of the knife or your fingers, lift up and pull out the vein.

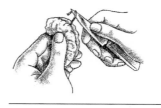

Spices

For the best flavor, grind whole spices with a mortar and pestle or in a spice grinder just before use.

Allspice This sweet spice has a flavor reminiscent of a blend of cinnamon, cloves and nutmeg. It may be purchased either as whole dried berries or ground.

Cayenne Pepper Very hot ground spice derived from the dried cayenne chili pepper.

Cinnamon The aromatic bark of a type of evergreen tree, this popular sweet spice traditionally flavors baked goods, and also finds its way into savory dishes in Greek and Turkish kitchens. It is sold as whole dried strips about 3 inches (7.5 cm) long—cinnamon sticks—or ground.

Cumin This pungent, yellowish brown spice, native to the Middle East, has a dusky, aromatic flavor. Sold ground or as crescent-shaped seeds.

Curry Powder Dutch and British traders first carried curry powder from India to Europe in the early 18th century. Most curry powders include coriander, cumin, chili powder, fenugreek and turmeric; other additions may include cardamom, cinnamon, cloves, allspice, fennel seeds, ginger and tamarind.

Ginger This intense sweet-hot spice comes from the rhizome of the tropical ginger plant. Whole fresh rhizomes, commonly but mistakenly called roots, should be peeled.

Nutmeg A sweet spice derived from the hard pit of the fruit of the nutmeg tree, this spice may be bought already ground or, for fresher flavor, whole, to be ground on a nutmeg grater (below), as needed.

Paprika Reddish ground spice derived from the sweet (mild) and hot forms of the dried paprika pepper.

Pepper For the fullest flavor, purchase this common savory spice as whole peppercorns and grind in a kitchen pepper mill. Black peppercorns, which have the most pungent flavor, are picked slightly underripe, and their hulls oxidize as they dry. Milder white peppercorns are fully ripened berries, husked before drying.

Red Pepper Flakes Coarsely ground flakes of dried red chilies, including seeds, which add mildly hot flavor.

Saffron This intensely aromatic, golden-orange spice, made from the dried stigmas of a species of crocus, is sold either as threads—the dried stigmas—or in powdered form. Look for products labeled pure saffron.

Sumac Sour in taste, with overtones of lemon and pepper, this purple powder is derived from the dried berries, and sometimes the leaves, of a nonpoisonous Turkish species of the sumac shrub.

Terrine

A word based on *terre,* "earth," terrine has two meanings in French kitchens. It is a deep, straight-sided ovenproof dish of earthenware, porcelain or glass. The term also refers to mixtures of puréed or chopped poultry, meat, seafood or other ingredients cooked and molded in such containers, then sliced to serve as a first course.

Tomatoes

Introduced from the New World to Italy in the mid-16th century, tomatoes were not popular in Italian kitchens until the 18th century. Today, they find their way into every course of the meal there except dessert.

The most familiar variety, and those that offer the best quality year-round, are Italian plum tomatoes, also known as Roma or egg tomatoes. Canned whole plum tomatoes are the most reliable for cooking; those designated San Marzano are considered the finest. At the peak of summer, firm, sun-ripened beefsteak tomatoes are an excellent choice for using fresh. Ripe tomatoes are also dried in the sun and submerged in olive oil or packaged dry; the latter may be reconstituted by soaking them in cool water.

TO PEEL FRESH TOMATOES
Bring a saucepan of water to a boil. Using a small, sharp knife, cut out the core from the stem end and cut a shallow X at the tomato's base. Submerge the tomato for about 20 seconds in the boiling water, then remove and cool in a bowl of cold water. Working from the X, peel off the skin, using your fingertips or the knife blade.

TO SEED TOMATOES
Cut them in half crosswise and squeeze to force out the seeds.

Truffles

Highly aromatic yet subtly flavored, this variety of wild fungus adds distinction to a wide range of savory dishes. The Périgord region of France is the source of what are considered the finest black truffles. Fresh truffles are available in late autumn and winter; they are also sold in jars and cans (whole or in pieces). Peel black truffles before using.

Vanilla Bean

The dried aromatic pod of a variety of orchid, the vanilla bean is a popular flavoring in French and other European desserts. Although vanilla's most common form is that of an alcohol-based extract (essence), the pod and the tiny seeds within it impart an intense vanilla flavor.

TO REMOVE VANILLA SEEDS
Using a small, sharp knife, split the bean in half lengthwise. Then, using the tip of the knife, scrape out the tiny seeds within each bean half.

Vinegars

The term *vinegar* refers to any alcoholic liquid caused to ferment a second time by certain strains of yeast, turning it highly acidic. Vinegars highlight the qualities of the liquid from which they are made. *Red wine vinegar*, for example, has a more robust flavor than vinegar produced from white wine. *Sherry vinegar* has the rich, nutlike flavor of the popular fortified wine of Spain. *Balsamic vinegar*, a specialty of Modena, Italy, since well before the 11th century, is made from reduced grape juice and is aged and blended for many years in a succession of casks made of different woods and gradually diminishing in size. The result is a tart-sweet, intensely aromatic vinegar prized by chefs.

Zest

The thin outer layer of a citrus fruit's peel contains most of its aromatic oils, which can provide lively flavor to both sweet and savory dishes. You can remove the zest with a simple tool known as a zester, drawn across the fruit's skin to cut the zest in thin strips; with a fine hand-held grater; or in wide strips with a vegetable peeler or a paring knife held almost parallel to the fruit's skin.

Zucchini

A squash of the New World, the slender, cylindrical green zucchini long ago found its way into Italian kitchens. Seek out smaller zucchini, which have a finer texture and tinier seeds than more mature specimens. Italian cooks who grow them in their own gardens take care to save the delicate blossoms, stuffing them for an antipasto.

INDEX

INDEX

INDEX

PHOTO CREDITS

Food Photography: Peter Johnson
Assistant Food Photographer: Dal Harper
Food Stylist: Janice Baker
Assistant Food Stylists:
Amanda Biffin, Liz Nolan, Alison Turner

Photography on pages 1–11, 122–123 and 228–229:
Steven Rothfeld

Cover Photography: Daniel Clark
Stylist: Pouké
Assistant Stylist: Samantha Campbell
Prop Stylist: Carol Hacker, Tableprop